American Policy in Nicaragua

HENRY L. STIMSON'S
AMERICAN POLICY IN NICARAGUA
THE LASTING LEGACY

 Markus Wiener Publishing, Inc.
New York & Princeton

For information write to
Markus Wiener Publishing, Inc
114 Jefferson Road
Princeton, N.J. 08540

Library of Congress Cataloging-in-Publication Data

Stimson, Henry, Lewis, 1867–1950.
    [American policy in Nicaragua]
    Henry L. Stimson's American policy in Nicaragua ; the lasting legacy / introduction and afterword by Paul H. Boeker ; plus essays by Andres Perez and Alain Brinkley.
    Originally published as: American policy in Nicaragua.
    Includes bibliographical references.
    ISBN 1-55876-036-9 (cloth)—ISBN 1-55876-037-7 (paper)
    1. United States—Foreign relations—Nicaragua. 2. Nicaragua—Foreign relations—United States. 3. Nicaragua—History—Revolution, 1926–1929. 4. Stimson, Henry Lewis, 1867–1950—Views on Nicaragua. I. Title.
E183.8.N5S8 1991
327.7307285—dc20   91-18265
                                                 CIP

Cover Design by Cheryl Mirkin

Printed in the United States of America on acid-free paper

Contents

Acknowledgements

The contributors to this book and the publisher gratefully acknowledge permission granted to use material in this volume:

The New York Times for *Bad Luck in Nicaragua.* Original publication date: July 20, 1927. Copyright © 1927 by the New York Times Company. All rights reserved. Reprinted by permission.

Brandt and Brandt Literary Agency and CBC Publications for, *Latin-America at War with the Past,* by Carlos Fuentes. Copyright © 1985 by the CBC Lecture Series Publications. All rights reserved. Reprinted by permission.

The New York Review of Books for *The Good Old Days,* by Alan Brinkley. Original publication date: January 17, 1991. Copyright © 1991 by Nyrev, Inc. All rights reserved. Reprinted by permission.

Newsweek for *The Code of the WASP Warrior* by Evan Thomas, Thomas M. De Frank, and Ann Mc Daniel. Original publication date: August 20, 1990. Copyright © 1990 by Newsweek Inc. All rights reserved. Reprinted by permission.

Introduction

PAUL H. BOEKER

Henry Stimson had a remarkable and long public life. Forty years after his death in 1950, he is still the mentor of American statesmen who confidently use U.S. military power to enforce peace and punish aggressors.* Colonel Stimson, as he preferred to be called, held a long succession of jobs between his first cabinet post, as Secretary of War (1911–13) under President Taft, and his last, as Truman's Secretary of War (Spring through December 1945). For more than two generations thereafter his ideas shaped America's concept of its role in the world.

Colonel Stimson was a hero to both Democratic Secretaries of State, most particularly Dean Acheson, and to Republican ones, such as John Foster Dulles. Such strong internationalists respected both the Colonel's confidence that right and wrong could be divined in conflicts around the world and his willingness to use U.S. power on behalf of the right side. George Bush is not only one of Stimson's fans, but one of his best disciples. Both the invasion of Panama in 1989 and the rapid deployment of massive U.S. military power to the Persian Gulf in 1990—and into open war there in January 1991—would have left Colonel Stimson proud of Prescott Bush's son.

Henry Stimson's account of his four-week mission to Nicaragua in 1927 says something about Nicaragua—but more about the United States: the progressively expanding concept of the country's mission in the world held by its twentieth-century political leaders, and their willingness to use military force to fulfill it. Before World War I and again between the wars that readiness to use force to protect a broad concept of U.S. interests was largely confined to Latin America. After World War II it became a global mission. Stimson himself made the personal transition easily and helped his country make it as well.

---

*For a history of the books about Stimson see pages 120-121

The quest to use American power to stabilize other countries that were deemed important to U.S. interests began with exhilaration and a sense of clear mission, which turned with time to frustration and confusion. Some Americans came to question whether the interests needed to be so broadly defined and the mission so ambitious, and whether the problems of stability were indeed so tractable to American power and diplomacy.

Stimson's heady Nicaraguan mission, so enthusiastically related and eloquently justified in his personal account, is a microcosm of America's early growing pains with its expanding role. For more than three generations after Stimson's well-meaning effort, America's political leadership continued to grapple with the questions of the extent of its "vital" interests, its mission with regard to the stability of other countries touching on those interests, and the limits on America's use of power in trying to bring stability to other regions.

Stimson's account reflects the sense of America's ascendent power held by the country's political elite in a heady phase that would carry Stimson and his cohorts to self-confident exercise of world leadership. Yet the seeds of doubt were already sown in the frustratingly ephemeral nature of Stimson's achievement in bringing peace to Nicaragua and his own later efforts to limit the costs of his unraveling diplomatic triumph. Stimson's subsequent frustration as Secretary of State in dealing with Nicaragua's still unsolved problems parallels the maturation of a nation trying to do good in a world that is not plainly good and bad, or as straightforward in its acceptance of U.S. ministrations as Americans would like to think.

The reprinting by Markus Wiener of *American Policy in Nicaragua* brings back to America a vivid reminder of the attitudes that enabled America to seize the role of leadership of the "free world" after World War II. Self-confident nationalists such as Henry Stimson were ready for an expanded American mission in the world even before the Second World War thrust this role upon a public much less anxious to take on the world's concerns. Stimson knew what to do, even if the people or the Congress were not so certain.

Henry Stimson was in every sense a scion of the "eastern establishment" that ran America before World War II. Phillips Academy at Andover, Yale and Harvard Law School, gave him all the right credentials. At Yale he made the prestigious secret society of Skull and Bones, an honor he took very seriously. He returned in later years to initiate personally other classes of new members, including that of George Bush in 1947.

Stimson became, early on, a member of the law firm of Elihu Root, a lion of the Republican establishment and former Secretary of both State and War. Stimson was closer still to Teddy Roosevelt, a Long Island neighbor and friend who first appointed him U.S. Attorney for the Southern District of New York. With these two mentors, Stimson shared an idealistic and expansive internationalism and a willingness to use military power in its service.

Military service in time of war was an obligation to men like Stimson. Before America's entry into World War I, he followed his own calls for America's preparedness and intervention by volunteering, although almost 50 years old, as an officer candidate. He received a quick commission after truncated officer's training, and later served briefly in combat in France. He was surely the only former Secretary of War in U.S. history to be commissioned subsequently as a lieutenant. Mustered out as a short-order Colonel, Stimson found his combat experience exhilarating and war to be a challenging game of wits.

The subtle and wily craft of diplomacy was one to which the Colonel turned his hand only as he approached his sixtieth birthday in 1927. Calvin Coolidge asked his trusted friend to go to Nicaragua to "investigate and report" (p. 18) on a persistent civil conflict that kept re-igniting like one of those trick birthday candles despite repeated efforts to blow it out. In 1909 those efforts had prompted President Taft to send U.S. Marines to Nicaragua, where they stayed until 1925 to assure that the faction on top at the moment did not give any European power or the Japanese the right to build a second transoceanic canal—in Nicaragua.

The U.S. had, at least on paper, gained this right for itself in perpetuity in the 1914 Brian-Chamorro Treaty, and did not intend to allow any insurgent government of Nicaragua a second thought. Throughout the first long period of the Marines' presence in Nicaragua, the U.S. generally backed the Conservative faction against the rival Liberals in a seemingly endless internal struggle that was more about power than political philosophy. Coolidge had withdrawn the Marines in 1925 when he thought a brokered coalition government with a Conservative president, Carlos Solorzano, and Liberal vice-president, Juan Sacasa, had brought reconciliation and stability.

But alas, a Conservative rival of Solorzano, Emiliano Chamorro, overthrew the coalition and fighting resumed.

In 1926 Coolidge sent the Marines back to the Central American nation ostensibly "for the protection of American and foreign lives" (p. 12). But he came under increasing public and congressional criticism for sending them back into a country wracked by apparently endless and bloody internal conflict.

Coolidge initially saw this as an operation with limited objectives, and thus left the military man on the scene, Admiral Julian Latimer, in charge of it. Latimer arrived at Bluefields on Nicaragua's Caribbean coast in August 1926, where he secured the consent of the rival factions fighting there to set up a neutral zone for the protection of foreigners; the Admiral subsequently established another neutral zone at the Pacific port of Corinto. Latimer went on to put 175 marines at the U.S. legation in the capital, Managua, and assigned more to guard the railway from the capital to the port at Corinto, which put them more in harm's way.

Coolidge had protested that "we are not making war on Nicaragua any more than a policemen on the street is making war on passers-by." (Current, *Secretary Stimson,* p. 30). But the passers-by were shooting at each other and the Marines were in danger of being caught in the cross fire.

Secretary of State Frank B. Kellogg, no doubt concerned that a friend of the President's was stepping on his turf, wanted Stimson's upcoming mission to be one of fact-finding, and reporting of his conclusions and recommendations to Washington (i.e., to Kellogg). For Stimson's benefit Kellogg cabled the U.S. mission in Managua on the eve of Stimson's arrival that "the Stimson mission should not be characterized in any sense as an act of mediation" (Current, p. 30). But Coolidge was looking for help with the political problems he faced at home, and this gave his friend Stimson latitude to take his efforts to solve Coolidge's Nicaragua problem as far as he could. Stimson's limited mission was thus destined to become one more U.S. try at installing a stable Nicaraguan regime friendly to U.S. interests.

While Coolidge's basic instructions to Stimson were "to investigate and report," Stimson claimed that Coolidge added an oral footnote "that if I should find a chance to straighten the matter out he wished I could try to do so" (p. 18). For Stimson, this opening was all he needed to invert the priorities for his mission to make straightening out Nicaragua the objective from the beginning. Straightening out Nicaragua was indeed the objective to which Stimson turned his extraordinary energy and self-confidence from his first day there. He approached the task with a can-do positivism that was at the same time admirable and naive.

In 1927, Stimson did not doubt that it was the business of the U.S. to bring stability to Nicaragua. He accepted fully his mentor Teddy Roosevelt's extension of the Monroe Doctrine to the obligation to enforce stability in Latin American republics. Roosevelt's logic leapt to the conclusion that only such stability would ensure that no European power would have any reason to intervene in the hemisphere. In justifying the U.S. role in Nicaragua, Stimson quoted Teddy Roosevelt, "We cannot permanently adhere to the Monroe Doctrine unless we succeeded in making it evident . . . that in as much as by this doctrine we prevent other nations from interfering on this side of the water, we shall ourselves in good faith try to help those of our sister republics which need such help toward peace and order" (Current, p. 33).

The additional interest of the Panama Canal created for Stimson a clear U.S. need to enforce stability in all of Central America and the Caribbean, the "vital" approaches to the Canal. These interests were to Stimson so strong and clear as to broach no doubt. "The national safety of our own country has, however, imposed upon us a peculiar interest in guarding from foreign influence the vital sea route through the Caribbean Sea and the Panama Canal" (p. 48).

With no doubt about either the U.S.'s right or his own authority to straighten out Nicaragua, Colonel Stimson set right to it. He presumed to have complete authority to do whatever was needed, virtual carte blanche. "No envoy ever received wider latitude or more loyal support" (p. 18). In fact, much of the "latitude" was presumed and some of the "loyal support" compelled by Coolidge's need to stay up with what Stimson had already done or committed him to.

With 64 years of hindsight, it is easy to criticize Stimson's failure to see how deeply divided were Nicaragua's many competing factions, even after his reconciliation of those whom he considered the main actors. Yet 64 years later one still has to admire a diplomat who had a complex tactical mission and worked at it with extraordinary energy and some success. One also has to respect a statesman who had a sense of the use of power for diplomatic ends, which is, even on the small stage of Nicaragua in the 1920s, breathtaking.

As a good lawyer, Stimson started by briefing himself thoroughly. "My first effort on arrival was to put myself in touch with all responsible sources of public opinion in order that I might get at the underlying facts of the situation" (p. 20). He learned his brief well and his own recapitulation in chapter 1 of the background of the immediate conflict is impressive. But as sophisticated as the Colonel became about Nicaraguan politics, his understanding of the civil strife was too simplistic. With his legal background he saw the dispute as one between two parties, Liberal and Conservative, whose balanced deal, in the form of the coalition government of Solorzano and Sacasa, had been upset by Emiliano Chamorro's coup of 1925.

In more cruel reality, Nicaragua had been riven by a struggle for power since the beginning of the century, one in which factions had become more personalized and diverse than Liberals and Conservatives. Chamorro's coup was one phase of a continuing struggle in which many pretenders never conceded their claim on power to the person momentarily on top, nor accepted an impartial process for choosing a successor other than themselves.

Stimson thus drew conclusions based on his talks with Conservative President Adolfo Díaz and the Liberal field commander, José Moncada, which did not apply to other factions. Thus he concluded: "The people of both parties were friendly to the United States, and were looking to us for active assistance to get them out of this deadlock and its distressing consequences (p. 23).

And again: "I found the leaders of both parties earnestly seeking our intervention and asserting the paramount interest of the United States in the establishment and maintenance of orderly and responsible government throughout Central America (p. 23).

And further: "The form of assistance which all parties desired and were agreed upon was that we should supervise the conduct of their coming national election in October, 1928."

And still further: "In their recognition of government-controlled elections as the fundamental will of their system, these Nicaraguan leaders were in agreement. . . ."

All of these conclusions may have applied to Conservative President Díaz, who could not succeed himself and had no brief for his Conservative rivals and to Liberal General Moncada, who expected to, and did, win the election of 1928. But few or none of these conclusions applied to the other factions and sub-factions.

None of Stimson's conclusions applied to the leader of one violent liberal faction, Augusto Sandino, a significant actor whom Stimson never met—probably because Moncada did not want him to. Sandino was militantly and bitterly anti-U.S. and committed to fighting the U.S. Marines indefinitely, no matter how the Liberal/Conservative strife was settled. His objective was to pursue his own fight for power and to rid Nicaragua of American influence. Sandino thus had no interest in participating in the election of 1928, and no reason to recognize its result. Augusto Sandino did not fit Stimson's simplified framework of the Nicaraguan conflict. Sandino was dismissed by Stimson as "a bandit," although Sandino had enough support in the countryside to fight on until 1933. He remained a strong factor in Nicaragua until another "Liberal" faction leader, Anastasio Somoza, had him murdered in 1934. That both Somoza and Sandino fought at one time or another under the Liberals' banner indicates how little unity this party had.

Another key Liberal politician, Juan Sacasa, also did not accept continued U.S. occupation to supervise the elections.

Despite the inaccuracy of Stimson's version of the problem, U.S.-supervised elections were a reasonable step toward a reconciliation, even if they were not capable of being the fundamental solution Stimson hoped they would be.

Having decided on the essential solution—U.S.-supervised elections—Stimson in cold logic laid out "certain requirements" to make fair elections possible: (1) "peace and a general amnesty"; (2) "complete disarmament . . . of the entire population"; (3) "a new and impartial police force."

With a stunning positivism, Stimson set out to make all of these certain requirements happen, in someone else's country—and in one month's time. He decided "to follow the straight and simple course of driving at the main object of securing a fresh and fair start in 1928 and not to try to play politics in the meanwhile" (p. 29).

Stimson did, to be proper, cable Washington his views on the importance of American supervision for the 1928 election, and received a reply indicating that "the president would be willing, on the request of the Nicaragua government and under Nicaraguan law, to recommend a commission for the supervision of this election."

But with this nod from Washington, Stimson pressed his mediation much further than these pale instructions would cover, including committing the President to use of force to back up his straight-ahead drive for a peace between warring Conservatives and Liberals as well as a U.S.-supervised election.

He first got President Díaz to agree to a cease-fire, and delivery of arms by both sides to the U.S. Marines; a general amnesty and organization of a new police force under American officers; and supervision of the 1928 elections by the Marines. Quite a heavy role for the United States, for starters.

Stimson then met the Liberal commander in the field, General Moncada, at Tipitapa and quickly got him to agree to all these terms except Díaz's remaining in office until the elections, a condition Stimson himself actually insisted upon, probably to avoid a struggle over a new provisional president and the possible ascension of some-one more ambitious than Díaz. Moncada protested that his troops would accept Díaz staying on until elections only if the United States insisted upon it in clear terms.

Whereupon Stimson, in one of U.S. diplomacy's clearest exercises of shear chutzpa, called in his secretary to dictate a letter to Mon-cada which asserted that Stimson was authorized to say that the President of the United States intended to supervise the 1928 elec-tions, that Díaz staying on until then was insisted upon by the U.S., that a general disarmament was necessary and that U.S. Marines were to accept the arms of both sides and "to disarm forcibly those who will not do so" (p. 33).

The last clause, which virtually committed the U.S. to go to war in Nicaragua if the Liberals did not turn over their arms, was almost an afterthought by Stimson. "I included the last sentence not as a threat to Moncada's organized and loyal troops . . . but as a needed warning to the bandit fringe" (i.e., Sandino). With this powerful threat in hand, Moncada got all of his troops, except Sandino and his faction, to accept the full terms Stimson had extracted from Díaz, as well as the expanded role of the U.S. Marines.

Moncada, for whom Stimson developed deep respect and admira-tion during their talks at Tipitapa, clearly misled Stimson on Sand-ino's motivations and following. Moncada, according to Stimson, told him that Sandino, "having promised to join in the settlement, afterward broke his word and with about 150 followers, most of whom were Honduran mercenaries, had secretly left [for Honduras]." Moncada further swayed Stimson to a conclusion that Sandino was not important by telling Stimson that Sandino had earlier returned to Nicaragua from 22 years in Mexico only "in order to enjoy the opportunities for violence and pillage." Sandino's character and motivations can still be debated, but obviously he had a much larger political following for his continued campaign against U.S. forces in Nicaragua than Moncada admitted, or Stimson recognized. And in his stated cause of ridding Nicaragua of U.S. occupation forces, Sandino had a cause that galvanized sufficient popular support to feed his growing guerrilla bands and help them elude the U.S. Marines and the National Guard for five years. Thus, fighting continued even as Stimson sailed home in mid-May 1927. With the "The Peace of Tipitapa," all was not nearly so settled as Stimson concluded in the account of his apparent diplomatic triumph in Nicaragua, which was originally run by the *Saturday Evening Post,* and appears in Chapter II of the book here re-printed.

Stimson concluded his account with the following sanguine epilogue and forlorn hope: "As we sailed away there remained with me as an earnest of the hopeful future of Nicaragua the memory of two patriotic men, one a 'Conservative' and one a 'Liberal,' each willing to sacrifice personal ambition and party interest to the higher welfare of his country and each willing to trust in the honor and good-will of the United States—Adolfo Díaz and José María Moncada."

American Policy
in Nicaragua

BY
HENRY L. STIMSON

Contents

Chapter I

The Historical Background

To understand the history of our relations to Nicaragua, it is necessary for us first to grasp certain geographical, racial and historical conditions of that nation. We Americans, in considering a foreign political problem are very prone to assume that the conditions which form the background of that problem are the same as our own. In the case of Nicaragua no worse error could be made.

The land area of Nicaragua is almost the same as that of the state of New York, but its population consists of less than 700,000 souls. The bulk of this population is settled in the great plain lying near the Pacific Ocean, where the most healthful climate is found and where the principal products of coffee, sugar, tobacco, corn and cattle are raised. This western portion of the country presents a pleasing aspect to the North American visitor, with open farming land interspersed with beautiful trees and cities of considerable size and antiquity. The Atlantic Coast, on the other hand—appropriately known as the Mosquito Coast, although it received this name from that of a tribe of Indians—where the rainfall is nearly double that on the west, is covered with a dense and unhealthy jungle. The population there is comparatively scanty and the occupation of the people confined to working a few small mines, to logging operations for mahogany and to the raising of bananas.

There are literally no lines of communication between these two districts, no railroads or even highways, nothing but jungle trails and tropical rivers by which to thread the difficulties of the mountainous barriers which lie between the two coasts. In the south lies Lake Nicaragua, the largest body of fresh water between Lake Superior and Lake Titicaca, in Peru. Seventy-five years ago, this lake with its outlet into the Atlantic, the San Juan River, formed one of the great trade routes from our eastern states to California, and Commodore Vanderbilt operated lines of steamers over its waters. Now that is all over. Since the opening of the Panama route, first by rail and then by canal, this Nicaraguan transcontinental route has been completely abandoned. To-day the lake lies practically deserted. No transcontinental commerce moves over its waters, although, next to Panama, it still marks the route which offers the easiest line for the construction of an interoceanic canal.

Nicaragua and its four Central American sisters—Guatemala, Salvador, Honduras and Costa Rica—were discovered, conquered and settled by Spanish adventurers early in the sixteenth century. The white conquerors, instead of driving off the Indian inhabitants, as happened in North America, enslaved them and intermarried with their women, and the present population is the result of that mingling. According to the census of 1920, the population of Nicaragua is 17 per cent white, 3 per cent pure Indian, 9 per cent negro and 71 per cent mixed—mainly Spanish and Indian. About 72 per cent of this population is illiterate. The negroes are mainly confined to the Atlantic Seaboard, having immigrated from the West Indies, Spanish law, customs, language and predilections prevail throughout the nation.

During the 300 years that these five countries were held as colonies by Spain, their population suffered much from oppression and violence.

> The Indians, who continue to form the bulk of the population, were deprived of their own religious and moral customs and were given in their place a Christianity which was imposed upon them by force and of which, because of the cruelty and licentiousness of their conquerors, they saw only the worst side. The oppression and violence which characterized the communities of the isthmus during their early history long prevented their social life from acquiring stability and made brute force rather than conscience and public opinion the ruling principle in private as well as public affairs.*

During those centuries they were also kept in commercial isolation. They were permitted to trade with no nation but Spain, and with her only under grievous and burdensome restrictions. Agriculture

---

The Five Republics of Central America, by Doctor Dana G. Monroe, page 12.

and industry were hampered and export made difficult or impossible by burdensome regulations and taxes. Furthermore, their chief cities and principal communities were situated on the Pacific side of the isthmus and therefore communication of any sort with Europe was slow and difficult. In 1822, when they threw off the yoke of Spain, they had had practically no intercourse with the outside world and their only government had been three centuries of despotism, broken now and then by unsuccessful revolts of the Indians against their masters.

When they became free from Spain our government recognized them as independent nations, and a year later, in 1823, by the Monroe Doctrine, we announced to the rest of the world that they were to remain free and were not to be subject to further European colonization. Using our American Constitution as their pattern, these nations thereupon chose for themselves probably the most difficult form of independent government—that of representative republics based upon manhood suffrage.

Under these circumstances it naturally soon became evident that they were not yet fitted for the responsibilities that go with independence, and still less fitted for popular self-government. Union with Mexico was first tried and soon ended. A federated union of the five republics was then attempted and lasted only a few years. Since then, for nearly 100 years, each of the five nations has been working out its own problems of government separately, and in its efforts following out much the same course of struggle, trial and failure. Forms of self-government embodied in their constitutions soon proved unworkable to their inexperienced populations and in all the countries the result was a concentration of practically all the powers of government in presidential dictators.

> An able president, in a Central American republic, exercises an absolute power for which it would be difficult to find a parallel anywhere in the civilized world. He is not restrained, like the absolute monarchs of Europe and Asia, by dynastic traditions or religious considerations, and he has little need to consider public opinion so long as he retains the good will of the army and of the office holders who owe their positions to him. He can often reelect himself for term after term and he is responsible to no one for the exercise of his authority or for the management of the public revenues. The country is so small that he can and does extend his control to matters of minor and purely local importance, even interfering with his fellow citizens' personal affairs and family relations, without regard for the most

sacred rights of the individual. It is in his power to exile, imprison or put to death his enemies, and to confiscate their property, while at the same time he can enrich and advance his friends.*

The central cause of the breakdown of popular government in these countries lay in the failure in their hands of the system of popular election. The percentage of illiteracy among the voters in each of the countries was overwhelming, and great masses of the Indian population had for centuries occupied a position little if any better than serfs or slaves. It was easy therefore for them to be controlled by fraud or threats or force. Consequently, in each of the five nations, it developed that the results of elections were habitually controlled by the man or men who held the machinery of government, including the army and the police.

The constitutions adopted, though largely modelled upon our own, have departed from our system by giving to the central government very great and concentrated powers over the departments and municipalities into which the nation was divided. The heads of the departments, who correspond to the governors of our states, instead of being elected by the voters of the departments, are, in Nicaragua, and I believe in most if not all the other four nations, appointed by the president of the republic; and this is true of most of the other local officers. There is therefore very little local self-government, that great school of democracy.

Out of these conditions it was easy for the system of dictatorships to develop, and instead of the people choosing their ruler by a free election, it soon became the universal rule for the president and his associates to dictate the result of the national elections. It is the literal truth that Nicaragua has never known a free election in our sense of the term. In later years there have been slight signs of improvement. A better public opinion on the subject has developed and the means used by the government to control the result of the election have of late sometimes not been so crude and violent as in the past; but I believe it remains literally true that no Nicaraguan election has ever produced a result which was contrary to the wishes of the man or party which was in control of the government.

Under such conditions the only way left to these people to dispossess from the government a man or a party which was in control

*The Five Republics of Central America, by Doctor Dana G. Monroe, page 39.

of it was by force. In default of a violent revolt on the part of the people against their government, that government remained indefinitely in power. Revolution thus became and for nearly a century has constituted a regular part of their political system.

The situation produced a vicious circle. The people, having been driven to violence in order to relieve themselves from the oppression of a dictator, have never cultivated the habit of peacefully abiding by the result of an election. They have come to realize that an election meant nothing. On the other hand, the revolutionary habit, once acquired, easily becomes habitual and inveterate, and the evils of continual revolution inevitably tended to concentrate into the hands of the government more and more arbitrary power.

In Nicaragua the evils of the situation are accentuated by the fact that the population is not homogeneous, but is divided into local and racial factions. True party government is easiest where people are homogeneous and divide politically merely upon issues of policy or principle. But in Nicaragua, although they have from the beginning had two great parties, known respectively as the Liberal and Conservative parties, these parties represent geographical and probably racial divisions and are not based upon any real differences of political principle. Thus from the foundation of the government, the city of Leon has been the head centre of the Liberal Party and the city of Granada the head centre of the Conservatives, and this division extends throughout the rural territory surrounding these cities. Managua, the capital, was founded later than the two others and placed between them in an attempt to occupy a neutral position.

I was told by an American scientist who has lived for many years in the country, in charge of the work of sanitation conducted there by the Rockfeller Foundation, that in his opinion this division between the two great parties took its origin historically in the racial differences of the two Indian tribes which inhabited the country before its conquest by Spain, and that there was a distinct Liberal versus Conservative watershed which could be traced running through the country. Whether this is so or not, it is certainly true that the differences between Liberals and Conservatives in Nicaragua are based largely upon local sentiment and are bitter beyond any party acrimony with which we are acquainted in the United States.

It is exceptional and difficult for a member of one party to live and do business in even a large city controlled by the other, while in the rural districts the feeling is even more acute and demonstrative. It can be easily seen what an additional burden is placed upon the task of popular government when a nation is so divided that the people of one locality look upon those of another almost as natural enemies.

As a result of these political conditions, the history of Nicaragua during the past sixty or seventy years presents a picture of successive periods during which one or the other of the two great parties was successful in holding the reins of government. Each of these periods was terminated by a revolution which placed the other party in power, and very often during the incumbency of one of the parties attempts at revolution would occur which were suppressed.

Thus from 1863 to 1893 the Conservatives held the reins of government. They were better organized than the Liberals, their leaders being composed of a few prominent families of Granada closely related by ties of blood and friendship. During that period, as a rule, they did not seek to continue a single man in power as president for many terms; but by mutual consent within this oligarchy of powerful families, they determined which of their members should succeed in holding the reins of government.

Revolutions against them were attempted a number of times, but none of them were successful until one in 1893 placed José Santos Zelaya, a Liberal, in the presidency. He remained in office for seventeen years, until 1910, when a revolution occurred which again placed the Conservatives in power. Zelaya's reign as dictator prior to 1910 had been a ruthless one. There had been many attempted revolts against him prior to the successful one and he had suppressed them with great severity. As his long term of power progressed it became characterized more and more by tryanny and oppression over his enemies. Consequently, after his deposition in 1910, the country was in a condition of turmoil and unrest worse than any which it had known for many years.

During the period of violence which accompanied and immediately followed the deposition of Zelaya, the American Government sent its naval forces to Nicaragua to protect American life and property on both the east and west coast. In 1912 these forces were twice drawn into serious combat with revolutionary bodies, on one occasion the marines taking by assault the difficult and almost impregnable hill of Masaya. After these forces were withdrawn a legation guard of 100 marines was left at the capital, Managua, on the request of the Nicaraguan Government, for the purpose of assisting by its presence to stabilize the country. It remained there until August, 1925, some fourteen years, without taking part in any fighting or violence. But probably in part owing to the moral impression produced by the presence of these 100 men, no very serious or successful attempt occurred at revolution during the time that they were there.

The Conservatives remained in power after the deposition of Zelaya from 1910 until 1924. This party again followed its group or family system of having each president after his term succeeded by another chosen by the group.

EFFORTS OF THE UNITED STATES TO ASSIST IN THE PURIFICATION OF ELECTIONS AND THE DISCOURAGEMENT OF REVOLUTIONS

As I shall point out later, the United States, ever since we recognized their independence, has in many ways endeavored to lend its assistance to the five Central American countries in their progress along the difficult road to orderly self-government. Here it is relevant to recall only some of the more recent efforts. In 1907 Mr. Roosevelt's Administration invited their representatives to a conference at Washington, where, with the assistance and advice of American representatives, mutual treaties of peace and amity were entered into by the five Central American nations, seeking to remove several of the chief causes of revolutions. Among other things, these nations agreed with one another not to recognize any government "which may come into power in any of the five republics as a consequence of a coup d'état or of a revolution against a recognized government so long as the freely elected representatives of the people thereof have not constitutionally reorganized the country."

Again, in 1923, another conference was held at Washington in which this mutual agreement not to recognize governments which might come into power by revolution or violence was renewed and made even more specific. And the United States itself, though not a party to the treaty, announced that it would follow the same course of conduct in according or withholding recognition.

Of course, such a mutual covenant not to recognize a revolutionary government did not get at the root of the evil. So long as the custom of government-controlled elections continued, revolution offered the only means of deposing the party in control of the government. Under existing conditions, revolution was an essential part of the system, and to forbid revolution simply tended to perpetuate the power of the party or individual who happened to be in control of the government.

These facts were self-evident and were recognized among the Nicaraguans themselves. As far back as 1920 the United States, through the Department of State, began to use its influence to try to reach the root of the evil and assist the Nicaraguans to purify their elections. With the approach of the election of that year the Department suggested to President Emiliano Chamorro the advisability of a reform in the electoral laws in order to insure a more nearly popular election. To secure such a reform it suggested that an expert should be sent from the United States to make a study of the system and suggest possible revisions in the law. President Chamorro, however, rejected this advice, claiming that the existing law was sufficient and uttering personal assurances that the election would be free. When, however, the registration and election came off, disorder and violence prevailed, and, as usual, the party favored by the government won.

Two years later, however, in 1922, the Nicaraguan Government accepted the recommendation of the State Department and appointed Doctor H. W. Dodds, of Princeton, as an expert to study the electoral situation. Doctor Dodds drafted an electoral law and that law was passed by the Nicaraguan Congress, although not until changes in it had been made which seriously weakened its integrity. The Liberal, or opposition, Party formally requested the United States to supervise the presidential elections to be held under this law in 1924, but President Martinez, being in control of the government, refused to join in the request.

Nevertheless, election reform was in the air. It was known that the American State Department was keenly interested in having the election go off in a fair and free manner, and that unless this took place the American Government might not recognize the legality of the president who should be declared elected. Finally the moderate Conservatives and the Liberals united on a coalition ticket composed of Carlos Solorzano, a Conservative, as candidate for president, and Doctor Juan Sacasa, a Liberal, as candidate for vice-president. The extreme Conservative faction presented an opposition ticket headed by a former president, Emiliano Chamorro. The coalition ticket was declared elected by a vote of 48,072 to 28,760 for the Chamorro ticket; but although the election had been comparatively free from overt violence, charges were insistently made that the government had aided the victorious ticket by widespread fraud and these charges were so current and widespread that the incoming administration entered office without either prestige or strength.

THE CHAMORRO COUP D'ETAT

For many years the United States had been seeking to withdraw its marines from Managua, but had been restrained by the importunities of the Nicaraguan Government. Many months prior to the 1924 election our government gave notice that the marines would be withdrawn on January 1, 1925, immediately after the inauguration of the new administration. On the urgent request, however, of President Solorzano we were prevailed upon to leave them there a few months more in order that his administration might have time to become steady in the saddle. The marines were then withdrawn on August 4, 1925.

Order lasted just three weeks thereafter. The friends of General Chamorro, the defeated extreme Conservative candidate, had been making preparations for trouble. President Solorzano had appointed a coalition cabinet composed of both Liberals and Conservatives. On August 25, while the Liberal cabinet officers were attending a banquet, they were seized and locked up. Thereafter the Chamorro conspiracy rapidly progressed. On October 25 his supporters seized the Loma, the fortress which overlooks the city of Managua, and the possession of which dominates the capital. Vice-President Sacasa and subsequently President Solorzano left the country, claiming to be in fear of their lives. The membership of Congress was reconstituted by expelling eighteen Liberal and moderate Conservative members and their places were filled by adherents of Chamorro. He was then elected by Congress as a designate, or substitute, for the presidency and assumed the functions of that office on January 16, 1926.

All this was done over the protest of the American Government and against its warning that under the policy of the Washington conferences of 1907 and 1923 Chamorro could not expect to be recognized as a legitimate government either by us or by the other four Central American republics. He, however, persisted in his purpose; and as he came into possession of a full treasury resulting from the long period of peace while our marines were in Managua, he succeeded for nearly ten months in holding his own against the Liberal revolutions which promptly broke out against him. The first such revolution broke out in May and was quelled. By August the situation had again become so disturbed that we were obliged to send naval vessels to Bluefields and Corinto to protect Americans at those points. This action was taken only after many repeated requests had been received from different parts of the United States for the protection of American lives and interests.

During the entire period of Chamorro's incumbency our government never ceased its moral pressure to induce him to withdraw. The representations of our chargé d'affaires at Managua were so insistent as to bring forth angry protests from the dictator. On January 22, 1926, and again on August 27, 1926, our secretary of state addressed to the Nicaraguan Government formal communications expressing disapproval of Chamorro's action in violating the treaties of 1923, which he himself had signed as a delegate. By October the combined pressure caused by the disapproval of this country which prevented him from raising any additional money by foreign loan, the increasing vigor of the revolutionists and finally dissatisfaction within his own party, the Conservatives, began to tell even upon Chamorro, who is an extremely determined and self-willed man, and he became ready to yield.

A conference was held during that month at Corinto on board the *U.S.S. Denver,* to which both Chamorro's government and the Liberals sent delegates to try to arrive at a settlement. This proved unavailing, and on October 30 Chamorro turned over the reins of government to Senator Uriza, who had been appointed the second designate by Congress.

THE ELECTION AND RECOGNITION OF DIAZ

The United States refused to recognize Uriza as president on the ground that he had been elected by the same illegal Congress which elected Chamorro. Thereupon a new extraordinary session of Congress was convoked. The eighteen senators and deputies who had been expelled by Chamorro from the previous Congress were invited to return and resume their seats. Of these, three returned to their seats and six others were represented by duly qualified alternates who had been legally elected in 1924. This Congress thereupon, on November 10, elected Adolfo Diaz as first designate. At this session fifty-three members of Congress were present out of a total membership of sixty-seven. Of these, forty-four voted for Diaz and two for Solorzano the balance abstaining from voting.

The Nicaraguan Constitution provides in Article 106:

> Art. 106: In case of the absolute or temporary lack of a President of the Republic, the office of Chief Executive shall devolve on the Vice-President, and in default of the latter, in one of the emergency candidates in the order of their election. In the latter case, if the Congress is in session, it shall be its duty to authorize the entrustment of the office to the Representative whom it may designate, who must fulfill the requirements for President of the Republic.*

At the time of this election President Solorzano was in California and Vice-President Sacasa in Guatemala, the latter having been out of the country nearly a year. Thereupon, on November 17, the United States Government extended recognition to President Diaz.

I think the foregoing simple statement of the facts will dispose of many of the thoughtless and baseless criticisms that have been uttered against the action of our government in Nicaragua. Some have not hesitated to charge that we have intentionally sided with the Conservatives and against the Liberals; they have even gone so far as to assert that our naval forces were used for the direct purpose of promoting the candidacy of President Diaz.

The facts are that we accorded our recognition to a coalition administration elected in 1924 containing Doctor Sacasa, a Liberal, as its vice-president; that when this administration was overthrown by the Conservative, Chamorro, we not only refused him recognition but used every effort consistent with diplomatic usage to persuade him to withdraw and reconstitute a legal government. When our

---

*From *Foreign Relations*, edition of 1918.

ships were sent to Nicaragua in August they were not sent to support any administration, but to protect American lives and property. Chamorro was then still in office and we were doing our best to get him out. Diaz had not been proposed as a candidate by anybody, Nicaraguan or American. Even when Chamorro finally resigned we did not recognize Uriza, to whom he delivered the reins of government, but declined to do so and it was not until every effort had been made to restore the legal *status quo* created by the election of 1924, and a properly reconstituted Congress had in the manner provided by the constitution elected Mr. Diaz as a designate, that we finally extended to him the recognition of our government.

It may be well also to remember here that the American officer who is vested by our American Constitution with the duty of determining which claimant in a foreign government is legitimate is the President of the United States and no other. Neither the Senate nor Congress shares that duty. When the president in good faith has decided, as he did in November, 1926, that a given foreign government is legitimate and is recognized as such by us, so far as our government is concerned the process is ended. His action can no more be officially reviewed on the floor of the Senate than it can in the pages of this book.

The president's decision was not only rendered in good faith but was, in my opinion, perfectly correct according to the facts. Diaz was elected designate by an overwhelming majority of a Congress which had been reconstituted so that its membership was identical with that legally created by the general election of 1924. The action of this Congress therefore could not be rightly claimed to be tainted by the coup d'état of Chamorro, nor could it be rightfully said that Diaz was disqualified in any other way. True, he was a Conservative, but the legally elected Congress was also Conservative in complexion. In former days he had been a political friend of Chamorro, but as I was reliably informed in Nicaragua, he had advised against Chamorro's coup d'état. That he was not a part of a Chamorro conspiracy is further indicated by the fact that the person whom Chamorro had chosen to succeed himself was not Diaz but Uriza, whom we refused to recognize.

When Diaz had peacefully and without violence been thus seated in office and had come into undisputed control, as he did, of the regularly organized government, occupying all the chief cities and practically all the territory of Nicaragua except the wild and uninhabited district where the revolution against Chamorro was still being waged he was evidently both *de jure* and *de facto* the ruler of Nicaragua.

Even if we should attempt to go behind the action of the reconstituted Nicaraguan Congress and interpret for ourselves the Nicaraguan Constitution, instead of following the interpretation which that Congress adopted, we could not produce the result that Sacasa was the lawful president. For if we should disregard Sacasa's absence from the country on the ground that he had been illegally driven away by Chamorro, exactly the same thing had happened to Salorzano, the president. The latter, quite as much as the former, was the victim of Chamorro's violence, and if we were to insist that any absentee should be seated in office regardless of his absence, and regardless of the views of the Nicaraguan Congress, it must necessarily have been Salorzano and not Sacasa. Our recognition of Diaz as the legitimate president was immediately followed by that of Great Britain, France, Germany, Italy and Spain; also by that of the neighboring Central American countries of Salvador, Guatemala and Honduras.

Not until all this had happened did Sacasa appear on the scene. He had personally visited Mexico, seeking material and moral assistance for his cause. On December 1, 1926, two weeks after our recognition of Diaz had been proclaimed to the world, he landed at Puerto Cabezas, a small town on the wild eastern coast of Nicaragua, immediately adjoining the boundary line of Honduras, which thus offered a convenient refuge in case of attack, and surrounded by a small group of followers, proclaimed himself the constitutional President of Nicaragua and the commander in chief of the revolutionary forces. He was then immediately recognized by Mexico as the President of Nicaragua.

Undoubtedly it was the sovereign right of the Republic of Mexico to recognize as President of Nicaragua whomever she chose; but having regard to all the circumstances of the case and the time and manner in which it was done, I think it would be difficult for any friend of Mexico to say that, as between our recognition of Diaz and her recognition of Sacasa, hers was not the more provocative action;

or that it was not the more violative of the spirit of the convention of 1907, of which her government with our own had been a sponsor and promoter.

PROGRESS OF THE REVOLUTION AND LANDING OF AMERICAN MARINES

Arms and munitions were shipped from Mexico to the revolutionists even before Mexico had recognized Sacasa as president. These were carried from Mexico to Nicaragua by four successive vessels, the steamships *Foam, Concon, El Tropical* and *Superior,* the first of these ships proceeding in August and the last in December. On the other hand, our government had, in October, 1926, placed an embargo on the shipment of arms and munitions to all parties in Nicaragua and had requested the other Central American states and Mexico to join in this embargo with a view to minimizing the bloodshed. The four Central American countries agreed to follow our suggestion and to cooperate in the embargo, Mexico declined. As to this, President Coolidge said in his message to Congress on January 10, 1927:

"As a matter of fact, I have the most conclusive evidence that arms and munitions in large quantities have been on several occasions since August, 1926, shipped to the revolutionists in Nicaragua. Boats carrying these munitions have been fitted out in Mexican ports, and some of the munitions bear evidences of having belonged to the Mexican Government. It also appears that the ships were fitted out with the full knowledge of and, in some cases, with the encouragement of Mexican officials, and were in one instance, at least, commanded by a Mexican naval reserve officer."

It was not until after it had thus become abundantly clear that the revolutionists were receiving assistance from Mexico that our government decided to lift its embargo and permit the Nicaraguan Government on its part to purchase arms and munitions. Otherwise we should have been unfairly siding against and hampering the efforts of the very government we had recognized as legitimate defending itself against its assailants.

With the aid of these Mexican arms and munitions, the revolution gained in violence and spread. Soon after he came into office, President Diaz formally notified our government that, owing to this Mexican assistance, it would be impossible for the Nicaraguan Government to protect the lives and interests of American citizens and other foreigners residing in Nicaragua. Shortly afterward the British, Belgian and Italian Governments sent us formal notice to the same effect and requested us to extend our protection to their citizens in Nicaragua.

Finally, in February, 1927, the British Ambassador in Washington notified our secretary of state "that the hostilities between the rebels and government troops have now resulted in a situation which threatens the safety of British lives and property in Corinto, Leon, Managua, Granada and Matagalpa," and after reminding our government that the British Government looked to us for protection to their British subjects, he informed us that they had decided to send a man of war to the west coast of Nicaragua, hoping that the presence of this vessel might have a moral effect on the situation and would be a base of refuge for British subjects.

In response to these requests from our own citizens and the governments of other countries notifying us that foreign lives and property were in danger, and also in response to the warning of the Nicaraguan Government itself that it could not protect such lives and property, our marines were landed in Nicaragua. Discretion as to how this well-known duty of protection should be carried out was properly left to our naval representative on the spot, Admiral Latimer. He performed it in the way by which such protection has commonly been maintained in similar cases—namely, by establishing neutral zones within which there should be no fighting and where consequently such foreigners and their property might be safe. On January 8, a guard of 175 men was placed at Managua for our legation, and marine guards were also placed along the railway which forms the sole route of communication between Managua and the sea.

In taking this step Admiral Latimer proceeded with special care to avoid infringing upon the rights of either of the combatants. Thus, when he arrived at Bluefields in August, 1926, where the early fighting was taking place, finding it necessary to declare a neutral zone there for the protection of American and foreign lives, he obtained the consent of both the warring parties to the arrangement, and this consent was subsequently ratified in writing by both of them on October 26, 1926. The same course was subsequently followed in the establishment of a neutral zone at Corinto.

Criticism has been made that our government deliberately established these zones for the purpose of interfering with the operations of the revolutionists by preventing them from capturing cities which they would otherwise have taken. Such accusations are easily made in the heat of conflict, and it is no doubt often simpler for a military commander to obtain his military objective if he does not have to conform to the usages of international law and spare the lives of neutrals. But that our naval commander had any other purpose than to carry out his plain duty of protection in the establishment of these zones will not be believed by anyone familiar with him or the situation. That he did not side with the Conservatives as against the Liberals is sufficiently indicated by the fact that Sacasa himself was conspicuously benefited by the establishment of the neutral zone at Puerto Cabezas, under the protection of which he remained until the end of the war, issuing therefrom freely his revolutionary edicts and pronunciamientos.

To summarize the situation and its causes as it existed in March, 1927, when I was requested by the president to go to Nicaragua:

A coalition Conservative-Liberal Government having been lawfully established in 1925, our government removed from Managua the legation guard which had been there for fourteen years and endeavored to leave Nicaragua to its own resources for the maintenance of order. Thereupon Chamorro, the defeated Conservative candidate, immediately overthrew the coalition government by violence. Pursuant to the policy of the treaties agreed upon among the Central American states, with our approval and that of Mexico, we refused to recognize this Conservative Government of Chamorro and endeavored to persuade him to withdraw. Chamorro refused and defied us, remaining in office for nearly a year. Revolutions broke out against him which he was able to suppress or defeat so long as his money lasted. Finally, and chiefly through the failure of his finances, he was forced to resign and a legal government was reconstituted under Diaz, which we then recognized. Subsequently Mexico recognized the revolutionary government of Sacasa. On notice not only from our own citizens but from many foreign governments that American and foreign lives and property were in danger, we sent our naval forces to Nicaragua to protect them. This last took place while Chamorro was still in office.

In March, 1927, Diaz, the Conservative president, was in complete possession of the populous western portion of Nicaragua, including the capital, Managua, and the principal cities of Granada, Leon, Chinandega and Corinto. The revolutionists, partly because of the skill of their commander, Moncada, and partly by reason of the arms and munitions and money furnished from Mexico, had captured many of the smaller towns on the Atlantic Seaboard and had made their way through the mountainous interior until they had come in contact with Diaz' main forces in the interior, not far from the town of Matagalpa; fighting had been stubborn and losses extremely heavy.

The long continued disorder and violence had also produced a general disintegration in the social fabric of the country; semi-independent bands of marauders were taking advantage of the situation to plunder even the settled districts. Our minister had reported to Washington that a general condition of anarchy was probably approaching.

Chapter II

The Settlement of 1927

On March 31, 1927, on the suggestion of the State Department, I was requested by President Coolidge to go to Nicaragua as his special representative to investigate for him the situation in that country, to confer with our Minister, Mr. Charles C. Eberhardt, and Admiral Julian L. Latimer, commanding the naval forces there, and to bring back my views for the use of our government. I was expressly given the utmost latitude with reference to observations on the policy theretofore adopted. The State Department not only put me under no restrictions as to comment or criticism, but, on the contrary, invited it. The president's only instructions other than to investigate and report were that if I should find a chance to straighten the matter out he wished I would try to do so. No envoy ever received wider latitude or more loyal support. If errors of judgment were committed, the fault thereof lies at my door.

Although I had been intrusted with somewhat similar missions to Latin America when I was secretary of war, I had never been to Nicaragua, and, as it happened, had never in my public or professional life come in contact with any of its political or business problems. So far as ignorance could free it from prejudices or commitments, my mind was a clean slate.

My party consisted of Mrs. Stimson and myself, with Consul General William Dawson as interpreter. We sailed from New York on April 9 on the Chilean steamship *Aconcagua.* At the Pacific end of the Canal we were met by the United States cruiser *Trenton,* which took us 700 miles north to the Nicaraguan port of Corinto.

One of the controlling features of the Nicaraguan problem is the difficulty and slowness of its communication with the outside world.

Its large cities and main population lie near the Pacific Coast, where its only considerable seaport is that of Corinto. Regular liners are scarce on that coast; there is nothing to compare with the frequent service established by the United Fruit Company on the Caribbean side of the Isthmus, and passengers and mails going to and from Corinto must often wait two or three weeks for a liner or else travel by small freight steamers and tramps. As a consequence, the outside world receives very little direct news from Nicaragua except what comes through the expensive medium of cables and radio.

During the recent revolution the agents of Doctor Sacasa, the revolutionary chief, who maintained their posts near the Atlantic Seaboard not only at Puerto Cabezas in Nicaragua but in Costa Rica, Guatemala, Mexico and the United States, had far easier and cheaper communication with the American press than the Nicaraguan Government, whose mail communications had such a roundabout and slow journey to travel.

I found when I came to conduct my own investigation that this comparative superiority of facility enjoyed by revolutionist propaganda in reaching America had quite seriously warped the accuracy of our American news, inasmuch as most of the political statements which reached the American public came from revolutionary sympathizers, many of whom had not visited Nicaragua for years and consequently had no first-hand knowledge of existing conditions and opinion.

From Corinto the only railroad in the country, a narrow-gauge line, runs 130 miles southeasterly, parallel to the coast, touching the principal cities of Chinandega, Leon, Managua, the capital, and finally Granada on the border of Lake Nicaragua.

At Corinto we were met by Minister Eberhardt and Admiral Latimer and proceeded at once by rail to the capital, a journey of approximately 100 miles. That the country was in the grip of war was apparent even from the car windows. The portion of the land through which we passed was evidently of great fertility. There were long stretches of open farming country interspersed with park-like vistas of beautiful trees, but the fields were uncultivated and little farming was going on. A large portion of the city of Chinandega was in ashes. Almost every man or boy whom one met either in the country or cities was armed. It was a common sight to see a farmer driving his cattle or leading his pack horse with a military rifle strapped across his back, while the butt ends of revolvers and automatics produced telltale creases in the garments of such male Nicaraguans as one met or did business with in town.

The total absence of improved lines of communication in Nicaragua has exercised great influence on its history. Other than the railway, there were literally no roads connecting these important cities except narrow rutted trails over which oxen with difficulty pulled the heavy Nicaraguan carts. In the rainy season most of these become impassable for anything except pack trains. Two improved roads lead out of Managua, the capital, in opposite directions, continue for a few miles and then stop. Motor transportation is impossible anywhere except in the dry season, and then only over a few roads and with great difficulty.

The Atlantic Coast of Nicaragua was distant from us much less than 200 miles as the crow flies, but it takes longer to get there than to go from New York to San Francisco, and the only way of going was by sea through the Panama Canal, unless one was willing to travel on foot through the jungle or to follow down a tropical river in a canoe.

METHOD OF INVESTIGATION

My first effort on arrival was to put myself in touch with all responsible sources of public opinion in order that I might get at the underlying facts of the situation. I first conferred with our American representatives on the ground, Minister Eberhardt and Admiral Latimer, as well as General Logan Feland, who commanded the landed forces. I then immediately called on the president and held conferences with him and the members of his cabinet. I then sought to meet the responsible leaders of public opinion of all parties and factions. I visited Granada, which is the historic centre of the Conservative Party, and held conferences with the leading men of that city. I visited Leon, which is the corresponding centre of the Liberal party, and held conferences with their leaders there. Day after day, for several weeks, I spent my mornings at Managua, receiving calls from such gentlemen as wished to give me their views upon the situation and its possible remedies.

It was comparatively easy to get the responsible views of the Conservatives, who were well organized and in possession of the government. It was more difficult with respect to the Liberals, many of whose leaders were in exile or actually fighting in the revolutionary army. But fortunately many responsible Liberal leaders remained in the country, and as it became clear that I wished to get their views and that they would not be punished or persecuted by the government for visiting me and giving them to me, they came more and more easily and talked with me.

GENERAL RESULTS OF INVESTIGATION

As the result of this work, the following general conclusion gradually became clear in my mind:

First, as to the military situation and conduct of the war: The principal armies of the government and of the revolutionists were confronting each other in the wild, mountainous country near Muy Muy, between fifty and seventy-five miles northeast of Managua. At the time I left New York, cable dispatches had reported important victories by the government forces over the revolutionists. I soon found, however, that these reports had been greatly exaggerated and that, though the government army had apparently forced back its opponents, the latter were not disorganized and soon afterward under their skilled leader, Moncada, they appeared again on the flank of their enemies at Boaco, consideraly nearer to Managua.

Government garrisons occupied all the principal cities and towns in the neighborhood of the railways, and occasionally these garrisons were attacked or threatened by small groups of rebels operating independently. Some of these groups professed to be Liberals acting in coöperation with Moncada; others were mere guerrillas or bandits taking advantage of the war to prey upon the country. One of the former groups, under a leader by the name of Parajon, had attacked the city of Chinandega a couple of months before my arrival, and after bloody and desperate fighting, had been driven off by the government forces. But in the course of the fighting a large portion of the city had been destroyed by fire.

The armies of both sides were largely recruited by conscription among the lower classes of the population. Unfortunate men were hauled from the logging camps on the Atlantic Coast by the Liberals or from their homes in the cities in the west by the Conservatives and forced into the respective armies to fight for causes about which they knew nothing. I myself saw boys of eleven and twelve side by side in the ranks with men old enough to be their grandfathers. Even women were to be found in both armies. But practically all in the rank and file came from the lower strata of the population and were of either Indian or mixed blood.

As a result of this system of conscription, there was a constant stream of desertions from both armies, gradually filling the country with unorganized but armed men who constituted a source of disorder and banditry. Many of them found it much easier to live on the country than to work, and the possession of weapons as well as the disorganization of authority gave them abundant opportunity to do so.

On the other hand, when the armies came into contact they fought bravely and with great bitterness, and the losses in proportion to their numbers were large on both sides. Prisoners were not being taken by either side, and unmistakable evidence came to me that during the Chinandega fighting the wounded were butchered with great brutality.

The conditions of the climate and country where the battles were fought served also to render the fate of the wounded terrible beyond description. Flocks of vultures filled the air ready to pounce upon any victims unable to defend themselves. Except the slightly wounded, very few reached the hospitals that had been established in Managua.

In general, the military situation was one of deadlock. Both armies fought well on the defensive; neither possessed the organization or discipline for effective continuous offensive action. The Conservative forces were the more numerous; the Liberals had, under Moncada, the more skilful leader.

Under these circumstances, it was abundantly clear that a pacification of the country could not be looked for from the efforts of either army, and time was working rapidly toward a disintegration of all authority into a condition of anarchy. This last tendency would have been infinitely more rapid except that the presence of our marines, wherever they were located, indirectly lent assurance to the law-abiding portions of the populations—much as the mere presence of a big policeman tends to stabilize conditions when the air is full of rowdyism.

That the law-abiding and peaceful part of the population was thoroughly weary and sick of war also became clear beyond any peradventure. On this the expressions of the women to my wife, who accompanied me and who met many representative Nicaraguan women, were quite significant. Though they are not invested with suffrage, Nicaraguan women play an important part in their communities, and the women of all parties whom we met, without exception, were against the war. Even close relatives of prominent revolutionary leaders were outspoken in their demand that their kin should not allow legal or constitutional questions to stand in the way of a fair compromise and an early peace.

To enforce this desire for peace, the rainy season was approaching, bringing with it the time for planting the annual crops and also making the movement of armed forces more difficult. Unless the war could be stopped in time for planting the new crop in June, another whole agricultural year would be lost. These factors served to emphasize the importance of an early settlement and also contributed to make it more possible.

Another general feature in the situation which became perfectly clear was that the people of both parties were friendly to the United States, and were looking to us for active assistance to get them out of this deadlock and its distressing consequences. This was a surprise to me. I had expected to find the Conservatives friendly because of the general impression that their political fortunes had, ever since 1912, been favored by the presence of our legation guard of marines in Managua. I had expected to find a corresponding resentment on the part of the Liberals and that perhaps the chief political stock in trade of that party would be anti-Americanism. I had been prepared for this not only by the outgivings of some of the Liberal propagandists in the United States but also by the assertions of American critics of our Nicaraguan policy.

I consequently tested this phenomenon with particular care, trying to make allowances for all misleading factors. As a result, I found the leaders of both parties earnestly seeking our intervention and asserting the paramount interest of the United States in the establishment and maintenance of orderly and responsible government throughout Central America.

These sentiments were expressed to me not only by the moderate Liberals who were living in the country but my men who were in active revolution. They were expressed to me by the Sacasa delegates when I met them later. General Moncada, the head of the revolutionary forces in the field, in former times had put himself on record publicly in support of the right of the United States to intervene in Nicaragua to assist in the establishment of order and liberty.

In the next place, the form of assistance which all parties desired and were agreed upon was that we should supervise the conduct of their coming national election in October, 1928. Under the Nicaraguan Constitution, their president is elected every four years, on the same year as our American president. Their Congress consists of a Senate and House of Deputies; one-third of the Senate and one-half of the house is elected every two years.

The leaders of all parties readily admitted that Nicaragua had never had a really free election; that the government habitually controlled the result and that the habit was so inveterate and ingrained that they could only hope to obtain a fresh fair start through outside assistance in supervising the conduct of their polls. The Liberals, being out of control of the government machinery, were even more emphatic than the Conservatives in demanding that the supervision should be thorough and effective, and that if undertaken by Americans, these should be given sufficient police power to prevent fraud and intimidation on the part of the authorities.

In their recognition of government-controlled elections as the fundamental evil in their system, these Nicaraguan leaders were in agreement with thoughtful students of Central American politics, and that they should thus unite upon this basic problem was in itself an encouraging feature of the situation. On the other hand, the difficulties and dangers of such supervision were manifest. A year previously I had made a personal study of the American attempt to supervise the plebiscite in Tacna-Arica and was thoroughly familiar with the way in which the patient and earnest efforts of General Pershing and General Lassiter to hold a fair election had been thwarted by the fact that the police power over the territory was in the hands of one of the parties, and that the American commissioner had not sufficient authority to maintain order and prevent intimidation. I was determined therefore not to recommend to President Coolidge that he assume any responsibility for such supervision unless at the same time the American representatives who conducted the election were given sufficient power to make good.

In applying the problem of holding a fair election to existing conditions in Nicaragua, certain requirements were clear: There must first be peace and general amnesty. There must be then a complete disarmament, so far as possible, of the entire population, in which at the time every man was going about with his hand metaphorically on his pistol pocket. Finally a new and impartial police force must be created to take the place of the forces which the government was in the habit of using to terrorize and control elections. These forces included both the army and the old local police. The government in Nicaragua is so centralized that it not only controls the national army but its power reaches directly down into every department and municipality and controls the local police.

An effort had been made, two years ago, to establish an impartial national constabulary under the instruction of a retired American officer recommended by our government. The effort had failed, and under the Chamorro régime the constabulary had been debauched and diverted from its nonpartisan status largely because the power of the American officer had been limited to instruction and not command. Under the existing situation it was clear that to render impartial and effective service in protecting the polls such a constabulary must be created, instructed and temporarily commanded by Americans who, being members of our active military forces, had their future record to consider and were above local temptation. This meant practically that it should be so instructed and officered temporarily by men of our Marine Corps. Fortunately several precedents for the success of such a constabulary exist in the Philippines and in Haiti.

These conditions were drastic, but they were demanded by a drastic situation. They pointed out the only road by which a bloody and devastating revolution could be stopped and ballots substituted for bullets in determining whether Conservatives or Liberals should hold the reins of government. Furthermore it was legitimate to hope that if a generally admitted fair election could once be held, it might serve as a guide and pattern toward which the minds of the Nicaraguan people might turn in the future, and that having been shown by Americans that such an election was possible, they would be encouraged in the future to adopt permanently a system of free elections with their own efforts. The saving of a nation from anarchy; the termination of a century-old political vice which had destroyed its attempted democracy; the setting of that nation upon the road to a possible orderly self-government—all seemed to me to be a goal worthy of every possible effort.

Of course, such a plan must be based wholly upon the assumption that the Nicaraguan Government itself would request this assistance and would itself enact the Nicaraguan laws under which Americans, whose names would be suggested by our president, would be appointed by the President of Nicaragua to the various positions of supervision and control.

If those conditions were fulfilled, many international precedents authorized the rendering of such assistance to a sister nation on the part of our chief executive. In fact, an already existing law of our own Congress, under which we have frequently acted in the case of Latin-American nations, authorizes the President of the United States to detail officers of the Army and Navy to assist other nations in their military and naval establishments.

In reaching all these conclusions I had the invaluable help and coöperation of Mr. Eberhardt and Admiral Latimer—as, indeed, was the case throughout my stay in Nicaragua. No step was ever taken or decision reached except after full discussion among us three, and every step taken I think without any exception met the approval of all.

Before taking the steps hereafter narrated, I had, of course, cabled to Washington our views as to the importance of American supervision for the 1928 election as an essential element in obtaining a peaceful settlement and received a cable indicating that the president would be willing, on the request of the Nicaraguan Government and under Nicaraguan law, to recommend a commission for the supervision of this election.

CRYSTALLIZING THE SITUATION

All these matters were fully discussed with President Diaz and members of his cabinet and met with their concurrence. On April 22 President Diaz placed in my hands the following memorandum of peace terms which he was willing should be suggested to the Liberals:

1. Immediate general peace in time for the new crop and delivery of arms simultaneously by both parties to American custody.

2. General amnesty and return of exiles and return of confiscated property.

3. Participation in Diaz's cabinet by representative Liberals.

4. Organization of a Nicaraguan constabulary on a nonpartisan basis commanded by American officers.

5. Supervision of election in 1928 and succeeding years by Americans who will have ample police power to make such supervision effective.

6. Continuance temporarily of a sufficient force of marines to make the foregoing effective.

Liberal leaders in Managua had already communicated with Doctor Sacasa at Puerto Cabezas and suggested that he either come himself to meet me or send delegates for that purpose. I thereupon handed to them a copy of those proposed peace terms, telling them that I felt confident that President Diaz would make a settlement on that basis and that I thought it was a fair and generous proposition. At the same time I told them that it was postulated upon Mr. Diaz remaining in office until the completion of his present term in 1928, and this fact, together with the peace terms, was then cabled to Doctor Sacasa by the Managua Liberals.

REASONS WHY IT WAS DEEMED NECESSARY FOR DIAZ TO COMPLETE HIS UNEXPIRED TERM

Mr. Diaz himself, in one of his conferences with me, expressed his own readiness to retire voluntarily, if such retirement were essential to a peace settlement. The result of my investigations, however, convinced me that only through his remaining in office was an immediate peace settlement possible. Under the Nicaraguan Constitution he was ineligible to be a candidate in the election in 1928 to succeed himself. The situation in his case, therefore, could not be complicated by personal ambitions.

He was so convinced of the necessity of American supervision for that election that in order to make it entirely fair he was ready to surrender all the traditional power of the presidency which had been heretofore used to influence and control election results. He was willing to disband the army; he was willing to take the necessary executive and financial steps to establish an impartial constabulary and to appoint as the officers thereof Americans recommended by our president. He was ready to advocate legislation—and in Nicaragua presidential advocacy of legislation usually means the enactment thereof—to provide for boards of election with American chairmen who should preside over the ballot boxes and command the services of the constabulary to prevent disorder and intimidation. In other words, in order to secure a fair election, he was ready to withhold the traditional powers of his office and make himself a virtual figurehead in respect to election control.

All these matters had been fully discussed with him, and his intelligent approval and coöperation were assured. His record in international relations with us showed that his word could be relied upon. We could be sure of these essential conditions in no other way than through Diaz remaining in office.

Suggestion has been made that the proper course to have followed would be to have both Mr. Diaz and Doctor Sacasa retire in favor of some neutral substitute. That suggestion is based upon complete ignorance of Nicaraguan conditions. No such neutral existed or could possibly exist in Nicaragua. For days I sat listening to suggestions of substitutes for Diaz and found behind every candidate suggested an ulterior expectation of partisanship. Neutrality might be achieved by the appointment of an American or other foreigner as chief executive—or, in other words, by the establishment of what would amount to a foreign receivership of the government—and some critics have not hesitated to suggest that course. But obviously it would have both violated the Nicaraguan Constitution and transgressed the executive powers of the American president to appoint such a man.

Our peace settlement must necessarily be carried out under the Nicaraguan Constitution, and to obtain any substitute for Diaz under that constitution would have involved fatal delay and created immediately new political controversies even worse than those which had arisen over the legitimacy of the Diaz presidency.

Under the Nicaraguan Constitution, any successor to Diaz must be elected by the Congress. The legally reconstituted Congress which had elected Diaz in November, 1926, had expired by limitation of term in December, 1926; and owing to the revolution, congressional elections had not been held in several of the most important Liberal districts during the year 1926. The surviving membership of the old Congress, where terms of office had held over, was therefore necessarily strongly Conservative in political complexion. To attempt to elect a successor to Diaz by that rump Congress would inevitably bring violent and just objections from the very Liberals who opposed Diaz. To hold new elections to fill the vacancies was impossible until there should be peace.

Therefore, in any attempt to change, we would have been held powerless in the grip of inexorable conditions. In the meanwhile, with every day that passed, anarchy crept nearer. At any moment a crisis might arise under which our marines might be drawn into a clash with one side or the other and the situation immeasurably complicated.

It seemed to me clear, therefore, that the only way out was to follow the straight and simple course of driving at the main object of securing a fresh and fair start in 1928 and not to try to play politics in the meanwhile.

This was all the more clear in that the retention of Diaz did not really constitute a source of danger of oppression to the Liberals. In conversation with me, Liberal leaders freely admitted his magnanimity to his political opponents. This characteristic went to an extent which in the eyes of his own party constituted his conspicuous political weakness. Liberal leaders told me over and over again that Diaz was the Conservative most acceptable to their party.

But they had been fighting him; the Diaz issue had become a political slogan. Their honor, they said, prevented them from voluntarily signing any settlement which retained him even temporarily. The climax of their argument was reached when an earnest Liberal, who had been quite zealous and useful in attempts at a compromise, suggested seriously that if Mr. Diaz would only change his name the whole difficulty would be solved!

CONFERENCE WITH SACASA DELEGATES

On April 27 I received word that Doctor Sacasa, though declining to come himself, had appointed Doctor Rudolpho Espinosa, Doctor Leonardo Arguello and Doctor Manuel Cordero Reyes as his delegates and that they were on their way from Puerto Cabezas on the American destroyer *Preston*. Espinosa was Sacasa's foreign minister and chief adviser, Arguello was a well-known Liberal leader, and Reyes was Sacasa's private secretary. The *Preston* made a record-breaking trip of less than three days round through the Panama Canal, and the delegates were landed at Corinto and reached Managua late in the evening of April 29.

During the two following days Mr. Eberhardt and I were in conference with these delegates. The atmosphere of the conference was friendly and cordial. I outlined my views as to the situation and the suggested peace terms. They expressed general concurrence in my diagnosis of the evil of government-controlled elections and in the proposition for a supervised election in 1928 as the remedy.

They vigorously disclaimed any anti-American feeling on the part of Liberals or any hostile understanding with Mexico. They asserted that their party recognized that the United States had a legitimate zone of interest and influence extending as far south as Panama and that they considered this fact natural and beneficial in its results to Nicaragua. But they were absolutely silent as to the single point of President Diaz's unexpired term, and at the close of two days I came to the reluctant conclusion that they would not or could not expressly agree to that indispensable condition. The fact, however, that they had come to confer with me with full notice as to my own position on that point, as well as their cordial attitude on all other questions, rather inclined me to the belief that Sacasa's opposition to this one point might, in the last extremity, prove to be only formal.

At the close of the second conference they told me they thought we had progressed as far as we could without conferring with the Liberal commander in the field, General Moncada, and asked me if I could put them in communication with him. I welcomed this as an opportunity for a conference with Moncada myself, and told them so; and that if they desired it, I would try to get into communication with him; and that if he was willing to confer between the lines of the contending forces, I would go myself with them and after their conference with him would be glad to talk with him myself.

Accordingly they wrote a letter to Moncada, asking either for a conference or that he would send a representative to meet them. Admiral Latimer selected three American officers to take this message through the lines to Moncada, and I reënforced it by sending also a copy of the Diaz peace terms which we were discussing and an urgent invitation that General Moncada should come himself and meet us all personally.

CONFERENCE WITH GENERAL MONCADA

Major Humphreys, Lieutenant Commander Moran and Lieutenant Frisbie, who carried these messages to Moncada, had a difficult and dangerous mission. Passing through the lines of Central American armies in actual combat is not without hazard, but they succeeded in reaching Moncada's hitherto unknown headquarters, delivered their message and persuaded the general to return with them to the conference. A forty-eight hour truce between the contending armies was arranged for that purpose. On the afternoon of May 3d I received a message that he would meet me at Tipitapa early the following morning. Tipitapa is a small village on the river connecting Lake Managua with Lake Nicaragua and constituted at that time one of the outposts of the Conservative forces, although their main army lay somewhat farther to the northwest near Tuestepe. Accordingly, early the next morning, with the Sacasa delegates and with Latimer and Eberhardt, I drove out to Tipitapa.

I felt that much depended upon this conference. Moncada represented the vital force of the revolution and for many months he and his army had been in the mountains and virtually out of communication with the world, including even his nominal chief, Sacasa. For many years he had been an outstanding figure in Nicaragua both as a soldier and as a man of letters. Though a Liberal, he had not hesitated to oppose the Liberal tyrant Zelaya in 1909. He had been a friend to United States influence in Central America, and now, as a man of fifty-six, he had won the respect of all military observers by conducting this difficult campaign at the head of his troops through the jungles and mountains that separated his present position from his point of departure on the Atlantic Coast. I also felt that having personally shared the sufferings and losses caused by the revolution, he might be less technical in approving a substantially just compromise than the civilian leaders of his party. I was not disappointed.

When in the early morning of May 4 we drove into Tipitapa, Moncada and the three American officers met us there. They were a bit weary from a difficult journey down from the mountains which had lasted until late into the night, but the general was at once ready for business. I turned over to him the three Sacasa delegates and told him that I should be glad to have a conference with him myself after he had finished with them. In about fifteen minutes he came out of the little inn where they had conferred and was ready to meet me.

He and I sat down under a large blackthorn tree near the dry river bed. He spoke English with unusual simplicity and directness, so no interpreter was needed. In less than thirty minutes we understood each other and had settled the matter. He had read the peace terms and fully approved them—all except for unexpired term of Diaz, which he said he could not in honor ask his army to accept, as it had been fighting against Diaz all winter. But though he might out-manœuvre and sometimes beat Diaz's armies, he frankly admitted that neither he nor any Nicaraguan could, without the help of the United States, end the war or pacify the country; so that the situation would necessarily grow worse each month. If I would assure him that we insisted on Diaz as a necessary condition to our supervision of the election, he would not fight the United States. He said he did not wish a single life to be lost on that issue between us. If I would give him a letter to that effect, he would use it to persuade his army to lay down its arms.

In short, the gist of the situation was that while he felt he could not, in view of past history, voluntarily make such a settlement, if our government was ready to accept the invitation of the Nicaraguan Government to supervise the election of 1928 and insisted on Diaz finishing out his term as a condition of that acceptance, he would yield to that decision and do his best to persuade his army to do so.

According to his request, I then and there called in my secretary and dictated the following letter, which was given to him:

TIPITAPA, May 4, 1927.

GENERAL JOSÉ MARIA MONCADA,
    TIPITAPA

Dear General Moncada: Confirming our conversation of this morning, I have the honor to inform you that I am authorized to say that the President of the United States intends to accept the request of the Nicaraguan Government to supervise the election of 1928; that the retention of President Diaz during the remainder of his term is regarded as essential to that plan and will be insisted upon; that a general disarmament of the country is also regarded as necessary for the proper and successful conduct of such election; and that the forces of the United States will be authorized to accept the custody of the arms of those willing to lay them down, including the government, and to disarm forcibly those who will not do so.

Very respectfully,

HENRY L. STIMSON.

I included the last sentence not as a threat to Moncada's organized and loyal troops, who, I was confident, would follow their leader's direction, but as a needed warning to the bandit fringe who were watching for any sign that we were not in earnest in order to indulge their taste for pillage once the government troops had laid down their arms and there remained no force in the country other than the Americans able to restrain them.

On Moncada's suggestion, the Sacasa delegates were called in and told of my decision. After a few moments' consultation, they told me that Sacasa would not resist the action of the United States. Moncada soon afterward returned to his army and in a few days informed me by message that he had been invested with full authority to conclude our negotiations.

In the meanwhile, without waiting for this message, President Diaz had taken certain steps which greatly aided the successful termination of the settlement. On May 5 he proclaimed an immediate general amnesty and permitted all his political enemies to return freely to the country. He proclaimed the freedom of the press and gave to Moncada express permission to issue through the press a general proclamation to the Liberals. He gave public notice that the membership of the supreme court, which had been illegally disrupted by his predecessor, General Chamorro, would be restored to its original status. He agreed to appoint Liberal *jefes politicos,* or governors, at the heads of the six Liberal provinces of the country in place of the Conservatives who then occupied those positions. Subsequently he appointed several of Moncada's former generals to those positions.

On May 11 we met Moncada again at Tipitapa. He asked me for assurances on several points that had been raised by his army and I then dictated and gave him the following letter:

TIPITAPA, NICARAGUA
May 11, 1927.

GENERAL JOSÉ MARIA MONCADA,
　　TIPITAPA.

Dear General Moncada: I am glad to learn of the authority that has been placed in you by your army to arrange for a general disarmament. I am also glad to make clear to you and to your army the attitude of the President of the United States as to this matter. In seeking to terminate this war, President Coolidge is actuated only by a desire to benefit the people of Nicaragua and to secure for them a free, fair and impartial election. He believes that only by such free and fair elections can permanent peace be secured for Nicaragua. To insure this in 1928 he has consented to the request that American representatives selected by him shall supervise the election. He has also consented to assign American officers to train and command a nonpartisan national constabulary for Nicaragua which will have the duty of securing such a fair election and of preventing any fraud or intimidation of voters. He is willing also to leave in Nicaragua until after the election a sufficient force of marines to support the work of the constabulary and insure peace and freedom at the election.

As further evidence of the good faith of the American Government and of the present Nicaraguan Government in this matter, I am glad to tell you what has already been done. It will answer the questions contained in the letter of your soldiers which you have shown me. General amnesty has already been granted by the President of Nicaragua. I have recommended to President Diaz that the Supreme Court be reconstituted by the elimination of the illegal judges placed in that court under Sr. Chamorro. President Diaz has already called upon those judges for their resignations and I believe that those resignations will be obtained. I have already advised that the Congress be reconstituted by the holding of special elections in those Liberal districts where elections were not held in 1926, under conditions which will insure that the Liberal voters will be amply protected in their rights. I have also recommended that members of Congress illegally expelled by Sr. Chamorro, whose terms have not yet expired, be reinstated. I have been assured that this will be done.

I have recommended that Liberal *jefes politicos* be appointed in the six Liberal districts of Bluefields, Jinotega, Nueva Segovia, Esteli, Chinandega and León. I have been assured that this will be done.

In short, I have recommended that steps be taken so far as possible to restore the political condition as it existed in Nicaragua before the Chamorro *coup d'état* and I believe that so far as possible it will be done.

I hope that these steps will assure you and your army of the fairness of the United States Government and its desire to see peace, justice and freedom reëstablished in Nicaragua without any unfairness or favoritism toward any party, but being regardful of the rights of Liberals and Conservatives alike.

　　　　　　　　　　　　　Very respectfully yours,
　　　　　　　　　　　　　HENRY L. STIMSON.

He assured me that this letter would be fully satisfactory to his army and then himself formally dictated the following statement:

> The Liberals cannot believe that the United States Government, through the personal representative of President Coolidge, will give a promise which it will not fulfill.
>
> Once again the Liberals place their confidence in the United States. The leaders of the army will try to convince their men that this promise of fair elections will be fulfilled. The central point which the army wishes to be assured of is that the United States will do its best to give Nicaragua a fair election in 1928.

He then returned to his army and on the following day I received a telegram signed by him and by all his chieftains except Sandino formally agreeing to lay down their arms and asking that American forces be immediately sent to receive them and "guarantee order, liberty and property." This was done. The Diaz government had agreed to pay the soldiers of both sides ten dollars for every rifle or machine gun turned in and in this way solved the question of back pay or pensions for both sides. Within a week more than 9000 rifles, 296 machine guns and nearly 6,000,000 rounds of ammunition were turned in to the United States marines from both Conservative and Liberal forces.

The semi-independent bands of guerrillas, including the aggressive force of Cabulla, which had been operating in the neighborhood of the city of Chinandega, followed Moncada's example and turned in their arms. The only exception was Sandino, one of Moncada's lieutenants, who, as Moncada told me, having promised to join in the settlement, afterward broke his word and with about 150 followers, most of whom he said were Honduranean mercenaries, had secretly left his army and started northward toward the Honduras border. I was told that Sandino had lived in Mexico for twenty-two years, where he served under Pancho Villa, and only came back to Nicaragua on the outbreak of the revolution in order to enjoy the opportunities for violence and pillage which it offered.

A force of marines and of the new constabulary constituted under the peace settlement were subsequently sent out after Sandino into the wild country of the north. On July 16 Sandino's force, augmented by other lawless individuals who had drifted in the interval to him, attacked a much smaller group of marines and constabulary at Ocotal, near the Honduras border, and were repulsed with severe losses. Later cable dispatches from our minister indicate that Sandino's following has now practically dispersed.

In contrast with the sensational statements of some of our own press, the following public statement issued by General Moncada after the affair at Ocotal fairly describes the Sandino incident:

> Existing on money from both natives and foreigners and merchants at Jinotega, as he had done before under threats of pillage and bloody reprisal, he—Sandino—interned in the mountains, took foreigners in the army and dedicated his time to murdering his enemies, both Conservatives and Liberals. He proved extremely cruel to prisoners, to whom life was never pardoned. I will not approve such a kind of war. I will never accept it. . . .
>
> In order to defend the cities of Jinotega, Esteli and Ocotal, the American command sent marines and soldiers of the Nicaraguan National Guard. Eighty-seven men of these mixed forces existed at Ocotal when it was attacked by Sandino and an overwhelming force. Sandino threw himself against them with all his army. The defenders resisted heroically for sixteen hours. . . .
>
> Sandino suffered great losses, exceeding 400 men. This, of course, has not been murder. There was an armed conflict in a legitimate defense. We Liberals are greatly sorry for the death of our brothers, but it is our duty to deny all contact with mercenaries, censuring such a war lacking in ideals. In Nicaragua the Liberals greatly desire peace and are confident of the word of the President of the United States given to us through his personal representative, Mr. Stimson. All the other Liberal chiefs except Sandino complied with their duty.

The final announcement of our settlement met with general demonstrations of joy and satisfaction in Nicaragua. Of course, a few extreme politicians on each side were displeased. Some Conservative leaders thought Diaz altogether too generous; some Sacasa extremists thought Moncada a traitor. But there was no mistaking the general feeling of the people. There was an immediate rush of the peasants in both armies to get back to their farms in order to be in time to plant the new crop.

In Managua, when Moncada entered the city, after his troops had laid down their arms, there was a popular demonstration of Liberals as to a victorious general and the Conservatives good-naturedly stood aside and permitted the festival. There were also general manifestations of gratitude to the United States. Far from being the victim of any hostile demonstration, I received marked expressions of their goodwill from both sides.

The University of Granada, a hotbed of conservatism, conferred an honorary degree upon me, while on the same day, by invitation, I addressed the assembled chiefs of the Liberal army. These generals, side by side with their former bitter enemies, the Diaz cabinet, were at the railroad station to bid our party farewell when we left Managua on May 16.

Coupled with these incidents were many little evidences of friendly good-will from both sides, which only a warm-hearted Latin-American people know how to give. As we sailed away there remained with me as an earnest of the hopeful future of Nicaragua the memory of two patriotic men, one a Conservative and one a Liberal, each willing to sacrifice personal ambition and party interest to the higher welfare of his country and each willing to trust in the honor and good-will of the United States—Adolfo Diaz and José Maria Moncada.

Chapter III

Landmarks of Our Policy in Future

In preceding chapters I have attempted to describe the development of our American relations to the Republic of Nicaragua, leading up to and culminating in the settlement which was negotiated last May. Under that settlement the devastating war between the Nicaraguan Government and the revolting Liberals was terminated, and as a part of the settlement our president undertook to assist in the supervision of the coming election in 1928 in order that the question of which party should control the government thereafter should be decided by peaceful instead of warlike methods. In assuming this responsibility toward our sister nation, President Coolidge was actuated by the hope not only that peace would be reëstablished in Nicaragua but that a permanent constructive step was being taken which would assist that country in maintaining in the future an orderly and independent government.

His action has already been criticised in some quarters as an encroachment upon the sovereignty of Nicaragua and an act of selfish imperialism on our part. For myself, I believe that his action follows well-known principles of law and amity recognized among nations, and not only will not impair the independence of Nicaragua but will conduce toward placing it upon an assured foundation. If I am right in this respect it is important that the situation should be recognized and understood among our own people as well as among our Latin-American neighbors. This problem has the peculiar difficulty of all problems in international relations. In such problems, with mutual confidence, everything can be accomplished; without mutual confidence, nothing. Therefore the common interest of all concerned depends upon establishing a condition of mutual understanding coupled with good-will and confidence. This is especially important where, as here, the differences between us and our Latin-American neighbors in language, racial temperament, habits and customs so easily make for misunderstanding.

Let me therefore try to outline certain general landmarks which seem to me to be clear and to govern what has been done in the past as well as to guide what is to be done in the future.

I

In the first place, it is perfectly clear that our relations with Nicaragua, as with all Latin-American nations, must proceed on the strict assumption of their continued existence as independent nations and with scrupulous regard for that independence. We recognized them all as independent nations more than a century ago, and in the language of President Monroe, we took that step "on great consideration and on just principles acknowledged." More than that, we then and there served notice on the rest of the world that these nations were to remain independent and were thenceforth "not to be considered as subjects for future colonization by any European powers."

The Monroe Doctrine, far from being the assertion of any rights on our part over these American neighbors, was a solemn assertion of a duty on our part toward them. It conferred on us no claim to suzerainty over them. It placed us under an obligation toward them to respect their independence, and it double-tied that obligation by its notice to Europe that we regarded Latin-American independence as so important to us that we were ready to fight for it. Therefore those who speak of our establishing a protectorate over any of these American nations would impute to us a readiness to violate a national obligation taken in the most formal and deliberate manner.

A century has now passed since this announcement was made and this attitude assumed—a century of independent existence on the part of these nations, with its struggles, sacrifices and sacred traditions. They have become deeply proud of their national existence and would be keenly resentful of any suggestion of a threat to deprive them of it.

II

On the other hand, it is only proper that our Latin-American neighbors, in approaching this question, should keep in mind our long and honorable fulfillment of this obligation. For a century we have been the scrupulous protector of their independence, not only against Europe but sometimes even against themselves. This last is particularly true in respect to the republics of Central America. On more than one occasion has one or the other of them come to us with proposals for annexation or for a cession to us of portions of their territory and we have declined the offer.

The first of these offers came in 1822, when the Emperor of Mexico, Iturbide, was trying forcibly to annex the five Central American republics to Mexico. The Congress of Salvador, on December 2 of that year, passed a formal resolution for annexation to the United States and sent a commissioner to Washington to urge favorable action thereon. During the past fifty years Guatemala, Costa Rica and Honduras have all sought to cede or sell to us coaling stations, naval bases or wireless stations on their coasts or islands.

The number of occasions when we have stood between the independence of Latin-American nations and danger from Europe or from each other makes a catalogue so long that only a few typical instances can be repeated here. In the early years of their independence our influence was constantly used to intercede with Spain in order that that country should finally recognize the independence of her former colonies. In 1865 it was the threat of our power which obtained the withdrawal of French imperialism from Mexico and resulted in the downfall of the Emperor Maximilian. It was our friendly influence which resulted in 1859 in treaties providing for the return by Great Britain of the Belize territory to Guatemala, the Bay Islands to Honduras and the Mosquito Coast, including Greytown, to Nicaragua. In 1895 it was the pressure of our government which secured the submission to arbitration of the boundary dispute between Great Britain and Venezuela and which in 1902 and 1903 procured the successful solution by arbitration of disputes between Venezuela, Germany, Italy and Great Britain.

If during all this century we had been guilty of imperialistic designs upon these smaller countries, our surest means of gratifying those designs would have been to promote and foster such disagreements and quarrels as now and then broke out between them and thus avail ourselves of the chance to fish in troubled waters. Instead of that, our influence has uniformly been used for peace. For more than forty years our State Department has been seeking to solve the long-standing dispute between Chile and Peru over the possession of the province of Tacna-Arica arising out of the war between those countries in 1879—a dispute which has frequently threatened the peace of South America.

A quite common form of disagreement between American nations has been a dispute over a doubtful boundary line. At the present moment the friendly efforts of the United States are being exerted to secure the settlement of such a boundary question in no less than five cases—between Peru, Colombia and Brazil; between Haiti and the Dominican Republic; between Panama and Costa Rica; between Nicaragua and Honduras; and between Honduras and Guatemala. Better evidence of our constantly pacific policy could hardly be offered.

Nor have our efforts been confined to cases of disagreement or quarrel. Our government, particularly during late years, often has been asked and has granted its assistance in matters requiring expert advice—matters of sanitation, finance, economic development or military instruction. Examples of such cases are General Gorgas' visit to Guayaquil, Ecuador, for yellow-fever prevention; the mission of another health specialist to Chile; of a police expert to Panama; of experts on financial administration to Colombia, Peru and several other countries; military or naval missions of instruction to Brazil and Peru. Our Government Schools of Agriculture and our Military Academy at West Point are open for instruction to their young men.

Quite apart from this governmental work, the Rockefeller Foundation, during the past few years, has spent more than $1,000,000 in Central America alone, in teaching the people of those five republics the laws of sanitation and how to combat hookworm, malaria and other tropical diseases. On my recent stay in Managua, the capital of Nicaragua, I was able to drink pure water because the Rockefeller Foundation had thus assisted in the establishment of a proper water supply for that city.

It is, I think, a fair statement that since our recognition of the independence of these nations, and particularly in later years, as modern improvements in steam communication have brought the countries of the world closer and closer together, our American influence, both public and private, has been uniformly and intelligently used to help them in the better performance of all those activities and responsibilities upon which the maintenance of independence and of world peace so largely depend.

III

In this connection it is interesting to note that the two matters which have been principally seized upon by our critics in Latin America as evidencing a contrary and imperialistic policy on our part took place three-quarters of a century ago and largely under an influence which no longer exists in the United States. Our alleged spoliation of Mexican territory at the time of the Mexican War and the popular encouragement given in this country to the filibustering expedition of William Walker to Nicaragua eight years later have been the two incidents most commonly used by hostile critics to offset the long and honorable record to which I have referred.

Both these took place at a time when negro slavery was a real and dominating power in the United States, seeking to acquire new territory under the Southern sun for the furtherance of its peculiar interest; and it was among the adherents of that slave power that the Mexican War and the Walker Expedition received their most ardent support.

Not only has negro slavery long since been washed out in the blood of a great Civil War but there has taken place much more recently an almost equally great change of public sentiment in the United States militating against any policy of imperialism. I refer to the change of public sentiment toward American self-government which has been recently embodied in our new immigration laws. Our former loose optimism has disappeared. We recognize now more adequately the real difficulties of popular government and the danger to that institution of trying to blend into our nation a too rapid influx of citizens having political experiences and traditions entirely different from our own.

This radical change of popular feeling shown as to immigration sets itself equally against the incorporation into our nation of new territory already occupied by men and women of different language and political habits. The United States has ceased to be an absorbing power.

IV

Our real attitude toward the sovereignty of Latin-American nations is most convincingly and adequately shown by the principles and rules of order which have governed the successive Pan-American Conferences as well as the Pan-American Union. These two great institutions were founded upon our initiative nearly forty years ago. To go into the details of the beneficent work which they have been accomplishing ever since would be impossible within my present limitations. But for the purposes of this book it is sufficient to remind the reader that in the conduct of these conferences the principle of the legal equality of the participating states, from the greatest to the smallest, is recognized to the fullest extent, and action is taken only by unanimous consent. This absolutely precludes the idea or use of force. No majority of states can conclude a minority even of the smallest and weakest. This is in striking contrast to the Concert of Europe, where only the great powers were admitted on a basis of equality; as well as to the constitution of the League of Nations, where the Council is similarly controlled by the great powers.

Through these Pan-American instrumentalities our country and its neighbors, for nearly half a century, have been working toward a Pan-Americanism based upon the legal equality of independent nations and having for its ideals certain common conceptions of political action. Their effort has been thus described by an eloquent Peruvian, Señor Francisco Garcia Calderon:

"Though the North American is Protestant and the Ibero-American is Catholic; though they speak different languages and respond to a different logic, yet they derive from like lands, from a uniform system of government, from a growth free from secular traditions, from the absence of rigid castes, from a community of generous principles, such as arbitration and the love of peace, and from general enterprises of utility, an active Pan-Americanism, theory and militant reality, practical crusade and romantic apostleship."

V

While the foregoing résumé indicates the principles and methods which have governed our attitude toward the sovereignty and independence of Latin-American nations in general, there are certain geographical considerations which impose upon us a very special interest as to how certain ones of these nations fulfill the responsibilities which go with sovereignty and independence. I refer to those Central American nations whose territory lies adjacent to and in a naval sense commands the great sea route from our Eastern to our Western states via the Caribbean Sea and the Panama Canal.

This situation does not arise out of the Monroe Doctrine but from certain broad principles of self-defense which govern the policy of the United States, as well as of all other nations which are in any way dependent upon the sea. These principles in part underlie the Monroe Doctrine, although they were not at all created by it. They bear a very much closer and more tangible relation to what I may call, for want of a better name, our Isthmian policy than they do to the Monroe Doctrine itself.

The most peculiar characteristic of the Western Hemisphere is the narrow isthmus which connects the two continents of North and South America. Human hands have found it possible to create in the Panama Canal a narrow passage for seagoing vessels. In so doing they have created a vital artery for both the commerce and the naval defense of the United States.

Long before the Panama Canal was built our statesmen recognized the vital and revolutionary part which it would play in our foreign relations. The same geographical feature which made its construction possible by human hands now renders its destruction possible by the same means. And its destruction in time of war or by hostile hands after our commerce and civilization have become adapted to it and dependent on it would be a grave and possibly fatal source of danger to the United States.

The same result would be produced by hostile occupation of territory commanding the seagoing approaches to the Canal which converge from both our coasts. Consequently for more than half a century and ever since construction of the Canal became an imminent event, it has become a cardinal part of our national policy that such a canal across the Isthmus must be entirely under the control and defense of the United States. This principle was clearly stated by

President Hayes in a message to Congress on March 8, 1880, when he said:

> The policy of this country is a canal under American control. An interoceanic canal across the American Isthmus will essentially change the geographical relations between the Atlantic and Pacific Coasts of the United States and the rest of the world. It will be a great ocean thoroughfare between our Atlantic and Pacific shores and virtually a part of the coast line of the United States. Our merely commercial interest is greater than that of all other countries, while its relations to our power and prosperity as a nation, to our means of defense, our united peace and safety, are matters of paramount concern to the people of the United States. No other great power would, under similar circumstances, fail to assert a rightful control over a work so closely and vitally affecting its interest and welfare.

As President Hayes thus pointed out, our policy toward this great sea route through the Canal does not rest upon any attitude of mind which is peculiar to us; it is simply the application of principles and policy which would govern any other nation in a similar situation. Thus Great Britain has a somewhat similar interest in the sea route to her possessions in India and Australia through the Straits of Gibraltar, and we now know from recently published documents that in 1911, when Germany threatened a possible encroachment upon Morocco near that sea route at Agadir, Great Britain was ready to fight Germany in order to prevent such a peril. The sea route to India is no more vital to Great Britain than the sea route through Panama is to us.

VI

Out of this principle of national self-preservation follows the corollary of our interest in the stability of the independent governments resting along the borders of the Caribbean and the Eastern Pacific. If those independent governments do not adequately fulfill the responsibility of independence; if they fail to safeguard foreign life within their borders; if they repudiate lawful debts to foreign creditors; if they permit the confiscation within their borders of lawful foreign property—then, under the common usages of international life, the foreign nations whose citizens and property are thus endangered are likely to intervene in Central America for the legitimate protection of such rights. History clearly shows that such intervention often leads to continuing control.

The failure therefore of one of these republics to maintain the responsibilities which go with independence may lead directly to a situation imperilling the vital interest of the United States in its sea-going route through the Panama Canal. Out of this situation has followed our national policy—perhaps the most sensitive and generally held policy that we have—which for half a century has caused us to look with apprehension upon even the perfectly legitimate efforts of European nations to protect their rights within this zone.

The Monroe Doctrine, as stated by its author, was aimed only against the extension of European government to this hemisphere in the shape of efforts at colonization; no such attempt might be involved in an effort by a foreign power to protect the lives or property of its citizens in Central America; yet American national policy has properly recognized the danger, and American opinion has been sensitive to any such attempt when it takes place in this peculiar isthmian zone.

This vital policy has underlain the successive efforts of our government to protect the Caribbean Sea from such encroachment, both by securing our own naval protection of it and by forestalling causes for foreign intervention. Establishment of our naval base at Guantánamo is an instance of one of the former steps. The provisions of the Platt Amendment restricting Cuba from incurring foreign debts beyond her ability to pay; the treaty with San Domingo assisting that republic to refund her foreign debt in 1906 at a time when Germany was threatening intervention; the treaty with Haiti for the purpose of assisting in the establishment of order in that sorely vexed republic—all are instances of the latter class of precautionary steps.

VII

The natural result arising from such a situation is that if we will not permit European nations to protect their customary rights within this zone, we must, to a certain extent, make ourselves responsible for this protection. To a certain extent, at least, we must assume the attitude of seeing that American countries within this zone fulfill their obligations as independent nations to the outside world.

This Isthmian policy is often confused with the Monroe Doctrine, which had its origin in part in a somewhat similar national interest of the United States against encroachment of European nations in this hemisphere, and this resulting obligation devolving upon us is sometimes spoken of as a corollary of the Monroe Doctrine.

President Roosevelt well stated the entire situation, including its resulting obligation, in his Chautauqua speech on the subject in 1905:

> We cannot permanently adhere to the Monroe Doctrine unless we succeed in making it evident, in the first place, that we do not intend to treat it in any shape or way as an excuse for aggrandizement on our part at the expense of the republics to the south of us; second, that we do not intend to permit it to be used by any of these republics as a shield to protect that republic from the consequences of its own misdeeds against foreign nations; third, that in as much as by this doctrine we prevent other nations from interfering on this side of the water, we shall ourselves in good faith try to help those of our sister republics which need such help upward toward peace and order.

These sentences contain the gist of the situation. They also show the true character of this duty which we have assumed. It is in no way an encroachment upon the independence of the Central American countries. On the contrary, it contains a recognition of and an assurance of that independence. For the efforts of the United States, when invoked in such a situation, are aimed solely at assisting those nations adequately to perform the duties of independence which they have assumed and which we have recognized.

VIII

Nicaragua is also related to this Isthmian policy of the United States in a peculiar way not common to its four Central American sisters. It contains within its boundaries the transisthmian route, which, by common consent is, next to the Panama route, most feasible for an interoceanic canal. Sooner or later, though not within the lives of this generation or possibly the next, a second canal will be constructed through the isthmus by that route, and this canal when completed will necessarily command the same dominating strategic relation to the safety of the United States as the present one at Panama.

By the Bryan-Chamorro Treaty, ratified in 1916, Nicaragua granted to the United States the permanent and exclusive right to construct such a canal. Any lodgment of a possibly hostile foreign influence upon the territory of Nicaragua would therefore in a double sense be perilous to the safety of the United States.

IX

The general principles which stand out from the foregoing analysis of our relations to Latin America are as follows:

Whatever steps we take in Central America must not be in derogation of the rights of those republics as independent nations. A long unbroken course on the part of our government toward them, however, indicates that there is no danger of such dishonorable repudiation of our recognition of their independence 100 years ago, but that, on the contrary, during that century we have been assisting them in every possible way to guard and protect their independence.

The national safety of our own country has, however, imposed upon us a peculiar interest in guarding from foreign influence the vital sea route through the Caribbean Sea and the Panama Canal, and therefore in seeing to it that no cause for foreign intervention may arise along the borders of that route. To protect this interest we are excluding foreign nations from exercising even well-recognized rights of redress against Central American and Caribbean republics whose territory commands that route, and in consequence we have incurred an obligation to see that these foreign nations are protected against injury arising from the failure of those American republics in the exercise of their responsible duties as independent nations. This obligation can be performed without infringement of the indpendence of these American republics. In fact, its purpose is to assist and develop that independence, and it should be performed in that way and with that purpose.

X

In the light of this analysis and of these principles, I believe that the history of our recent action in Nicaragua, as I have set it forth in my preceding articles, makes it clear that in no way have we transgressed upon the sovereignty and independence of the government of our sister nation. Every step which we have taken has been upon the earnest request of the Nicaraguan Government. More than that, the principal step which we propose to take—namely, to assist in the supervision of the national election of 1928—is one which we have been formally requested to take not only by the government itself but by the opposition party to that government. General Moncada, who was formerly the commander-in-chief of the revolutionary forces and is now the duly elected political chief of the Liberal Party, has joined in the request of the government that we should so assist in this election, and his action has, I believe, the concurrence of the entire present directorate of that party in Nicaragua.

I believe therefore it is entirely accurate to say that our presence in Nicaragua today is for the purpose of taking an action which we have been requested to take by the government and which has the cordial concurrence of the opposition party in Nicaragua. Such an entire concurrence in any political object is a rare event in a Central American country.

In the next place, the purpose of our action, far from being in derogation of the rights and interests of Nicaragua as a sovereign and independent state, is to promote that independence and sovereignty in the most effective way. We are to assist her to hold for the first time in her history as a republic a free and fair election of her president. She has asked us to do this; her statesmen have freely admitted the prevalence of the ancient evil of government-controlled elections which has destroyed her democracy, and they have asked our president to assist them in eradicating this evil and starting them afresh upon the road of order and of peace. Can anyone say that this great constructive step is an impairment of her sovereignty?

XI

Our promise thus to help Nicaragua has been made in the highest spirit of fellowship and coöperation. The difficulties and dangers that will surround the attempt are perfectly evident. We shall be made the target of the criticism of those who are unsuccessful at the election, but we have decided that the chance of rendering such needed assistance is worth the risk. The promise is a sacred one and will be carried out in that spirit. President Coolidge, in nominating General Frank R. McCoy for the position of chairman of the National Board of Elections which is to be created by the Nicaraguan Government, has given the best possible pledge of this purpose. No better-qualified person for such a task, by virtue of long experience in Cuba, Central America and the Philippines and an honorable record in the fulfillment of difficult tasks, could be found in the United States.

It is to be hoped that the election will not only accomplish the immediate result of determining which of the two great Nicaraguan parties shall control the government for the next four years, but will serve also as a guide and precedent for the future. It is perhaps too much to hope that a single free election will at once terminate evil political habits accumulated through a century, but it can at least serve as a demonstration of what is possible and a pattern for future accomplishment. Furthermore, it can serve to bring into closer mutual confidence our own representatives and those of Nicaragua.

The events of the past three months, since the settlement was agreed upon, thus far indicate the promise of such an outcome. The banditry and violence which at the time of my visit in May we feared would for many months be an inevitable sequel of the war have quieted down and disappeared with surprising rapidity. The new nonpartisan constabulary is developing efficiency with admirable speed and winning high praise from its American instructors. The illegally disrupted supreme court has been reconstituted to its former legal membership; President Diaz, in a spirit of marked magnanimity, has voluntarily turned over to his Liberal opponents the governorships of the six Liberal provinces, and thus far the spirit which has been maintained after such a bitter war is a remarkable earnest of hope for the future.

XII

This book has been immediately concerned with the political aspect of the Nicaraguan problem. My mission was primarily concerned with that aspect. But it would be shortsighted to close without calling to the attention of the reader the fact that no solution of these political problems which I have discussed can be complete or final without an attempt at the same time to help Nicaragua to solve the economic problems which underlie them.

Nicaragua to-day is an almost wholly undeveloped country. She not only has no transsisthmian railroads or roads of any kind but even the highways in the more populated portion of the country are rudimentary. Much of the acrimony and bitterness which have stained her politics is accentuated by this fact—by the inability of one community easily to communicate with another.

Her industries and manufacturies are undeveloped; her artisan population is scanty; there is almost no middle class between the cultivated leaders of politics and the ignorant peons or peasants; though she is preëminently an agricultural country, even her agricultural methods are primitive and obsolete. For improvement in all these vital directions she has no capital. Moreover, the havoc and destruction wrought during the recent war have resulted in claims against her government for compensation to those damaged amounting to many millions of dollars. Her treasury has no funds for the payment of these claims, a large part of which are due to small farmers and other Nicaraguans whose property has been taken during the war, and many of whom are thus left destitute.

The intelligent leaders in Nicaragua, both on the side of the government and in the opposition party, recognize these evils and urged upon me the necessity of our help in terminating them. They know that no permanent political reform can be accomplished without the solution also of this problem. They realize that Nicaragua today lacks one of the principal foundations for a democratic government in that she has no well-developed middle class of artisans and workers from whose influence and out of whose problems come the usual activities of democracy.

Such a middle class cannot come into existence until the industries of the country are developed. These industries cannot be developed without capital, and capital can be obtained only by foreign loans coupled with a reform of their fiscal system, including particularly their system of taxation.

The present financial methods of the Nicaraguan Government are inefficient and corrupt. For nearly fifteen years the collection of her customs has been supervised by an American collector of customs under an agreement made between her government and the representatives of the holders of her foreign debt, and this work has been so efficiently carried out as to bring out in glaring contrast the shortcomings which have marked the collection of her other revenues.

In short, not only has she no capital for needed improvements but she cannot raise the money necessary to pay the interest on loans borrowed for such capital, by taxation under her present methods. As one Nicaraguan put it to me: "Our system of internal taxation has been simple—when the Conservatives are in power the Liberals pay the taxes; when the Liberals are in power the Conservatives pay them." Another, a member of the high commission, told me that he believed an honest and effective system of assessment and collection of these internal taxes would increase the internal revenues of the country by 50 per cent.

Much of this situation is evident at a glance to any visitor to the country. Nicaragua is in the same need to-day, both of inside fiscal reform and of outside capital to develop her resources, that we were after our American Revolution, when we borrowed so freely from Europe and when our credit was saved by the fiscal reforms of Alexander Hamilton. The only obstacle to satisfying this obvious need is the fear of unfounded and reckless criticism.

The only thing that stands in the way of Nicaragua procuring on fair and proper terms the money universally recognized as necessary, as well as the help to reform her fiscal methods which she also requires, is the fear on the part of those who must help carry out such a program that the cry will be raised in this country that our government is going into "dollar diplomacy" and that we are exploiting a helpless republic.

When I came to investigate it I found that this was precisely what had happened seventeen years ago, when our State Department attempted to help Nicaragua after her revolution of 1909 and 1901, when she was in an even worse condition than now. I found that then the State Department, in order to help Nicaragua to get her money on the most favorable terms and to keep her out of the hands of less scrupulous bankers, had persuaded two of the foremost banking firms of America to undertake the rehabilitation of her finances. Although the result of their work has been highly successful; although the depreciated currency was brought to par; although the war claims were cut down from over $13,000,000 to less than $2,000,000; although the principal of her foreign debts was largely paid off and the interest rate thereon reduced to 5 per cent and a surplus produced which enabled the Nicaraguan Government to buy from the foreign stockholders the country's only railroad—yet the criticism and outcry excited among politicians were such that after a few years one of these banking firms withdrew from all further participation in Nicarguan affairs and respectable bankers now hesitate to lend their assistance.

This is not the way intelligently to help a friendly small republic which is in financial difficulty. No one asks that our government should be free from criticism in its foreign relations. But our government has a right to ask that the criticism leveled against it by its own citizens in respect to those foreign relations shall be responsible and based upon a reasonable amount of investigation of the facts. That has not been the case in the past in respect to the criticism leveled at our Nicaraguan policy.

After a careful and practically uninterrupted study of that policy for the past five months, I feel that not only have we no cause to be ashamed of that page in our history but that it contains the record of a long, patient and intelligent effort on the part of this country to do an unselfish service to a weak and sorely beset Central American state. Such an effort ought to have the widespread commendation of our people. It should be helped to its consummation by their approval and not hampered by their disapproval.

Sixteen years ago, when Secretary of State Knox had first announced his policy of assisting Nicaragua in the maintenance of republican institutions by assisting in the reform of her fiscal system, General Moncada, the present leader of the Liberal Party, thus announced his approval:

> It is to be hoped that the spirit of the Knox note may be raised to the dignity of a principle of government, like the Monroe Doctrine, and that it may be proclaimed frankly in the face of the entire world. There are no reasons for concealing this tendency of American politics, as no power can object to the reign of order and liberty.

A year later, when Mr. Knox visited Nicaragua, Mr. Diaz, then and now the leader of the Conservatives and now president of the country, in welcoming Mr. Knox said:

> As an admirer of that policy [of the Knox note] by reason of its evident results in other fortunate Latin countries, I live in the firm intention of accepting that friendly influence so long as I myself have any influence in the destinies of my country. . . . We are weak and we need your strong help for the regeneration of our debilitated land. The hand which your Government generously and fraternally extends to us, I accept without reserve or fear, for I know that it belongs to a

people which has made a religion of liberty, and, educated in and for freedom, loves its independence above everything and respects the independence of others.

A policy of helpfulness, which was thus accepted by Nicaragua in the same spirit in which it was offered by our government, should not be poisoned and rendered of no effect by ignorant or partisan attacks in the United States.

Afterword by
Paul H. Boeker

The Painful Aftermath

As he sailed home from Nicaragua in May 1927, Stimson had, as he saw it, ample reason to be satisfied that he had straightened out Nicaragua, and thereby assured that the U.S. Marines could be brought home for good. The Marines just had to stay through October 1928 to supervise the country's first fair elections and to train the Nicaraguan officers to replace themselves in the new nonpartisan constabulary. And, of course, the Marines had to disarm Augusto Sandino's "outlaws." The leadership of both the Liberal and Conservative parties were satisfied with the accords mediated by Stimson.

"The civil war in Nicaragua is now definitely ended. . . . Among the Nicaraguans themselves bloodshed has substantially ceased," Stimson announced to the *New York Times* two days before his departure from Managua. (*New York Times,* May 17, 1927). And on his return to New York, Stimson asserted with only slightly less confidence: "This situation is now practically entirely ended" (*New York Times,* May 23, 1927). In the book version of his account of the mission to Nicaragua, which Scribners published in the fall of 1927, Stimson concluded boldly that "Under that [May 1927] settlement the devastating war between the Nicaraguan Government and the revolting Liberals was terminated (p. 38)."

But the repeatedly heralded end did not come. The Marines found themselves in continual combat with the faction of "the revolting Liberals" led by Sandino, who not only refused to be disarmed, but kept attacking the Marines at every opportunity. In July 1927 Sandino's forces, which Moncada in May told Stimson numbered perhaps 150 mercenaries and outlaws, suffered over 400 casualties, according to Moncada, in battle with the Marines at Ocotal. Despite these casualties, Sandino's forces grew, although they soon switched to guerrilla tactics from the large-force, head-on tactics that were so costly at Ocotal.

Stimson persisted in his view that Sandino was an "outlaw" and "bandit," "engaged in murder and pillage" against both Liberals and the Conservative Government. Sandino, of course, was brutal and in an armed struggle for power which shunned the electoral route. But his stridently anti-U.S. and anti-occupation stance attracted a substantial group of persistent fighters.

By July, when press reports of the battle of Ocotal highlighted significantly the increased bloodshed on both sides, U.S. domestic reaction to Stimson's diplomatic triumph was turning distinctively sour. Latin American opinion was also focusing not on Stimson's peace-making, but the continued occupation of Nicaragua by U.S. Marines. Among the more pointed criticism of Stimson and his diplomacy was the *New York Times,* which on July 20, 1927, ran the following editorial on Stimson's work, headed "Bad Luck in Nicaragua."

Napoleon did not like Marshals who were "unlucky," and President Coolidge might well have a distaste for those who have advised him for the past eight months in his Nicaraguan policy. President Green of the Federation of Labor spoke of it in Washington as "unhappy." It has been so almost from the first. Plans have miscarried and expectations have been frustrated. After Colonel Stimson made his trip to Nicaragua and succeeded in getting both political factions to suspend hostilities until after the next Presidential election in Nicaragua, which was to be supervised by agents of the United States Government, it was hoped and believed that things would quiet down. The only role assumed by our Government forces in Nicaragua was that of a policeman. But events this week show that the lot of an international policeman on foreign soil is distinctly not a happy one. When it comes to actual warfare, in which there are casualties in our marines, and a reported great slaughter among the Nicaraguans who attacked them, it seems as if ill luck were malignantly pursuing the whole venture.

The unfortunate affair is not greatly relieved by Secretary Kellogg's letter to the President of the American Federation of Labor. One of the unlucky aspects of the whole business is that the Pan-American Federation of Labor was meeting in Washington at the very time when these bloody occurrences were reported in Nicaragua. Violent speeches were naturally made by some of the Latin-American delegates, and a resolution of protest was to be drafted and sent to the

State Department. To Mr. Green Secretary Kellogg wrote that the affray had no political significance whatever; that the so-called General leading the Nicaraguans in an attack upon American marines is no better than a bandit chief, and his followers are "in effect nothing more than common outlaws." These epithets are applied apparently only because General Sandino and his men follow the customary practice of guerrillas in Latin America by looting as they go and living off the country. The same might be said of some of the leaders of armed forces in China. But they are not for that reason declared by our Government to be beyond the pale of the law.

Of course, we have assumed no such police power and police duties in China as we have in Nicaragua. It may well be that, considering the position which our Government had taken in Nicaragua, the fatal clash at Ocotal could not have been avoided. But it arouses fear lest further sanguinary encounters of the kind follow from time to time. If they do, they would come near completing the unlucky record.

The unluckiest thing of all is undoubtedly the bad impression, even if it is distorted away from the facts, which will be created in all Central and South America. Exactly the kind of thing has happened which Republicans charged upon President Wilson in 1920. In that year, Warren G. Harding in the course of his successful campaign for the Presidency made the following pledge in regard to his foreign policy:

Nor will I misuse the power of the Executive to cover with a veil of secrecy repeated acts of unwarrantable interference in domestic affairs of the little republics of the Western Hemisphere such as in the past few years have not only made enemies of those who should be our friends, but have rightfully discredited our country as their trusted neighbor.

This undoubtedly squinted at Mexico. It did not refer to Haiti or Santo Domingo or the previous occupation of Nicaragua by American marines, since that would have been to cast reproach upon acts by Republican Presidents. Nevertheless, Mr. Harding had a just sense of the danger of meddling in other nations, and the ill-feeling which our course in Nicaragua has so manifestly aroused among the republics to the south of us comes as if in fulfillment of his unconscious prophecy.

For almost a year after February 1928, Stimson was relieved from parrying continual public and congressional criticism of the U.S. role in Nicaragua by his appointment by Coolidge as Governor General in the Philippines. During this year the heady elements of Stimson's grand design to straighten out Nicaragua seemed to be haltingly falling into place despite Sandino's rebellion. The election of October 1928 took place on schedule, with U.S. military officers overseeing the voting. The winner was the Liberal José Moncada, who had signed Stimson's Peace of Tipitapa on behalf of the Liberal forces, and whose confidence in an electoral solution was thereby vindicated. After the elections the Marines continued to train the nonpartisan constabulary, in Stimson's terms, which was supposed to eventually allow the Americans to return home.

But in early 1929 Stimson returned to Washington, and the front line for public criticism, as Herbert Hoover's Secretary of State. From the outset of his tenure Stimson was embarrassed by the continuing civil conflict in Nicaragua and the continued presence of the U.S. Marines. The Congress grew increasingly hostile to the Marines' role in Nicaragua and pressed the new Administration to withdraw them. By 1931 the Congress was sufficiently upset with the Marines' war on Sandino to demand their immediate and complete withdrawal.

Hoover himself had clearly adopted a more conciliatory and less interventionist attitude than Coolidge toward Latin America. Hoover particularly wanted to bury the so-called Roosevelt corollary to the Monroe Doctrine. It fell to Hoover's Secretary of State, Stimson, to issue in 1930 a new policy memorandum on Latin America which specifically said that the Monroe Doctrine was not a basis for intervention in Latin American affairs to assure peace and stability. This must have been an uncomfortable step, given that Stimson's own book three years earlier cited Roosevelt's corollary as the justification for U.S. intervention in Nicaragua.

Stimson's response in Nicaragua to Hoover's policy was to promise withdrawal of the Marines in time, while continually narrowing their mission to protecting U.S. lives and training the constabulary, now called the National Guard, to take over. He basically wanted to preserve what he could of his 1927 peace, which he still, and to the end of his life, considered a good piece of work. In 1929 Stimson announced his intention to bring the Marines back, but they were not finally withdrawn until January 1933, in one of Stimson's last acts as Secretary of State.

Over the course of his four years as Secretary of State, Stimson tried to narrow the Marines' area of responsibility and to withdraw them from exposure to raids by Sandino's forces. He announced that U.S. citizens, rather than presuming protection of the Marines throughout Nicaragua, should leave the country or go to coastal towns where the Navy could protect them or, if necessary, evacuate them. In response to continuing congressional criticism and continuing Sandino attacks against U.S. citizens and property, Stimson in 1931 said: "The United States cannot undertake general protection of American citizens throughout that country with American forces. [To do so] would lead to difficulties and commitments which this government does not propose to undertake (Current, *Secretary Stimson,* p. 57).

This shrinking concept on Stimson's part of the U.S. role in Nicaragua was no doubt dictated by both Hoover's policy and congressional and public disillusionment with the absence of an end point for U.S. involvement and U.S. casualties. By 1933 over 100 U.S. Marines and over 4,000 Nicaraguans had been killed in the U.S. effort to pacify the country and put down Sandino's opposition to U.S. occupation and his challenge to the reconciliation and electoral process brokered by Stimson. Stimson was no doubt sobered and disappointed himself by the continuing strife in the Central American nation. By 1932 he was certainly willing to settle for less than straightening out Nicaragua and eliminating the Sandino challenge to the reconciliation of 1927 and the electoral politics he had relied upon to make it permanent. In particular, by withdrawing the Marines from Nicaragua in January 1933, with Sandino still in the field, Stimson clearly wanted to draw a line under the Nicaragua intervention. That line would leave Franklin D. Roosevelt free to form his policies toward the hemisphere without the Nicaragua entanglement and the Nicaraguans to find their own resolution of their persistent political rivalries.

That resolution was not long delayed, but it was not a stable one. As the Marines left in January 1933, Anastasio Somoza, with U.S. support, became commander of the National Guard, which Stimson had five years earlier foreseen as an apolitical, professional constabulary. Within a year Somoza had completed the job of turning the Guard into a thoroughly corrupted and brutal instrument for political domination by himself and his faction. In February 1934, Somoza's guardsmen assassinated Sandino, who had in February 1933 signed a truce with President Juan Sacasa, elected in a second and last U.S.-supervised election in 1932. With Sandino gone, Somoza's National Guard quickly wiped out the remnants of Sandino's forces and followers, then living in a semi-autonomous region that was supposed to be protected under the truce. Over the remainder of the Sacasa's term, power increasingly concentrated in Somoza's hands. Near the end of Sacasa's term in 1936, Somoza edged aside this last

legitimately elected president, rigged his own election and inaugurated himself as Nicaragua's dictator on January 1, 1937, launching a
dynasty of Somoza dictators that would last 42 years, with a few
front men occasionally and briefly in charge.

Why did Stimson fail to foresee this unhappy result? Stimson, first
of all, saw too much in the brokered election of 1928. The election
was a tactical solution to the rivalry between Moncada and Díaz and
their factions. But it did not establish electoral politics as the mechanism for resolving political competition in Nicaragua. This strategic
objective was not in sight because there was no consensus among the
political pretenders in that country to contain their rivalry within
electoral politics. Nicaragua remained a ring for personalized political rivalry, with no agreed limits on the means to be used in seeking
power or suppressing opponents after achieving it.

In this political arena, there was no chance that the new National
Guard, under Somoza or someone else, could remain a neutral force,
that the most powerful institution in the country could stay effectively above the partisan struggle, as Stimson's vision of an apolitical
constabulary envisaged. Stimson was wrong in his judgment of
Somoza, whom, like Diaz and Moncada, he saw in a much too kindly
light. But it would be wrong to see Somoza as Stimson's chosen
leader and solution for Nicaragua, although he endorsed his role as
leader of the National Guard.

Stimson's earnest, if ill-fated, effort was to institutionalize a process of fair elections that would themselves absorb all the rivalries
and tensions fueling Nicaragua's long political warfare. Somoza's
dictatorship repressed those tensions for a protracted period, but did
not resolve them. The rivals in another era, who looked to a sani-
tized vision of Augusto Sandino as their mentor, were thus left with
violence once more as the only means to pursue their claims. Stimson would not have been surprised by the violent end of the Somoza
dynasty, with the Sandinistas' victory in July 1979. His own 1927
brief on Nicaragua's violent past left a picture of where a regime such
as Somoza's was headed:

> Out of these conditions it was easy for a system of dictatorships to
> develop, and instead of the people choosing their ruler by free elec-
> tion, it soon became the universal rule for the president and his
> associates to dictate the result of the national elections . . . no Nic-

araguan election has ever produced a result which was contrary to the wishes of the man or party which was in control of the government.

Under such conditions the only way left to these people to dispossess from the government a man or a party which was in control of it, was by force. In default of a violent revolt of the part of the people against their government, that government remained indefinitely in power. . . . The situation produced a vicious cycle. The people, having been driven to violence in order to relieve themselves from the oppression of a dictator, have never cultivated the habit of peacefully abiding by the result of an election. . . . On the other hand, the revolutionary habit, once acquired, easily becomes habitual and inveterate, and the evils of continual revolution inevitably tend to concentrate into the hands of the government more and more arbitrary power (pp. 4–5).

After his Nicaragua mission and his service as Hoover's Secretary of State, Stimson went on to become a major architect of the U.S. role after World War II, both by virtue of his own service as Franklin Roosevelt's and Harry Truman's Secretary of War, and by virtue of his influence on the generation of foreign policy planners who provided the key figures in the White House and the Department of State after his death in 1950. Stimson represents a strong strain of U.S. foreign policy that is still very much alive in the 1990s. Some of the key notes of that strain were apparent in Stimson's first big diplomatic task in Nicaragua, for which he fortunately documented both his efforts and his reasoning so clinically in this small book.

The clearest keynote is strong nationalism, with an imperious edge. It was manifest to Henry Stimson that: the United States was more important than any place else and that clear conclusions should flow from that for others within our orbit as well as for the U.S. To Stimson the United States was naturally the dominant protecting power in this hemisphere. Latin America had to respect this role, and the U.S. had to play it.

In the last chapter of this book Stimson asserts a clear and sweeping U.S. sphere of influence in the Caribbean and Central America that would justify repeated military intervention in the region. "National preservation," he proclaims, determines "our interest in the stability of the independent governments resting along the borders of the Caribbean and the Eastern Pacific" (p. 45). His attitude to the independent republics in this zone of U.S. influence is unabashedly patronizing. "The failure therefore of one of these republics to maintain the responsibilities which go with independence may lead directly to a situation imperiling the vital interest of the United States in its sea-going route through the Panama Canal" (p. 46).

This expansion of allegedly vital U.S. interests to include the stability of little republics anywhere along the sea routes to the Canal did not die with Stimson. Versions of this concept provided a justification for U.S. military intervention in the Dominican Republic in 1968, in Grenada in 1984 and in Panama in 1989. Only with the establishment of democratically elected governments in all the region save Cuba, have the heirs of Stimson asked themselves whether the increased legitimacy deriving from democratic government takes away the justification for U.S. intervention.

U.S. policy in the 1980s continued to be troubled with the inherent dilemma in using force to establish democracy. Foreign intervention and promotion of democracy do not mix well still. As the U.S. found in Panama, intervention can remove a ruler, but it creates few incentives for the emergence of self-reliant, political institutions, democratic or otherwise. Stimson himself did not seem to pay much attention to the debilitating effect of continued foreign intervention on the capacity of domestic actors and institutions in Nicaragua to find solutions to their own problems, or on the capacity of the U.S. to advocate peaceful resolution of disputes and democracy as a mechanism for pursuing this happy result internally. He was uncomfortably aware by 1931 that U.S. Marines in Nicaragua presented an awkward precedent when it came to condemning Japanese intervention in China in the name of re-doing *that* country's politics. But deterring "aggression," unprovoked and unwanted intervention, was the precedent he wanted to protect, and to his dying day the U.S. 1927 intervention in Nicaragua was different.

Ironically, the United States has in South America more consistently pursued an indirect and institutional approach to promoting democracy, without the ready resort to intervention that has long characterized U.S. policy in Central America and the Caribbean. In South America U.S. advocacy of human rights and international pressure for fair elections has been effective both in terms of playing a modest, but constructive, role in South America's turn to democracy and in maintaining popular support for such an indirect role, based on moral suasion, for the U.S. Crucial to this approach has been the highroad advocacy of human rights, initiated by Jimmy

Carter but since quite firmly institutionalized in U.S. policy, as it is in the role of the UN and the Organization of American States.

This more subtle U.S. approach has obviously been only an ancillary factor in the impressive tide of democracy in South America, but it is one that has been widely credited with constructive impact by South America's own leadership and one that has contributed to warmer relations between the U.S. and Latin America. The broadly shared judgment of Latin America's leadership on this constructive role of U.S. policy since the late 1970s is reflected in the collection of interviews published in *Lost Illusions: Latin America's Struggle for Democracy, As Recounted by Its Leaders.* One has to conclude that in the delicate task of encouraging democracy in other lands subtlety works. And it will now work better than intervention in Central America and the Caribbean as well.

On the broader stage of U.S. policy, Henry Stimson was the forerunner of those advocating a strongly nationalist and assertive U.S. foreign policy that did not shy away from the threat and use of force. His bold personal threat of force at Tipitapa, to disarm the "revolting liberals" if they did not turn in their arms, was Stimson's approach to enforcing stability in a nasty world. He believed strongly, as he said in *American Policy in Nicaragua,* that "the mere presence of a big policeman tends to stabilize conditions when the air is full of rowdyism" (p. 22). And the presence of a big policeman is, of course, the threat of the use of force.

Where the mere presence of policemen and the threat of force were not adequate, Stimson was comfortable with the use of U.S. power to punish the aggressor. He was a vocal advocate of U.S. entry in the Second World War before Pearl Harbor. He was not comfortable with the constraint on U.S. action implied by collective peacekeeping through the United Nations, or, earlier, the League of Nations. The U.S. should be free to act when it needed to act. "We are forced to act in the world as it is, not in the world as we wish it were, or as we would like it to become." (Current, *Secretary Stimson,* p. 250).

In the 1990–91 crisis in the Persian Gulf, Stimson would be on the

---

Lost Illusions: Latin America's Struggle for Democracy, As Recounted by Its Leaders, by Paul H. Boeker, Markus Wiener Publishing, Inc., New York, 1990.

side of those convinced the U.S. needs to maintain the ability to decide upon and use military force on its own. He would probably be impatient with those seeking to constrain U.S. military and diplomatic options within a United Nations effort to enforce a collective judgment against the aggressor. On the global level and in Latin America, the disciples of Henry Stimson are thus still in the discussion of U.S. policy—arguing that U.S. interests extend to far corners of the globe, and that we need to enforce stability here and there. They are, however, rather forgetful of the endless complications that arose from the last effort to straighten out that other rowdy corner on our own.

Henry L. Stimson in Nicaragua

The Historical Context and Political Significance of his Mission

ANDRES PEREZ

There is a passage in the novel *One Hundred Years of Solitude* by Gabriel Garcia Marquez in which the patriarch Jose Arcadio Buendia decides that from now on it shall always be Monday.

"If a Latin American Rip Van Winkle had gone to sleep, say, in 1928, and woke up, he would have this extraordinary sense of deja vu: it is always Monday in relations between the United States and Latin America.

Where are we? Why is the president of the United States denouncing Mexico—I'm sorry, Nicaragua as the source of Bolshevik subversion in Central America?

Why is Honduras occupied by United States Marines? Why are warships in Caribbean waters demonstrating that diplomacy comes from the mouth of a cannon?

Who has decided all this?

Rip Van Winkle would answer: President Calvin Coolidge. This is 1928. This is Monday, so it must be Nicaragua."

Carlos Fuentes
Latin America: At War with the Past

C arlos Fuentes' assertion that "it is always Monday in relations between the United States and Latin America" is substantiated by the striking similarities that exist between the views expressed in Henry L. Stimson's *American Policy in Nicaragua,* first published in 1927, and the assumptions that have guided the US foreign policy in Nicaragua in the 1980s and 1990s. The image of the United States as the legitimate enforcer of democracy in Central America, the belief that the American technology of democracy can be transplanted to Central American countries regardless of their history and socioeconomic reality, and a shallow understanding of the phenomenon of democracy *per se,* are omnipresent features of the rationale underlying the United States' relations with Nicaragua throughout most of this century.

Stimson's account of American foreign policy in Nicaragua in the 1920s cannot be treated simply as an historical curiosity. *American Policy in Nicaragua* is a lucid political expression of the philosophy of pragmatism that has shaped American thinking about Latin American issues in general, and about Nicaraguan political problems in particular during this century.[1]

Pragmatism was essentially an American invention facilitated by the emergence of the United States as a world power at the turn of the century.[2] It rationalized, justified, and reenforced the image of the United States as sitting "on top of the world."[3] Americans took the future for granted, and transformed the promise of American life into a secular faith to which all humanity was to be subjected.[4]

Pragmatism disregards history and the historical limitations to human will. Lewis Coser points out that pragmatism "does not insist upon antecedent phenomena but upon consequent phenomena; not upon the precedents but upon the possibilities of action."[5] Historical factors are not considered relevant to the pragmatic mind so much as the human will to shape the future according to preconceived designs.

Stimson was a pragmatist[6] who in 1927 believed that his lack of historical knowledge of Nicaraguan politics was not an impediment to his mission to investigate and, if possible, "to straighten" Nicaragua's problems.[7] He candidly acknowledged his ignorance and even presented it as an asset:

> Although I had been intrusted with somewhat similar missions to Latin America when I was secretary of war, I have never been to Nicaragua, and as it happened, had never in my public or professional life come in contact with any of its political or business problems. So far as ignorance could free it from prejudice or commitments, my mind was a clean slate.[8]

More than half a century later, President Ronald Reagan instructed former US Secretary of State, Henry A. Kissinger, to identify "what would be appropriate elements of a 'long-term United States policy that will best respond to the challenges of social, economic, and democratic development in the [Central American] region, and to internal and external threats to its security and stability.' "[9] Kissinger, like Stimson before him, had no serious understanding of the history of Central America. Moreover, he displayed an absolute contempt for Latin America's political history and had dismissed as irrelevant everything that happened south of the United States. The man whom President Reagan entrusted with the task of formulating the principles of a new American foreign policy in Central America pointed out to Gabriel Valdes, the Foreign Minister of Chile, in 1969 that politics in Latin America had no historical importance:

> Nothing important can come from the South. History has never produced in the South. The axis of history starts in Moscow, goes to Bonn, crosses over to Washington, and then goes to Tokyo. What happens in the South is of no importance.[10]

Besides its ahistorical orientation pragmatism is also characterized by its rejection of "truth" as an idea that can serve as an universal point of reference for political action. Pragmatism turned truth into a "social achievement."[11] Truth, according to the proponents of pragmatism, is made "by events."[12] It follows that those who have the capacity to shape events also have the power to create truth and thus, define what is right and what is wrong. Throughout the present century US economic and military power has often decided what is true and false, what is right and wrong, and what constitutes a legitimate government and what does not, in Nicaragua. For example, Secretary of State Philander C. Knox decided in 1909 that the armed movement launched by the Conservatives against the Liberal government of Jose Santos Zelaya represented "the ideals and the will of a majority of the Nicaraguan people more faithfully than does the Governmment of President Zelaya. . . ."[13] President Reagan continued the American tradition of determining Nicaraguan politics when he decided seventy five years later that the anti-Sandinista Contras were both the legitimate representatives of the Nicaraguan people, and "the moral equivalent of our [the American] Founding Fathers and the brave men and women of the French Resistance."[14]

Finally, pragmatism assesses the value of knowledge according to its instrumental and practical value. Dwight Waldo points out, that "impatience with the 'abstract' or 'theoretical' . . . characterize the pragmatic temper."[15] Stimson, Ronald Reagan, and Elliott Abrams were all pragmatists *par excellence*. They viewed democracy simply as a technological device that could be exported to, and implemented in Nicaragua in the same way fertlizers could be manufactured in the U.S. and used on Nicaragua banana plantations. Stimson, for example, suffered from no ambiguity when he asserted that "the central cause of the breakdown of popular government in these [Central American] countries lay in the failure in their hands of the system of popular elections."[16]

Long after Stimson, Washington has continued to see elections as the solution to the problems of social polarization and war in Central America. In so doing, American governments have chosen to ignore the lessons of their own political tradition, which shows that democracy in Europe and the United States is not only a formal mechanism for conflict resolution but also the expression of a social consensus in regard to the political organization of society. Thus, elections in liberal democratic societies are democratic "not because they . . . [are] *about* democracy, but because they . . . [are] *within* democracy."[17] A democratic consensus reflecting the balance of power within a country has to be established before the electoral technology of democracy can be functional.

To sum up, pragmatism has provided US governments with the rationale within which American foreign policy in Nicaragua has been formulated and implemented during most of this century. Convinced of their moral superiority and of the power of their political technology, American governments, in their self-declared role of international guardians of democracy, have ignored both the lessons of history in Nicaragua and the lessons of their own history. There is no doubt that, when it comes to Nicaragua, American government's historical amnesia has had an effect equal to or even more negative than that of selfishness and blatant self-interest.

The purpose of this article is twofold: first, to place Stimson's mission to Nicaragua in its historical context, and second, to offer an interpretation of the effects of American interventions on Nicaragua's political development. An historical analysis of Washington's role in Nicaraguan domestic politics shows that, but curtailing Nicaragua's sovereignty, the United States has severely reduced Nicaraguans' possibilities of achieving a durable political consensus based on the domestic balance of power within the country.

DEMOCRACY AND SOVEREIGNTY

Assessments of Nicaragua's prospect for democracy often ignore the particular conditions that have made possible the emergence of democratic practices and values in the liberal democratic countries of the world. Consequently, they fail to identify those particular aspects of Nicaragua's political development that might explain both the absence of a democratic tradition and the obstacles to democracy in Nicaragua.[18]

In the historical tradition of liberal democratic societies, democracy is both a set of formal procedures for the resolution of political conflict (elections being of paramount importance), and the expression of a social consensus with regard to the scope and form of legitimate political struggle and dissent.[19] These two dimensions of democracy are intimately linked because the effectiveness of democracy as a formal mechanism for conflict resolution depends to a large extent on the existence of a minimum social consensus regarding the rules that govern political competition. This consensus may be facilitated by the existence of a homogeneous political culture.[20] The more heterogeneous a society's values concerning the most desirable and best possible form of political organization and government, the more difficult the institutionalization of democratic political rules will be.[21]

Historically, consensus regarding the rules that govern political competition has been the outcomes of processes of institutionalization of the political order. These processes are guided, although not necessarily determined, by the elites that control the main institutions of society.[22] In long historical processes of negotiation, competition, and compromise, these elites manage to impose upon the rest of society a view of political reality that functions as a "collective will."[23] The process of institutionalizing a political order, then, refers to the continuous production and reproduction of a socially acceptable political reality.[24] This process involves the definition of the basic problems of human existence, the elucidation of possible answers to these problems, and the organization of institutional and symbolic structures for their solution.[25]

The process of institutionalization of the political order that gave rise to the political structures of those societies we identify today as liberal democratic had as a point of departure the establishment of sovereignty at the nation-state level. It is no accident that the development and consolidation of the theory and the practice of national sovereignty during the seventeenth and eighteen centuries was closely associated with the development and consolidation of democratic theory.[26] Modern democratic theories, as noted by Reinhold Niebuhr, "almost without exemption assume the autonomy of the national state."[27] F. H. Hinsley corroborates this view when he explains that,

> the rise of legislatures, the introduction of representation, the extension of suffrages and the insertion of constitutional features into the basis, the composition and the procedures of government—necessitated the notion that sovereignty resided in the body-politic as a means of preserving the pre-condition of effective action in and for the community, the sovereignty of the state.[28]

The formation of sovereign national states involved the organization of autonomous hierarchical structures of social relations within given territories.[29] Sovereignty, in other words, involves the right of a state to establish its own system of political domination within its boundaries. This right is recognized by international law, the main purpose of which is "the delimitation of the exercise of sovereign power on a territorial basis."[30]

The emergence of the modern principle of sovereignty is historically linked to the decline of the universal authority of the Catholic Church in Europe. The principle was originally developed to legitimize the concentration of "absolute" power and authority in the hands of the sovereign king. The concept later evolved "in the closer association of the developing state and the developing community which became inevitable when it was discovered that power had to be shared between them."[31] It is possible to argue from this perspective that the political systems of the liberal democracies of Europe have developed out of an historic struggle over the definition and interpretation of the concept of sovereignty. Hinsley explains:

> As the community became still more complex the thesis of the sovereignty of the ruler was challenged by the thesis of the sovereignty of the people, and even by the thesis that the state and the notion of sovereignty were dispensable.[32]

The emergence and evolution of liberal democracy can thus be understood as a by-product of the struggle between the elites who determined the nature and organization of political life and the social groups excluded from the decision-making process that affected their lives. The struggle was about the definition of political rights and political participation, the constitution of "the social contract," and the political mechanisms to change it.[33] Democratic consensus, from this perspective, is the expression of the balance of power among domestic political contenders.[34] Terry Lynn Karl has suggested that the recourse to democratic procedures has often been the result of the inability of political contenders to overpower their opponents.[35] That is, democratic political accommodation and compromise can result from the power contenders' recognition of their inability to fully succeed in their struggle for power.[36] Democracy, in this sense, becomes "a second best option"[37] for the competing parties.

Historically, the concept and the practice of sovereignty has imposed limits on both the form and the substance of political competition. The most important of these limitations is that political struggle must take place within the legal and physical boundaries of the state and with the resources available within these boundaries. Without this restriction, domestic political struggles would be left open to intervention by external forces with the capacity to change and distort the balance of power within the state. Recurrent external interference in the process of political competition in a country would make the achievement of a political consensus based on the correlation of domestic forces difficult, if not impossible.[38] Sovereignty, in this sense, does not simply regulate relations among states, but it also conditions the competition for power within states by establishing legal and territorial limits on the resources available to domestic power contenders. It is possible to argue from this perspective that the foundation upon which the political institutions of the liberal democratic societies are based is the balance of power among conflicting social forces within sovereign states rather than the *idea* of democracy. As Niebuhr points out,

> the prestige of a democratic government is clearly only partly derived from the idea that it speaks with the "consent of the governed." It must fashion equilibria of social and political power which will impress the people with its capacity to preserve order and to extend justice.[39]

Sovereignty is, then, the foundation of political order at the national level. It is the "legal container" in which the turbulence of domestic political competition finds a balance. This balance can become the foundation of a democratic political system. However, democracy is only one among many possible forms of political order. Sovereignty, in this sense, does not guarantee the emergence of a democracy, but it is a necessary condition for the articulation of the type of social consensus upon which democratic stability is built. Sovereignty, therefore, does not provide an unequivocal route to democracy, but it is a "necessary working assumption"[40] for its institutionalization.

SOVEREIGNTY, DEMOCRACY, AND ELECTIONS IN NICARAGUA

The most striking characteristic of Nicaragua's political development is the pervasive role played by external powers in the definition of its political agenda and in the resolution of the disputes among domestic power contenders. Foreign interventions have drastically reduced the possibilities for Nicaragua to achieve political stability and democratic consensus.

The most visible form of political conflict in Central America during the colonial period was between *Criollos* (Creoles) and the representatives of the Spanish Crown, who were perceived by the former as an obstacle to the exploitation of the New World.[41] This dichotomy evolved into political polarization between Liberals and Conservatives.[42] The Liberals, largely Creoles, favoured independence. They rejected "traditional Hispanic values and institutions, especially the Church, and espoused classical economic liberalism, opposing monopolies while encouraging private foreign trade, immigration, and investment."[43] The Conservatives, on the other hand, sought to preserve the *status quo*.[44]

The conservative sectors of Central America favored annexation to the newly formed Mexican empire as the best means of preserving the existing social order after independence from Spain in 1821. The Liberals, on the other hand, promoted the formation of an independent Central American federation. The predominance of the conservative forces after independence was demonstrated when they succeeded in annexing Central America to Mexico in January of 1822.[46]

The question of Central America's political organization was brought to the fore again after the dissolution of the Mexican Empire in 1823. The liberal forces of the region succeeded in establishing the *Republica Federal de Centroamerica* in 1824. The conservative forces actively opposed the liberal's federalist project, which finally collapsed in 1838.[46]

Great Britain was the most influential external power in the political development of Central America during the first three decades of its independent life, particularly during the federalist experiment.[47] This situation began to change in Nicaragua with the expansionist policies of the James Knox Polk Administration (1845–1849), the discovery of gold in California in 1848, and the emerging need for cross-continental transportation routes.[48] Gold fever in California made the Rio San Juan interoceanic route in Nicaragua a valuable asset, and consequently, it became a source of tension between Great Britain and the United States. In 1850, after difficult negotiations, the United States and Great Britain signed the Clayton-Bulwer treaty, which guaranteed cooperation between the two countries and established that neither of them would have exclusive control of the Nicaraguan interoceanic route.

The Clayton-Bulwer treaty marked the beginning of the decline of British influence in Nicaragua and the rise of the United States as the most important external force shaping the processes and results of political competition in that country.[49] From then on, Nicaraguan domestic politics would be shaped by American pressures to suit American interests and Nicaraguan political actors would be unable and often unwilling to resolve their differences within the legal and political boundaries of Nicaragua as a sovereign state. This became painfully evident during the civil war of 1854 between the Liberals and the Conservatives (or *Serviles* or *Legitimistas*) over the control of the state.[50]

The Liberals hired William Walker, a "filibuster" from Nashville, Tennessee, and fifty–five mercenaries to defeat the Conservatives.[51] Earlier, Walker had led a failed filibustering expedition aimed at transforming Lower California and Sonora into a new slave state.[52] In Nicaragua, however, he proved that he had what Richard Slotkin describes as a filibuster's most important qualification: "the ability to act swiftly and decisively, making the maximum use of temporary military advantage to create a political *fait accompli*."[53]

Walker's forces defeated the Conservative army and, with the collaboration of important members of the Nicaraguan elites, achieved control of the political life of the country. He changed the Nicaraguan electoral system that, since independence, had restricted political competition and political participation to a small segment of society and introduced the practice of direct elections.[54] This constitutional change allowed him to "run" for the presidency and become the elected head of the government in 1856.[55] As President, he made English an official language, promulgated laws to establish peonage and slavery in the country, and encouraged immigration from Europe and the United States. Walker argued that,

> The introduction of negro-slavery into Nicaragua would furnish a supply of constant and reliable labor requisite for the cultivation of tropical products. With the negro-slave as his companion, the white man would become fixed to the soil; and they together would destroy the power of the mixed race which is the bane of the country. The pure Indian would readily fall into the new social organization; for he does not aim at political power, and only asks to be protected in the fruits of

his industry. The Indian of Nicaragua, in his fidelity and docility, as well as in his capacity for labor, approaches nearly the negroes of the United States; and he would readily assume the manners and habits of the latter. In fact the manners of the Indian toward the ruling race are now more submissive than those of the American negro toward his master.[56]

These views were popular in many sectors of the United States society. William V. Wells, Consul-General of the Republic of Honduras, wrote in 1856:

That the effete and decadent descendants of the early Spanish colonists must eventually succumb and give place to the superior activity and intelligence of the Anglo-Saxon, none who have lived in Central America or Mexico will dispute. The term "Manifest Destiny" is no longer a myth for paragraphists and enthusiasts; the tide of American population, stayed on the shores of the Pacific, seeks new channels; and already the advancing step of the blue-eyed race is heard among the plains and valleys of Central America.[57]

Regardless of Walker's popularity in the United States, the questions that are most relevant to understanding Nicaragua's political development in the mid-nineteenth century are: How could Walker manage to radically alter the rules of political competition in Nicaragua? How could he have gained collaboration from important sectors of the country's elites?[58] Answers to these questions have to be found in the weakness of Nicaragua as a political formation; that is, in the absence of national values and national institutions and in the "predominance of regional and particular interests over national ones."[59]

Walker's presence in Nicaragua, and his expansionist ambitions, created fear among the members of the Central American oligarchies who united against the American adventurer and managed to drive him out of Central America in 1857. It is important to note that Walker's defeat was possible only with the assistance of Great Britain and Cornelius Vanderbilt.[60] The recourse to foreign assistance to combat Walker serves as a clear example of both Central America's weakness and Nicaragua's frailty as a nation-state.[61]

Walker's defeat represented the beginning of thirty-six years of oligarchical Conservative rule and relatively stable electoral politics in Nicaragua. The constitution of 1858 reintroduced the system of indirect elections that Walker had abolished, and reestablished capital and property requirements for participation in competition for public office.[62] During this period of oligarchical rule, the interests of the United States were protected and secured by governments who ruled Nicaragua in the same passive way in which they managed their haciendas.[63] These governments not only gave in to American acts of aggression, but also to violations to the national sovereignty by Great Britain and Germany.[64]

New tensions developed between the Conservative oligarchy and the Liberal elites as the latter faction's economic capabilities expanded with Nicaragua's integration into the international coffee market at the turn of the century. These tensions created the conditions for the Liberal revolution of 1893, led by Jose Santos Zelaya.[65]

Zelaya, who represented the interests of the elites associated with the coffee business, transformed the social and political structure of the country to suit its new economic reality. He developed the basic financial and physical infrastructure required to encourage the production, processing, and export of coffee. These changes were accompanied by a radical transformation of the country's legal structure and by the organization of a strong central state apparatus. Social services and a public education system were established concurrently with an extension of political participation through the introduction of universal suffrage.[66]

Zelaya was a nationalist dictator as well as a social reformer. In 1894, with the support of the United States, he recovered the British controlled areas of Nicaragua's Atlantic coast and reasserted the territorial integrity of the Nicaraguan state. The United States tolerated Zelaya's nationalism as long as it was directed against Great Britain, but the dictator's nationalism was considered an intolerable menace when it began to affect American interests in the region.[67] Cancellation of some concessions to American businesses in the Atlantic coast region, the rejection of the financial conditions imposed by American bankers, his decision to obtain financial assistance from the Ethelburg Syndicate of England, and more important, Zelaya's intention to negotiate the construction of a canal through Nicaragua with Germany and Japan, convinced Washington that the Nicaraguan government was a threat to American interests.[68] The American solution was to instigate Zelaya's overthrow by supporting an armed counter-reformist Conservative movement that won power in 1910.[69]

The persistence of Liberal nationalist forces in the country and the Conservatives' inability to consolidate their power after Zelaya's overthrow prompted the Americans to occupy Nicaragua in August of 1912. The American marines immediately forced the Liberal troops in Granada to surrender. Then, on the fourth of October of the same year, they launched a decisive attack against the troops commanded by General Benjamin Zeledon that were positioned on Coyotepe Hill, outside the city of Masaya.[70] Zeledon refused to surrender and died "in defense of his country, of his army, and of his race."[71] His body was paraded through the streets of Masaya and buried in the town of Catarina.[72] Years later, Augusto Cesar Sandino recalled these dramatic events:

> At that time I was a kid of seventeen and I witnessed the crushing of Nicaraguans in Masaya and other parts of the Republic by North American filibusters. I saw Zeledon's body buried in Catarina, a town near my own. His death gave me the key to our country's plight in face of North American piracy; so we see our war as a continuation of his.[73]

US-controlled presidential elections were held in 1912 and again in 1916, 1920, 1924, and 1928.[74] The Liberals were not allowed to participate in the 1912 and 1916 elections, which ensured victories for Conservative, pro-interventionist governments. The exclusion of the Liberals was in accordance with the US State Department's written disapproval of "any revival of Zelayaism."[75] Washington's decision to exclude the Liberals from political competition was ratified by Nicaragua in Agreement No. 4 of the Dawson Pacts signed on October 27, 1910.

The Liberals were allowed to participate in the elections of 1920 and were able to join a Government of Reconciliation following the elections of 1924, which were held within the framework of a new electoral law approved by the Nicaraguan Congress in 1923 and written by Harold Dodds, a political scientist from Princeton.[76] It is important to point out that by 1920 the Liberal Party had practically abandoned Zelaya's nationalist position.[77] Within ten years the United States had succeeded in changing the political orientation of the party. This process of political sterilization reached its climax two decades later when the Somozas took control of the political organization.[78]

The Government of Reconciliation was overthrown in 1925 by the conservative *caudillo* Emiliano Chamorro. The civil war started in 1926 and led to a new American occupation that lasted from 1927 to 1933. The United States never recognized Chamorro, who was forced to resign. Washington then installed Adolfo Diaz as the President of the country,[79] a decision that was forcefully denounced by Senator Burton K. Wheeler of Montana on March 6, 1927:

> Listen to this abject Diaz whine: "Whatever may be the means chosen by the State Department, they will meet with the approval of my absolute confidence." Mr. Coolidge evidently thinks that is proper language for the puppet he has placed at the head of a sovereign State to use, for he quoted it with evident satisfaction in his message to Congress.
>
> In its dual capacity as loan agent and guardian angel of certain New York bankers, our State Department has been using Diaz off and on ever since it assisted in fomenting the revolution in Nicaragua in 1909, which resulted in the overthrow of the Zelaya government. He is one of the two handy men. The other was Emiliano Chamorro. Of the two, Diaz is the easier to handle. Both are professional revolutionists, or what might better be called, in the light of the methods made use by certain international bankers in their illegitimate methods of dealing with small Latin-American countries, *baker-bandits*.
>
> There is a closer relationship between the business activities of certain New York banking houses and the bandit business in these little countries than can be really appreciated by one who has never looked into their interlocking activities.
>
> Neither Diaz nor Chamorro has any sense of public honour whatever. They regard treason as a perfectly legitimate get-rich-quick scheme. They see no reason whatever why, if by use of force and foreign money they can get into a position to sell out their country, they should not do so. If they ever had any scruples on the subject, they are long since dead. They have sold and delivered not only the material resources but the liberty and honour of their country so often, it has become a fixed habit with them.[80]

Henry Stimson arrived in Nicaragua the same year the American marines landed to support the Diaz government. He managed to pressure the Liberals and Conservatives into a compromise that resulted in the Stimson-Moncada pact, better known as the Tipitapa Pact or *Pacto del Espino Negro*. The terms of the pact were drafted by the Conservatives and conveyed to the Liberals by Stimson. They included:

> Immediate general peace in time for the new crop and delivery of arms simultaneously by both parties to American custody.

General amnesty, return of exiles and return of confiscated property.

Participation in Diaz's cabinet by representative Liberals.

Organization of a Nicaraguan constabulary on a nonpartisan basis commanded by American officers.

Supervision of election in 1928 and succeeding years by Americans who will have ample police power to make such supervision effective.

Continuance temporarily of a sufficient force of marines to make the foregoing effective.[81]

Jose Maria Moncada, the military commander of the Liberal forces, agreed with the terms of reference of the accord, with the exception of the accord's implicit acceptance of the continuation of Adolfo Diaz as President of Nicaragua until the end of his term. Moncada wrote in his records of these negotiations that he had pointed out to Stimson that the government of the United States was making a mistake in allowing the Conservative government of Diaz to continue in power until after the elections of 1928. According to Moncada, Stimson replied: "My government has recognized President Adolfo Diaz and the United States of America does not make mistakes."[82] Moncada answered: "The mistake has already been made and because of it, the American government will lose credibility in Latin America."[83] Stimson responded: "Peace is an imperative. I have instructions to achieve it through peaceful means or through force."[84]

Augusto Cesar Sandino, who had returned from Mexico in 1926 to join the Liberal forces, refused to accept the pact and went to the mountains to initiate his heroic anti-interventionist struggle. Sandino's cause was totally misinterpreted by Stimson who, in his account of the Liberal-Conservative settlement of 1927, wrote:

> I was told that Sandino had lived in Mexico for twenty-two years, where he served under Pancho Villa, and only came back to Nicaragua on the outbreak of the revolution in order to enjoy the opportunities for violence and pillage which it offered.[85]

The Liberals won the elections of 1928. Oscar Rene Vargas explains that this favored the United States for at least three reasons: first, a Liberal victory would have helped neutralize Sandino's cause; Moncada's election put the Liberal Party under the control of the United States who wanted to eliminate the possibility of a nationalist revival within the party; and third, the election of a Liberal government eliminated the need for the United States to support the unpopular Conservative Party.[86]

The Liberals were elected again in 1932. One year later the American marines ended their occupation of Nicaragua, an event that induced Sandino to negotiate a peace with the government of Juan Bautista Sacasa. He was assassinated in Managua in 1934 during those negotiations.

The regimes that emerged out of the US controlled elections of the post-Zelaya era proved to be fragile and artificial solutions to Nicaragua's domestic political problems. This was demonstrated by the instability and high levels of political disorder that prevailed in the country after 1910.[87] Those regimes did not represent the balance of power among the different sectors of Nicaraguan society. They were rather an expression of the United States' over-determinant power as it was exercised through Nicaraguan elites, who lacked the power and will to lead the economic and political development of the country.[88] The United States gained control of Nicaragua's political and economic life through these elites.[89] Furthermore, the Chamorro-Bryan Treaty of 1914 granted the United States perpetual rights on the construction of an interoceanic canal through Nicaragua, and a 99 year lease on the Gulf of Fonseca and the Corn Islands in 1914.

The American marines left behind the newly created *Guardia Nacional* as Washington's main instrument for the maintenance of social order in the country. The military institution was placed under the control of the ruthless Anastasio Somoza Garcia, the founder of the Somoza dynasty and the man who Franklin D. Roosevelt later described as Washington's "son of a bitch"[90] Walter LaFeber offers a telling portrait of the dictator:

> Not born to the elite class, he had made his way to Philadelphia where he studied advertising, met the young woman—the daughter of a wealthy Nicaraguan—whom he would marry and who gave him entry to Managua's power elite, and learned English so well that he often preferred it to Spanish. His love for the Phillies and Athletics made baseball a lifelong passion, ranking just below the accumulation of wealth and mistresses. He wormed his way up through Nicaraguan business and political circles until, in 1927, his ability to use English made him invaluable to Henry Stimson's mission.[91]

Somoza, in fact, made a favorable impression on Stimson, who recorded in his diary that "Somoza is a very frank, friendly, likable young Liberal and his attitude impresses me more favorably than almost any other."[92] In 1936 Stimson's favorite deposed President Sacasa and appointed himself the Liberal Party's official candidate for the elections of November of that year. He became the elected president of Nicaragua on January 1, 1937.

In 1939 Somoza initiated a process of constitutional reform that allowed him to extend his presidential term to eight years.[93]

Somoza then engineered the victory of his candidate, Leonardo Arguello, in the presidential elections of 1947. Arguello was over-thrown by Somoza less than a month after his inauguration. Somoza then installed a new president, deposed him, and finally took direct control of the government. The dictator's scandalous political be-havior forced the United States to criticize his electoral abuses. He responded by placing his uncle, Victor Roman Y Reyes, in the presidency. Washington accepted Somoza's concession.

Somoza was inaugurated again in 1951, this time for a period of six years. The constitution was changed before his term was over to allow him to run in the elections of 1957. Somoza's presidential career however, was almost over. On September 21, 1956 the dictator was assassinated by the Nicaraguan poet, Rigoberto Lopez Perez. Anastasio Somoza was dead, but the Somoza dynasty was just beginning.

Luis Somoza, Anastasio Somoza's oldest son, was immediately appointed president by the National Congress, with a mandate to finish his father's term. Luis then declared himself the official candi-date of the Liberal Party for the elections of 1957. He won these elections and ruled Nicaragua until 1963. His brother, Anastasio Somoza, Jr., kept control of the National Guard.

To diffuse domestic and international criticism, the Somozas ap-pointed Rene Schick as the official Liberal candidate for the elec-tions of 1963. Schick was elected president, Luis was appointed to the senate, and Anastasio maintained control of the armed forces.

In March of 1966 Anastasio announced his candidacy for the presidential elections of February 1967. He won the elections and was inaugurated for a four-year term. The constitution did not allow Somoza to run for the presidency in the elections of 1972. He stepped down temporarily while constitutional changes were introduced to facilitate his reelection. In the meantime, a Somoza controlled Junta of Government was formed to run the country.

Somoza was once again elected president in 1974, this time for a six-year term ending in 1981. Meanwhile, his son, Anastasio, was rushing through the ranks of the national armed forces as part of his process of preparation for the presidency of Nicaragua. The triumph of the Sandinista Revolution in July 1979 brought a dramatic end to the Somoza dynasty.

The Somozas' power was based on their control of the armed forces, the complicity of the economic elites that benefited from their rule, but above all on the political, economic, and military support of American governments who saw them as protectors of their interests in the region and as as bastions against communist penetration in Central America. In this sense, the Somocista regime was the expression of a domestic correlation of political forces overdetermined by the power of the United States. Elections, in this externally determined balance of power had no democratic significance since their results never reflected the political correlation of forces within the country. Constitutional reforms and the electoral technology of democracy were used by the Somozas as means of legalizing their illegitimate regime. Hebert Adam has shown in a different political context that legality can become a substitute for legitimacy and an effective guideline for the enforcement of order. According to Adam, "the separation of legality from legitimacy makes it possible to rule illegitimately with the aid of the law."[94]

The end of Somocista rule and the emergence of the Sandinista regime in 1979 provoked a similar reaction in Washington to that caused by the Zelaya government in 1909. Nicaragua's political future was once again uncertain and out of American control. The Carter Administration's response to the Nicaraguan events was to cooperate with the Sandinista controlled government in an attempt to influence the course of the revolution. The Sandinistas did not trust the Carter Administration and made no significant effort to establish a working relationship with Washington. In their anthem they had emotionally declared war against "yankees enemies of humanity."[95]

The coming into power of the Reagan Administration in 1981 and Washington's rapid adoption of a more aggressive approach towards Nicaragua made the Sandinistas realize that Carter and his relatively

flexible approach to Nicaragua might have represented a rare historical opportunity to establish a form of relation with the United States
that could be conducive to the development of national sovereignity
in Nicaragua. The Reagan Administration imposed an economic
embargo in Nicaragua and promoted a series of covert military
operations to overthrow the Sandinista government. More important,
a counter-revolutionary army was organized and financed by the
United States to allegedly defend freedom and democracy in Nicaragua.

The Sandinistas organized elections in 1984 in an attempt to
undermine Washington's justification of their support of the Contra
army. The United States refused to recognize the elections because
Washington anticipated a Sandinista victory. When the ballots were
counted, the Sandinistas had received 66.97 percent of the vote[96] in
elections considered fair and clean by many foreign observers.[97]
Washington labeled the elections a sham and continued its attacks
on the Sandinista government, still hoping that the Contras could
make the Sandinistas "cry uncle."

By 1988, it was clear to Washington that the Contra army was
unable to achieve a military victory. This conclusion forced the
United States to change its strategy and place more emphasis on
political methods to displace the Sandinistas. As William Robinson
and David MacMichael point out "the slogan in Washington changed
from 'support the freedom fighters' to 'democratization in Nicaragua.' "[98] Washington's new strategy coincided with the Es-
quipulas Peace Process and the Arias Plan, which focused on the use
of electoral mechanisms to achieve peace in the region. It was in the
context of this plan that the Sandinistas scheduled national elections
for February of 1990. As Peter Rodman, National Security Council
(NSC) representative, declared in his testimony to the "Bipartisan
Commission on Free and Fair Elections in Nicaragua," Washington
saw these elections as an opportunity "to test the Nicaraguans, to
mobilize all international pressure possible against [the Sandi-
nistas] . . . , to transfer the conflict in Nicaragua to the political
terrain."[99]

The United States began to provide technical and financial support to the opposition coalition *Union Nacional de Oposicion*
(UNO) while it continued to put military and economic pressure on
the Sandinistas. Throughout 1989 and 1990 the US Congress contrib-

uted $12.5 million to influence the Nicaraguan political process.[100] If the calculation is made for the five-year period before the election of February 1990, "the covert and overt support to Anti-Sandinista political groups in Nicaragua," according to Hemisphere Initiatives, "totalled $26.1 million."[101] Guillermo Cortes Dominguez calculates that the external support to the Anti-Sandinista opposition, including funding from sources other than American, between 1984 and 1989 was of $29.6 million.[102]

The results of the election of February 25 in Nicaragua are well known. The opposition coalition UNO won a clear victory over the *Frente Sandinista de Liberacion Nacional.* Washington happily accepted the results and proclaimed the advent of democracy in Nicaragua.[103] Democracy, however, is both a mechanism for the resolution of political conflict and the expression of a social consensus with regard to the scope and form of legitimate political struggle and dissent. The effectiveness of democracy, it was argued before, depends to a large extent on the existence of a minimal social consensus over the nature and organization of political life. From this perspective, the elections of February 1990 do not represent the advent of democracy to Nicaragua. They can only be regarded as a possible point of departure for the articulation of a minimum consensus about the organization of political life in Nicaraguan society. A lasting and substantive consensus, however, will only be achieved if Nicaragua's sovereignty is made effective.

DEMOCRACY, ELECTIONS, AND FOREIGN INTERVENTION IN NICARAGUA

The purpose of this article was to place Stimson's role in Nicaraguan politics in its historical context and to offer an interpretation of the effects of American interventions on Nicaragua's political development. Stimson characterized American foreign policy in Nicaragua as "a policy of helpfulness."[104] He explained that,

> After a careful and practically uninterrupted study of that policy for the past five months, I feel that not only have we no cause to be ashamed of that page in our history but that it contains the record of a long, patient and intelligent effort on the part of this country to do an unselfish service to a weak and sorely beset Central American state.[105]

Stimson's thought followed Washington's traditional justification for interventions in Nicaragua. For instance, the Department of State defended the military intervention in Nicaragua of 1912 in a manner that was consistent with Stimson's arguments:

> In discountenancing Zelaya, whose regime of barbarity and corruption was ended by the Nicaraguan nation after a bloody war, the Government of the United States opposed not only the individual but the system and this government could not countenance any movement to restore the same destructive regime. The government of the United States will, therefore, discountenance any revival of Zelayism and will lend its strong moral support to the cause of legally constituted good government for the benefit of the people of Nicaragua, whom it has long sought to aid in their just aspiration toward peace and prosperity under constitutional and orderly government.[106]

More recently, in his address to a Joint Session of Congress on April 27, 1983, President Ronald Reagan explained that the four basic goals of American foreign policy in Central America were:

> First: . . . [to] support democracy, reform, and human freedom. This means using our assistance, our powers of persuasion, and our legitimate "leverage" to bolster humane democratic systems where they already exist and to help countries on their way to that goal complete the process as quickly as human institutions can be changed.
> Second: . . . [to] support economic development.
> Third: . . . [to] support the security of the region's threatened nations. We do not view security assistance as an end in itself, but as a shield for democratization, economic development, and diplomacy.
> Fourth: . . . [to] support dialogue and negotiations—both among the countries of the region and within each country.[107]

The historical perspective of US involvement in Nicaragua's domestic politics provided in this article shows that American interventions, regardless of their motivations and short term results, have had a negative and enduring impact on Nicaragua's political development. By curtailing Nicaragua's sovereignty the United States has severely reduced Nicaraguans possibilities of achieving political consensus and democracy. The institutionalization of democratic consensus, which in liberal-democratic countries has been an expression of the correlation of forces among domestic power contenders, has never had a chance in Nicaragua. Throughout this century American governments, by their "acts of commission and omission"[108] have formed artificial domestic alliances, switched the internal correlation of power within the country, supported dictatorial and illegitimate governments, eliminated political forces and created new ones, to force Nicaragua's political evolution to conform to their geopolitical objectives, policies, and strategies in the region.

Determining the political development of Nicaragua has created a perpetual dilemma for American governments. American democratic traditions and institutions required that interventions in Nicaragua had to be justified by the same principles and ideas that rationalize political life in the United States. Thus, the principles of democracy had to be used to legitimize American interventions in the Central American country. However, Adam Przeworski notes that democracy creates uncertainty[109] and this does not play well with the overwhelming desire for certainty that the United States has traditionally shown in its relations with Nicaragua. Thus, American governments have conveniently interpreted and manipulated the meaning and the practice of democracy, and particularly the meaning and the practice of elections to overcome this dilemma. In so doing, they have severely reduced Nicaragua's ability to create a social consensus with regard to the rule that govern political life and political competition in that country. Elections in Nicaragua have therefore had little democratic significance. The overview of the history of political competition in Nicaragua presented in this article shows that elections in this country have been used either as a formal political ritual designed to legalize illegitimate regimes (the case of elections during Somocista rule) or as externally conditioned mechanisms designed to change the balance of power within the country (the case of the 1990 elections during Sandinista rule and those celebrated in the post-Zelaya period). In both cases, the logic of elections was dictated by US interests and power rather than by domestic forces.

The effect of US interventions in the political history of Nicaragua can be seen both in the fragility of its political institutions and in the political values of the country. American interventionism has created a political culture in Nicaragua that accepts as legitimate the use of external support to succeed in the national political struggle. The process of negotiation and compromise among domestic political groups that is essential for the development and consolidation of a democratic system has not matured in Nicaragua where political competition has traditionally been shaped by, and often decided in, Washington and the US embassy in Managua.[110]

The challenge for Nicaraguans continues to be, then, to articulate and institutionalize a basic political framework within which political parties can compete for power. This requires both a substantive change in the pragmatic and short-term rationale that has informed American foreign policies in Nicaragua and a change in the political culture of the Nicaraguan elites. However, the ultimate responsibility for the political development of the country resides with Nicaraguans. Governments and political groups in that country must learn to resist the temptation and pressure to utilize the power of external forces to avoid the kind of negotiation and compromise required to create a democratic consensus. This is imperative if we want to avoid the wasteful repetition of our tragic political history.

Notes

*Preliminary versions of this article were presented at the symposium "Towards Peace and Security in Central America" at Haverford College, April 20–21 1990, and at the Annual Meeting of the Canadian Association for Latin American and Caribbean Studies (CALACS) at York University, Oct. 11–14, 1990. The central arguments of the article were published in "Combinar mas que Elegir: El Reto del 25 de Febrero," *La Cronica,* #59, January 3–10, 1990, pp. 2–3, and in "Democracia y Soberania," *Barricada,* October 21, 1990, p. 3.

1. For an introduction to Pragmatism, see H. Standish Thayer, ed., *Pragmatism: The Classic Writings* (New York and Toronto: New American Library, 1970).

2. Guido de Ruggiero argues that "pragmatism was born in America, the country of 'business', and is *par excellence,* the philosophy of the business man." Guido de Ruggiero, *Modern Philosophy,* translated by A. Howard Hannay and R. G. Collingwood (New York: Macmillan, 1921), quoted in Don Martindale, *The Nature and Types of Sociological Theory* (Cambridge, MA: Riverside Press, 1960), p. 297.

3. Hans Gerth and Saul Landau, "The Relevance of History to the Sociological Ethos," in Maurice Stein and Arthur Vidich, *Sociology on Trial* (Englewood Cliffs, NJ: Prentice-Hall, 1963), p. 29.

4. Ibid.

5. Lewis A. Coser, *Masters of Sociological Thought: Ideas in Historical and Social Context* (New York: Harcourt Brace Jovanovich, 1971), p. 14.

6. See Godfrey Hodgson, *The Life and Wars of Henry Stimson, 1867–1950* (New York: Alfred A. Knopf, 1990). For a review of

this book see James Chace, "A Pragmatic Idealist." *The New York Times Book Review,* October 21, 1990, p. 3.

7. Henry L. Stimson, p. 18.

8. Ibid., p. 18.

9. Letter of presentation of the Report of the National Bipartisan Commission on Central America addressed to President Ronald Reagan of January 10, 1984 and signed by Henry A. Kissinger and the members and counsellors of the commission.

10. Henry A. Kissinger to Gabriel Valdes, Foreign Minister of Chile, June 1969, quoted in Policy Alternatives for the Caribbean and Central America (PACCA), "Changing Course: Blueprint for Peace in Central America," in Peter Rosset and John Vandermeer, *Nicaragua: Unfinished Revolution. The New Nicaragua Reader* (New York: Grove Press, 1986), p. 18. See also Seymour M. Hersh, *The Price of Power: Kissinger in the Nixon White House* (New York: Summit Books, 1983), p. 263.

11. Samuel Eliot Morison, Henry Steele Commager, and William E. Leuchtenburg, *The Growth of the American Republic,* 2 vols. (New York and Oxford: Oxford University Press, 1980), vol. II, p. 199.

12. William James, quoted in Ibid.

13. For portions of Secretary of State Philander C. Knox's letter of December 1, 1909 containing this statement, see The Department of State, *The United States and Nicaragua: A Survey of the Relations from 1909 to 1932,* Latin American Series, No. 6, Washington, 1932, p. 8.

14. Ronald Reagan, March 1, 1985, quoted in Peter Rosset and John Vandermeer, op.cit., p. 229

15. Dwight Waldo, *The Administrative State* (New York: The Ronald Press, 1948), p. 83.

16. Stimson, p. 4.

17. Giuseppe Di Palma, "The European and the Central American Experience," in Giuseppe Di Palma and Laurence Whitehead, *The Central American Impasse* (London and Sydney: Croom Helm, 1986), p. 36.

18. To argue in favor of an historical and comparative approach to the study of democracy in Nicaragua is not to argue that the European and North American historical experiences are the *only* routes to democracy. A comparative and historical approach is simply a means to identify differences and similarities in the *processes* of political development of different societies that might explain differences in the *outcomes* of those processes. Knowledge of the differences and similarities among the political processes and outcomes of different societies can be used to articulate strategies to achieve political objectives, including the objective of democracy.

19. For in-depth analyses of these two dimensions of democracy, see Robert A. Dahl, *A Preface to Democratic Theory* (Chicago: University of Chicago Press, 1956); Robert A. Dahl, *Polyarchy: Participation and Opposition* (New Haven: Yale University Press, 1971); Dankwart A. Rustow, "Transitions to Democracy: Toward a Dynamic Model," *Comparative Politics,* April 1970, pp. 337–366; Terry Lynn Karl, "Democracy by Design: The Christian Democratic Party in El Salvador," in Giuseppe Di Palma and Laurence Whitehead, eds., op. cit., pp. 195–217; Terry Karl, "Imposing Consent? Electoralism vs. Democratization in El Salvador," in Paul W. Drake and Eduardo Silva, eds., *Elections and Democratization in Latin America, 1980–1985* (San Diego: University of California Press, 1986), pp. 9–36; Giovanni Sartori, *The Theory of Democracy Revisited* (Chatham, NJ: Chatham House Publishers, Inc., 1987), pp. 89–92.

20. Giovanni Sartori, op. cit. p. 90.

21. Ibid.

22. For in-depth analyses of the concept of institutionalization see Samuel Huntington, *Political Order in Changing Societies* (New Haven: Yale University Press, 1968); Uriel Rosenthal, *Political Order: Rewards, Punishment and Political Stability*

(Alphen aan den Rijn: Sijthoff & Noordhoff, 1978), pp. 129–155; Lynne G. Zucker, "Institutional Theories of Organization," in *Annual Review of Sociology,* Vol. 13, 1987, pp. 443–464; Talcott Parsons and Neil J. Smelser, *Economy and Society: A Study in the Integration of Economic and Social Theory* (Glencoe, IL,: The Free Press, 1956), p. 102.

23. Antonio Gramsci, *Selections From the Prison Notebooks of Antonio Gramsci,* edited and translated by Quintin Hoare and Geoffrey Nowell Smith (New York: International Publishers, 1971), pp. 125–133.

24. For an in-depth analysis of this phenomenon, see Peter L. Berger and Thomas Luckman, *The Social Construction of Reality: A Treatise in the Sociology of Knowledge* (Garden City, NY: Doubleday and Company, 1966).

25. Shmuel Noah Eisenstadt, *Tradition, Change and Modernity* (New York: John Wiley and Sons, 1973), p. 121.

26. See Francis Harry Hinsley, *Sovereignty* (Cambridge and New York: Cambridge University Press, 1986), pp. 158–235; Max Beloff, *The Age of Absolutism: 1660–1815* (New York: Harper & Row, 1962), pp. 170–182; Crawford Brough Macpherson, *The Life and Times of Liberal Democracy* (Oxford and New York: Oxford University Press, 1977).

27. Reinhold Niebuhr, *Nations and Empires: Recurring Patterns in the Political Order* (London: Faber and Faber, 1959), p. 64.

28. Hinsley, op. cit., p. 223.

29. See Oscar Oszlak, "The Historical Formation of the State in Latin America," in *Latin American Research Review,* XVI, 2 (1981), pp. 3–10.

30. Robert Yewdall Jennings, *The Acquisition of Territory in International Law* (Manchester: Manchester U.P., 1963), p. 2, quoted in Jean Gottmann, *The Significance of Territory* (Charlottesville: The University Press of Virginia, 1973), p. 3.

31. Hinsley, op. cit., p. 222.

32. Ibid.

33. Charles Tilly has pointed out that "the European experience suggests that most of the transformations European states accomplished until late in their histories were by-products of the consolidation of central-control; that the forms of government themselves resulted largely from the way the coercion and extraction were carried out; that most members of the populations over which the managers of states were trying to extend their control resisted the state-making efforts (often with sword and pitchfork) and that the major forms of political participation that westerners now complacently refer to as "modern" are for the most part unintended outcomes of the efforts of European state-makers to build their armies, keep taxes coming in, form effective coalitions against their rivals, hold their nominal subordinates and allies in line, and fend off the threat of rebellion on the part of ordinary people." Charles Tilly, "Western State-Making and Theories of Political Transformation", in Charles Tilly, (ed.), *The Formation of National States in Western Europe* (Princeton: Princeton University Press, 1975), p. 633.

34. Rustow, op. cit., p. 352–355; Dahl, *A Preface to Democratic Theory,* op cit., p. 132–133.

35. Terry Lynn Karl, "Democracy By Design," op. cit.

36. Karl, "Democracy by Design," op. cit., p. 196.

37. Ibid., p. 195.

38. This is not to suggest that all forms of foreign intervention has historically been fatal to democracy. Recurrent forms of intervention, however, designed to shape the political development of a country to suit the interest of the interventionist power would make the achievement of political consensus difficult, if not impossible. For an analysis of foreign intervention and democracy see Robert A. Dahl, *Polyarchy,* op. cit., pp. 189–201.

39. Niebuhr, op. cit., p. 61.

40. Hinsley, op. cit., p. 223.

41. Severo Martinez, *La Patria del Criollo* (San Jose: EDUCA, 1979), p. 36.

42. For analyses of the particular ways in which liberal and conservative ideologies expressed themselves in Nicaragua, see Emilio Alvarez Lejarza, "El Liberalism en los 30 Anos," in *Revista Conservadora del Pensamiento Centroamericano,* Diciembre, 1964, # 51, Vol. 10, pp. 23–34; Diego Manuel Chamorro, "El Conservatismo de los 30 Anos," in Ibid., pp. 35–36; Franco Cerruti, *Los Jesuitas en Nicaragua en el Siglo XIX* (San Jose: Libro Libre, 1984); Chester Zelaya, *Nicaragua en la Independencia* (San Jose: Editorial Centroamericana, 1971).

43. Ralph L. Woodward, "The Rise and Decline of Liberalism in Central America: Historical Perspectives on the Contemporary Crisis," *Journal of Interamerican and World Affairs,* Vol. 26, No. 3, August 1984, p. 293.

44. Ibid.

45. Edelberto Torres Rivas, *Interpretacion del Desarrollo Social Centroamericano* (San Jose: EDUCA, 1980), p. 39.

46. Thomas L. Karnes, *Los Fracasos de la Union* (San Jose: ICAP, 1961), p. 98.

47. Great Britain's role in the formation and dissolution of the Central American Federation is controversial. Historians like Edelberto Torres Rivas argue that Great Britain was an obstacle for the consolidation of the federal experiment. On the other hand, Thomas L. Karnes absolves Great Britain of this charge. See Edelberto Torres Rivas, op. cit. and Thomas L. Karnes, op. cit.

48. Karnes, op. cit., p. 193.

49. Walter LaFeber, *Inevitable Revolutions: The United States and Central America* (New York: W. W. Norton & Company, 1984), p. 30. In the early 1880s the Clayton-Bulwer treaty was denounced by many prominent citizens of the United States as

unfair to the interest of their country. For illustrations of this view, see the speeches pronounced in support of William Walker's adventures in Nicaragua reproduced in W. V. Wells, *Walker's Expedition to Nicaragua* (New York: Stringer and Towsend, 1856), pp. 226–236.

50. Richard Slotkin, *The Fatal Environment: The Myth of the Frontier in the Age of Industrialization, 1800–1890* (New York: Atheneum, 1985), pp. 245–246. See also Juan Luis Vazquez, "Luchas Politicas y Estado Oligarquico," in Alberto Lanuza, Amaru Barahona, and Amalia Chamorro, *Economia y Sociedad en la Construccion del Estado en Nicaragua* (San Jose: ICAP, 1983), pp. 141–142.

51. Filibusters, as Richard Slotkin explains, "were private military expeditions, usually invited and organized by Latin American patriots-in-exile or embattled in-country partisans, whose aim was to use American manpower and firepower to achieve victory." Slotkin, op. cit., p. 243.

52. Morison, Commager, and Leuchtenburg, op. cit. p. 578; Slotkin, op. cit., p. 245.

53. Slotkin, op. cit, p. 244.

54. For a description of electoral procedures and regulations in Nicaragua before the elections of 1856 see Emilio Alvarez Lejarza, *Las Constituciones de Nicaragua: Exposicion Critica y Textos* (Madrid: Ediciones Cultura Hispanica, 1958), pp. 423–530.

55. For analyses of the illegitimate and fraudulent nature of this election see Edelberto Torres Rivas, "Guerra y Elecciones en Nicaragua," in Edelberto Torres Rivas, *Centroamerica: La Democracia Posible* (San Jose: EDUCA, 1987), pp. 78–81; Karl Bermann, *Under the Big Stick: Nicaragua and the United States Since 1948* (Boston: South End Press, 1986), p. 64; William O. Scrooggs, *Filibusters and Financiers: The Story of William Walker and his Associates* (New York: Russell & Russell, 1969), pp. 201–204.

56. William Walker, *The War in Nicaragua* (New York: S.H. Goetzel & Co., 1860), p. 261.

57. William V. Wells, op. cit., p. 13. Derogative descriptions of Central Americans were also common among British authors. For example, see Bedford Pim and Berthold Seemann, *Dottings of the Roadside in Panama, Nicaragua and Mosquito* (London: Chapman and Hall, 1869).

58. Karl Bermann asks this question and provides an answer to it: "How could a small handful of North American adventurers, virtually overnight, take control of an independent nation? Luck, superior armaments, the shortage of professional officers among the native troops—all these played a role, but were not decisive. The most important part of the answer lay in the conditions of Nicaraguan politics." Bermann, op. cit. p. 58. Edelberto Torres Rivas proposes a similar question: "We should inquire into the cultural, political, and economic meaning of the ritual by which authority was transferred from the Nicaraguan provisional President Ferrer to the American filibuster Walker. . . ." *Centroamerica: La Democracia Posible,* op. cit., p. 80.

59. Alberto Lanuza, "Economia y Sociedad en la Construccion del Estado Nacional," in Lanuza, Barahona, and Chamorro, op. cit., p. 100.

60. Morison, Commager, and Leuchtenburg, op. cit., p. 578.

61. LaFeber, op. cit., p. 30.

62. See the constitution of 1858 in Emilio Alvarez Lejarza, *Las Constituciones de Nicaragua,* op. cit., p. 531–555,

63. Jaime Wheelock, *Democracia y Dictadura* (Mexico: Fondo de Cultura Economico, 1980), p. 105; Edelberto Torres Rivas, *Centroamerica: La Democracia Posible,* op. cit., p. 82.

64. Wheelock, op. cit., p. 106. During the administration of General Tomas Martinez (1859–1867) Great Britain imposed upon the Nicaraguan government the Wyke-Zeledon treaty by which Nicaragua lost once again the control of the *mosquito* territory in the Atlantic coast. See Francisco Ortega Arancibia, *Cuarenta Anos de Historia de Nicaragua (1838–1878)* (Managua: Banco de America, 1975), p. 409–412. During the admin-

istration of Pedro Joaquin Chamorro (1875–1879) a German warship threatened the city of Corinto to demand financial compensation for the injuries suffered by the German consul during a fight with a Nicaraguan citizen. Ibid., p. 491–493.

65. Ibid. See also Oscar Rene Vargas, *La Revolucion que Inicio el Progreso: Nicaragua 1893–1909* (Managua: Consa, 1990). For a vivid description of the social and political life of Nicaragua in the period of the emergence of the Zelaya government, see Carlos Selva, *Un Poco de Historia* (Guatemala: Coleccion 'Los Clasicos del Istmo,' Ediciones del Gobierno de Guatemala, 1948).

66. Oscar Rene Vargas, *Elecciones en Nicaragua: Analisis Socio-Politico* (Managua: Dilesa, 1989), p. 163.

67. Amaru Barahona Portocarrero, "Estudio Sobre la Historia Contemporanea de Nicaragua," Avances de Investigacion, Universidad de Costa Rica, Ano 1977, No. 24, p. 9. Gregorio Selser casts some doubts on Zelaya's nationalism and anti-imperialism in *Nicaragua: de Walker a Somoza* (Mexico: Mex-Sur Editorial S.A., 1984), pp. 83–84.

68. Hector Perez Brignoli, *Breve Historia de Centroamerica* (Madrid: Alianza Editorial, 1988), p. 101. Wheelock, op. cit., pp. 107–108; LaFeber, op. cit., p. 46–47; Edelberto Torres Rivas, *Interpretacion del Desarrollo Social Centroamericano,* op. cit. p. 72. Richard Millet, *Guardians of the Dynasty* (New York: Orbis Books, 1977), p. 23.

69. Oscar Rene Vargas argues that the overthrow of the Zelaya regime, "castrated the possibility to consolidate a Nicaraguan nation-state." Oscar Rene Vargas, *Elecciones en Nicaragua,* op. cit., p. 142.

70. Millet, op. cit., p. 32.

71. Content of a letter by Zeledon to the commander of the American forces on September 19, 1912. In the letter, Zeledon protests "in the name of my country, my army and my race for the violation of Nicaragua's sovereignty." See Jaime Wheelock Roman, op. cit., fn. 9, pp. 110–111.

72. The following is the account presented by Richard Millet of the capture and death of General Zeledon:
Zeledon was captured by Nicaraguan government troops as he was fleeing from the battle. The Americans were immediately informed of this fact and asked what disposition they wanted made of the Liberal leader. Major Buttler telegraphed Admiral Southerland, asking for instructions. He informed the Admiral that "if you direct I can have Zeledon back here under guard or protected by my men in Masaya," but added that he "personally would suggest that through some inaction on our part someone might hang him." The Admiral's reply to this message had apparently been destroyed, but the final result is quite clear. The next day the Diaz regime announced that Zeledon had been killed during the battle. Peace, enforced by American bayonets, had returned to Nicaragua. See Millet, op. cit., pp. 32–33.

73. A. C. Sandino, *Manifiesto a los Pueblos de la Tierra y en Especial al de Nicaragua* (Managua: Tipografia La Prensa 1933), cited in Gregorio Selser, *Sandino* (New York: Monthly Review Press, 1981), p. 206, and quoted by Holly Scklar, *Washington's War On Nicaragua* (Toronto: Between the Lines, 1988), p. 3. See also Eduardo Galeano, *Memorias del Fuego III: El Siglo del Viento* (Mexico: Siglo Veintiuno Editores S.A., 1987), pp. 36–37.

74. For analyses of these elections see *The United States and Nicaragua: A Survey of the Relations from 1909 to 1932,* The Department of State, Latin American Series, No. 6, Washington, 1932. See also "Los Estados Unidos en las Elecciones de Nicaragua: Tres Modelos de Intervencion," *Envio,* Ano 3, No. 32, Feb. 1984, Managua, Instituto Historico Centroamericano; Vargas, *Elecciones en Nicaragua,* op cit.; Edelberto Torres Rivas, *Centroamerica: La Democracia Posible,* op. cit., pp. 81–86.

75. Letter of the Department of State to President Adolfo Diaz, in *The United States and Nicaragua: Survey of the Relations, 1909–1932,* op. cit., p. 21.

76. For analyses of these elections see Virginia L. Greer, "State Department Policy in Regard to the Nicaraguan Election of

1924," *Hispanic American Historical Review,* XXXIV (Nov. 1954). See also William Kamman, *A Search for Stability: United States Diplomacy Toward Nicaragua 1925–1933* (Notre Dame: University of Notre Dame Press, 1968).

77. Oscar Rene Vargas, *Elecciones en Nicaragua,* op. cit., p. 48; Bermann, op. cit., p. 178.

78. Oscar Rene Vargas, *Partidos Politicos y la Busqueda de un Nuevo Modelo* (Managua: CONSA, 1990), p. 77.

79. This was the second time Adolfo Diaz had been selected as President of Nicaragua by Washington. In 1911 he assumed the Presidency after President Juan Jose Estrada was invited to resign by Elliot Northcott, the American representative in Nicaragua. Diaz was an accountant of the La Luz and Los Angeles Mining Co. before he became president in 1911. The owners of this company were legally represented in the United States by Secretary of State Philander C. Knox's law firm. Selser, op, cit., p. 95.

80. Quoted in Rafael De Nogales, op. cit., pp. 111–112.

81. Stimson, pp. 63 and 64 of the 1927 edition (use pages of the Wiener's edition)

82. Jose Maria Moncada, *Estados Unidos en Nicaragua* (Managua: Coleccion "Ediciones Nicaraguenses de Cultura General," n.d.), p. 6.

83. Ibid.

84. Ibid.

85. Stimson, p. 35.

86. Oscar Rene Vargas, *Elecciones en Nicaragua,* op. cit., p. 99.

87. At least ten armed rebellions were launched against the Conservative governments between 1913 and 1924. Wheelock, op. cit., p. 112.

100   *American Policy In Nicaragua*

88. Amaru Barahona Portocarrero, *Estudio Sobre la Historia Contemporanea de Nicaragua,* op. cit., p. 12.

89. See Juan Luis Vazquez, "Luchas Politicas y Estado Oligarquico," in Lanuza, Barahona, and Chamorro, op. cit., p. 174–193. See also Oscar Rene Vargas, *La Intervencion Norteamericana y sus Consequencias: Nicaragua 1919–1925* (Managua: ECOTEXTURA, 1989).

90. Gregorio Selser, *Nicaragua de Walker a Somoza,* op. cit., p. 241.

91. LaFeber, op. cit., p. 68.

92. The Diary of Henry L. Stimson, Vol. VII, May 3, 1927, in Yale University Library, New Haven, CT, cited in Millet, op. cit., p. 55.

93. The chronology and data on elections celebrated under *Somocista* rule presented herein is mainly based on the account of the Somoza dynasty presented in Bernard Diederich's *Somoza and the Legacy of U.S. Involvement in Central America* (New York: E.P. Dutton, 1981) and Gregorio Selser, *Nicaragua: De Walker a Somoza,* op. cit.

94. Hebert Adam, "Legitimacy and the Institutionalization of Ethnicity: Comparing South Africa," in Paul Brass, ed., *Ethnic Groups and the State* (London: Croom Helm, 1985), p. 265.

95. The anthem of the FSLN says "we [Sandinistas] fight against yankees enemies of humanity".

96. *Envio,* "Los Actores del 90 en el Escenario Electoral del 84," Ano 8, Numero 98, Octubre 1989, p. 33, Managua, Instituto Historico Centroamericano.

97. *Envio,* "Analysis of 1984 Elections: The Elections Reagan Would Like to Forget," Special Edition, October 1989, Managua, Instituto Historico Centroamericano, pp. 3–5.

98. William Robinson and David MacMichael, "Intervention in the Nicaraguan Election," *Cover Action Information Bulletin,* #33, Winter, 1990, p. 32.

99. Peter Rodman, National Security Council (NSC) representative, May 10, 1989, Washington DC, quoted in Robinson and MacMichael, op. cit., p. 32.

100. William Robinson and David MacMichael, op. cit., p. 33.

101. Ralph Fine, David Kruse, Jack Spence, and George Vickers, "Hemisphere Initiatives: Nicaragua Election Update Number 2. Foreign Funding of the Internal Opposition," Boston, October 16, 1989, in Robinson and MacMichael, op. cit., p. 35.

102. Guillermo Cortes Dominguez, *La Lucha por el Poder* (Managua: Editorial Vanguardia, 1990), p. 266.

103. For analyses of the 1990 elections see Cortes Dominguez, op. cit.; John A. Booth, "Elecciones y Democracia en Nicaragua: Una Evaluacion de las Elecciones de Febrero de 1990," *Polemica,* Numero 11, Segunda Epoca, 1990, pp. 29–43.

104. Stimson, p. 54.

105. Ibid, p. 53.

106. The Department of State, *The United States and Nicaragua: A Survey of the Relations From 1909 to 1932,* op. cit., p. 21.

107. President Ronald Reagan: Address to Joint Session of the Congress (April 27, 1983), in Robert S. Leiken and Barry Rubin, *The Central American Crisis Reader* (New York: Summit Books, 1987), pp. 553–554.

108. Laurence Whitehead, "The Prospects for a Political Settlement: Most Options Have Been Foreclosed," in Giuseppe Di Palma and Laurence Whitehead, op. cit., p. 230.

109. Adam Przeworski, "Some Problems in the Study of the Transition to Democracy," in Guillermo O'Donnell, Phillipe C. Schmitter, and Laurence Whitehead, *Transitions from Authoritarian Rule: Prospects for Democracy* (Baltimore: The John Hopkins University Press, 1986), p. 57.

110. See Mark B. Rosenberg, *Democracia en Centroamerica?* (Costa Rica:CAPEL, 1985), pp. 16–18.

The Good Old Days

The Colonel: The Life and Wars of Henry Stimson, 1867-1950

ALAN BRINKLEY

I n 1976, Godfrey Hodgson, a British journalist with long experience covering American politics, published *America in Our Time,* a remarkable study of America's fall from the enormous power and confidence of the 1950s and early 1960s to the disillusionment of the post-Vietnam, post-Watergate era. Among the principal culprits in this tale of failure, Hodgson argued, was the foreign-policy "establishment," which had dominated American international relations throughout the postwar era, guiding the country from triumph to disaster.[1] Now, fifteen years later, Hodgson has written a biography of the man who by almost all accounts was the founder and patron saint of the postwar foreign policy establishment: Henry L. Stimson, one of the most widely revered American statesmen of the twentieth century, whose extraordinary public career spanned four decades and six presidencies.

Thirty years have passed since the last major study of Stimson appeared: Elting Morison's *Turmoil and Tradition,* an impressive biography authorized (and partially paid for) by the Stimson estate.[2] It is a measure of the aura surrounding Stimson that throughout those decades his reputation remained virtually untouched by the many harshly critical reassessments of modern foreign policy. Indeed to most chroniclers of recent American history, he is still what his protégé John McCloy often called him, "my hero statesman."[3]

Hodgson's study is still another indication of how successfully Stimson's historical reputation has weathered the years since his death in 1950. *The Colonel* is less thorough and less exhaustively researched than Morison's 1960 biography, but it is an important book nonetheless. Hodgson raises troubling questions about Stimson's understanding of what we now call the third world, discusses Stimson's racial and ethnic prejudices (largely ignored by Morison and other, earlier biographers), and pays particular attention to Stimson's central role in the decision to use atomic weapons against Japan. What most clearly distinguishes this book from its predecessors, however, is Hodgson's continuing interest in the idea of the American establishment and his effort to define its values. The skepticism that marked *America in Our Time* is still visible here, but Hodgson's opinion of the traditional foreign policy elite seems to have softened since 1976. In Stimson's notable career he discovers not only the weaknesses but also the strengths of the foreign policy establishment between 1920 and 1950.

That there was such a thing as an "establishment" in the United States had barely occurred to Americans in 1960, when Morison's biography appeared. Henry Fairlie had introduced the concept to England in 1955, in a celebrated essay on Britain's ruling elite in the London *Spectator*. But no one made the case for an American establishment until Richard Rovere's half-joking article about it in the *American Scholar* in 1961. By the mid-1960s, however, the concept had caught hold. "Since then," Hodgson noted in *America in Our Time*, "the idea that there is indeed an American Establishment, and that it exercises influence particularly over foreign affairs, has taken root in earnest and become part of the common coin of political debate."[4]

This idea was an article of faith to revisionist historians in the late 1960s and 1970s, who blamed that establishment for locking the United States into a rigidly anticommunist position which led to the Vietnam War; and to the far right, which saw the establishment as an elite conspiring to destroy freedom.[5] The same idea has appealed more recently to some "postrevisionists," who credit the establishment with the creation of a stable and intelligent postwar foreign policy that, on the whole, served the nation well from the beginning of the cold war to very near its end.[6]

Most definitions of the establishment rest on two interlocking sets of characteristics: one social and one ideological. Socially, the establishment was characterized by the privilege and self-conscious elitism of its members. Not all were born to wealth and influence, but those who were not usually attained both at a relatively early age. They had the help of connections made at prestigious prep schools (especially Andover and Groton), Ivy League colleges (particularly

Yale), and important law schools (mainly Harvard). Much of the social cohesion that lay at the heart of the idea of the establishment was, therefore, a result of shared educational experiences and old school ties. It was a result, too, of Wall Street, where almost everyone identified with the establishment worked for at least some time, either in a law firm or an investment bank; and of New York City, which provided a network of institutions—the Century Association, the Council on Foreign Relations, and others—that helped to preserve the sense of fellowship that began in college clubs and law-school seminars.

The ideological affinity that made the establishment an effective force in public policy was in many ways a reflection of these social characteristics. Establishment figures were almost always successful men (and, on rare occasions, women) who had inherited, or acquired, a sense of entitlement mixed with civic responsibility that in another time or place might have been called noblesse oblige. Although they were usually Republicans, they were rarely partisan and indeed looked with some misgivings upon electoral politics and elected politicians. (Relatively few establishment figures ever ran for public office, and even fewer succeeded.) A sound foreign policy, they claimed, must be insulated from politics and guided by disinterested people capable of distinguishing the national interest from individual interests. It was, therefore, the duty of such people to serve the nation when called; what went without saying was that prestige in their own circle came from such service.

Most of all, perhaps, establishment foreign policy rested on the assumption of America's right and duty to take a leading position in world affairs and on an almost unquestioned faith in the moral and practical wisdom of their nation's values and its capitalist institutions. When Winston Churchill described the Marshall Plan as "the most unsordid act in history," he was, perhaps unintentionally, expressing the establishment's sense of its goals: that there was a seamless connection between American national interest and the interests of the world.

The foreign policy elite deplored the chauvinism of the most militant internationalists as much as they detested isolationism. They also displayed a limited ability to understand social or political systems markedly different from their own. They were, therefore, always more successful in dealing with Britain and Western Europe (and even at times with the entrenched political leaderships of the Soviet Union and, later, China) than with the more volatile nations of the third world. They were skilled at doing business with "gentlemen," but often maladroit in dealing with less polished leaders. They prized stability and identified all but the most modest challenges to the status quo as "radicalism," and hence a danger.

In reality, of course, the establishment was never the coherent entity that its critics (and some of its defenders) claimed. Nor did its members have as much control over American foreign policy as popular myth suggests. Even when they dominated policy making, they had to contend with presidents, members of Congress, and competing bureaucracies with interests often very different from their own. And yet it is hard to look at the workings of postwar American diplomacy and not be struck by the intimacy, at times bordering on incestuousness, that has characterized its leadership. Occasionally the connections were literally ones of blood (the Bundys, the Dulleses). More often, they were ties of friendship. To an astonishing extent, the postwar foreign policy elite was bound together by its association with and loyalty to Henry Stimson.

"I was born in New York City on September 21, 1867," Stimson wrote in the preface to his 1948 memoir, *On Active Service in Peace and War.* "Less than nine years thereafter my young mother died . . . but the doors of my grandparents' house immediately opened and took us in to the loving care of the large family within."[7] Stimson says almost nothing about what he calls his "hard-working father," but in fact he was all but abandoned by him as well. For all the affection he undoubtedly received at home from his grandparents, Hodgson writes, "the little boy must have been cruelly bewildered by the double shock of his mother's death and his father's apparent rejection." Perhaps that was one source of Stimson's lifelong and, even by the standards of his own time, unusually intense loyalty to almost all the institutions that embraced him in his youth; they gave him a sense of acceptance and security that his distant and disapproving father seldom offered.

Throughout his long life, Stimson remained unwaveringly loyal to Andover, which he entered at thirteen, and which "opened to me a new world of democracy and of companionship with boys from all portions of the United States." His four years at Yale, he recalled, were "most important to my life, both in the character developed and in the friendships formed." Even decades later, he remained active in Yale's Skull and Bones society (and was present in the clubhouse one night in the spring of 1947 to initiate a new class of members that included George Bush). Harvard Law School, from which he graduated in 1890, created a "revolution in my power of thinking."[8] Later, as a rising attorney in New York, he developed similar lifelong attachments to his law firm, Winthrop and Stimson, to the Century Association, to the St. Hubert's Club in the Adirondacks ("a glorified summer camp for wealthy, old-family New Yorkers," Hodgson calls it). He built a country house on Long Island in 1903 and lived there until he died. Always finding time for riding and hunting, he sought to make his days (including, apparently, his long and successful but childless marriage) as stable and correct as possible.

Stimson developed similarly intense loyalties to several of the aristocratic heroes of his age: to Theodore Roosevelt, whose friend and neighbor he became, and whose political causes he championed until they conflicted with his own ambitions; and above all to the prestigious New York lawyer Elihu Root. Secretary of war, secretary of state, revered statesman, Root was to Stimson's generation what Stimson became to the generation that followed: an exemplar of the ideal of disinterested public service. Shortly after graduating from Harvard Law School, Stimson joined Root's law firm in New York and remained associated with it until he died. His relationship with Root—a man of stern rectitude and unwavering conviction—became one of the most important of his life, both because it immensely aided his advancement and because it provided him with a model for his own public career. Forty years later, he kept a copy of Root's collected writings within reach of his desk in the War Department. "Where others would later ask, 'What would Colonel Stimson have done?'" Hodgson observes, "no doubt Stimson asked, 'What would Mr. Root have done?'"

Although Stimson ultimately became one of the richest and most powerful members of the New York Bar, aggressively litigating complex cases in the courts for his corporate clients, he never much liked the practice of law (and seemed to suffer especially from the insomnia and hypochondria that afflicted him throughout his life whenever he was confined within the legal world). Unsurprisingly, therefore, he almost always leaped at opportunities to move beyond Wall Street. Theodore Roosevelt appointed him United States attorney for the southern district of New York in 1906. His success there led him into a hopeless race for governor in 1910, where his unfitness for popular politics quickly became clear. "His cultured accent," one journalist later wrote, "his uneasy platform presence, his cold personality, almost every detail of his manner betrayed his birth and breeding, gave his electorate an impression of a young aristocrat who condescends to rule. . . . The opposition press called him 'the human icicle.' " But those same qualities served him well in other worlds.

In 1910, he accepted an offer from William Howard Taft to become secretary of war (even though it precipitated a temporary rupture in his friendship with Theodore Roosevelt) and spent an uneventful but dignified two years presiding over the nation's small and, for the moment, unimportant army. He served briefly as an artillery officer in World War I (at the age of fifty-one), a crucial experience for men of his generation, who had grown up in the shadow of the heroes of the Civil War. "I have seen and felt real war now," Stimson wrote proudly at the time, "and been under more fire (little as it was) than many of the civil war 'patriots' . . . to whom we have so long looked up." He clung tenaciously to his military title and was known for the rest of his life as "Colonel Stimson."

In late middle age, Stimson had become a widely respected lawyer-statesman with an impressive record of official positions he had held but, as yet, no particularly striking accomplishments. He was a reliable man, of undeniable intelligence and unquestioned integrity, but also, perhaps equally important of utterly predictable values. Nothing he had confronted in his career to that point, and virtually nothing that would confront him in the far more important career to come, succeeded in shaking the stolid, Victorian morality that produced his memorable denunciation of modern espionage: "Gentlemen do not read each other's mail." Nor did his remarkable experiences ever challenge his extraordinary social isolation. His circle of friends and associates was defined by Andover, Yale, Harvard, the Century, St. Hubert's, and the Long Island aristocracy. Divorced people were never welcomed in the Stimson's house. Nor, on the whole, were Jews, with occasional exceptions such as Stimson's friends and protégé Felix Frankfurter. (Stimson once recommended against donating the proceeds of a bequest to Columbia University by citing, among other things, "the tremendous Jewish influence" there.) An avid hunter and outdoorsman, he made frequent trips into the wild and came into contact with many people very different from himself. But much like a British colonial official of the nineteenth century, he nevertheless stuck to his unwavering moral and social code.

In 1927, Stimson undertook his first major diplomatic assignment when he led an American negotiating team to Nicaragua to mediate a dispute between warring factions in that unstable nation, which had long been, in effect, an American protectorate. His mission was superficially successful, producing a ceasefire in the civil war and free elections supervised by the United States Marines. The lesson of the agreement was a simple one, Stimson observed in his memoirs.

> If a man was frank and friendly, and if he treated them as the equals they most certainly were, he could talk turkey with the politicians and other leaders of Latin America as he could with his own American colleagues. And they would not let him down.[9]

But the prerequisite for talking turkey was that the "politicians and other leaders" must embrace Stimson's own gentlemanly code. Not all did. The agreement he negotiated conspicuously excluded the rebel general Augusto Sandino, who went on to become the leader of a spirited guerrilla resistance and a revered hero to future generations of Nicaraguan revolutionaries. "It is hard to avoid the impression that there was an element of class consciousness in Stimson's evaluation" of Sandino, Hodgson notes. General José Moncada, the rebel leader with whom Stimson negotiated, was a man whose "manner and bearing" he greatly admired and whom Stimson later pronounced "as good as his word"[10] The rising politician Anastasio Somoza, graced with good manners and fluent English, impressed Stimson "more favorably than almost any other" and struck him as a "very frank, friendly, likeable young liberal." Sandino, by contrast, was more common (and more popular) and hence a "bandit . . . plainly unprincipled and brutal."[11] By any count," Hodgson notes, "it was a disastrous mistake to underestimate Sandino" and a "catastrophic mistake to be taken in by Somoza."

To the government in Washington, however, Stimson's Nicaragua mission was a huge success and propelled him to larger diplomatic assignments. Early in 1928, he became governor-general of the Philippines, where his subdued and tactful personal style made him immediately popular—particularly since it was such a welcome contrast to the swaggering bravado of his predecessor, General Leonard Wood, who had died suddenly the previous summer. But Stimson was no less an imperialist than Wood, no less certain of the redemptive value of American capitalism,[12] and at least equally committed to what Hodgson calls "the doctrine that the United States was justified in using its military and economic strength to protect those who might want to go to hell in their own way but ought not to be allowed to do so."

He spent less than a year in Manila, long enough to soothe the sensitive feelings of local politicians, but not long enough to do much else. When he returned home in March 1929 to become secretary of state in the Hoover administration, however, he was widely praised in the American press for his "brilliant" success.

Much of Stimson's four-year term in the State Department was dominated by the unsuccessful effort to find an effective American response to Japanese aggression in Manchuria. A committed internationalist, he was hamstrung and frustrated by the legislated neutrality of United States policy and found himself working to stimulate international opposition to Japanese aggression while unable to commit his own country to participate in any boycotts or sanctions that might result from his efforts.[13]. His principal contribution to American diplomacy was the 1932 "Stimson Doctrine," by which the United States refused to recognize "any situation, treaty or agreement . . . brought about by means contrary to the Pact of Paris"— that is, by war or the threat of war. Highly popular at the time, it had no practical effect.

Stimson was also alarmed by the growing instability in Europe and the increasing strength of totalitarian movements there. But he never developed as much mistrust and suspicion of the new European leaders as he did of their Japanese counterparts. He was, in fact, rather taken with Mussolini when he and Mrs. Stimson visited Italy in 1931. "He showed his attractive side," Stimson wrote after a Sunday outing in the Duce's new speedboat, "and we both liked him very much." Hodgson observes, "He shared with most white Americans of his generation a hierarchical view of the world's nations and peoples," in which Asians ranked consistently below Europeans—and Africans ranked lowest of all. (When Franklin Roosevelt asked him about the prospects of a new Haitian government in 1932, he replied: "I did not think it would stay permanently put and I asked him whether he knew any self-governing negro community which had stayed put.")

Presiding over American diplomacy in the early years of a great world crisis, Stimson displayed both the strengths and weaknesses of his approach to public life. He recognized the seriousness of the dangers of fascism and spoke eloquently of the possible costs of inaction. But he showed as well a striking lack of imagination—both in envisioning the likely consequences of the policy failures over which he reluctantly presided and in judging the worth of the leaders with whom he dealt. His leisurely and opulent travels through Europe in 1931 and 1932 were, as Hodgson uncharitably but not inaccurately describes them, a "rich man's holiday" which Stimson "was somewhat complacently enjoying . . . while the world was falling apart." In Germany, he was much impressed by Kurt von Schleicher, who helped prepare the way for the Third Reich. In France, he was drawn above all to Pierre Laval ("an able, forceful and I think a sincere man"), who was soon to become a notorious Nazi collaborator. Stimson was a skillful negotiator and a superb diplomatic insider when dealing with those he considered his social and moral equals. But only intermittently did he show much awareness that gentlemanly diplomacy had become obsolete as the international order that followed World War II was, in Ramsay MacDonald's words, "crumbling under our feet."

Had Stimson retired from public life in 1933, as he fully expected to do, he would be remembered dimly as a respected but relatively minor statesman of the early twentieth century. But his service as secretary of war during World War II earned him his large place in history. Hodgson appropriately devotes nearly half his book to the last five years of Stimson's official career.

Stimson's appointment to the war department in 1940 was in part a political ploy. Franklin Roosevelt believed that adding prominent Republicans to his cabinet would undercut his opposition in the

presidential election that year (just as William Howard Taft had lured
Stimson into his cabinet thirty years earlier to undercut the challenge from Theodore Roosevelt). But Stimson was attractive to
Roosevelt for other reasons, too. By 1940, he had become an outspoken advocate of a more internationalist foreign policy—including
aid to Britain. And he would give weight and stature to the
beleaguered war department, demoralized by years of bitter infight-
ing between the previous secretary, the feckless isolationist Harry
Woodring, and his wildly ambitious undersecretary, Louis Johnson.
Stimson cleaned house immediately. He assembled a stable of deputies drawn from his own social and professional milieu—a remark-
ably able group of younger men (Robert Patterson, John McCloy,
Harvey Bundy, Robert Lovett, George Harrison) who would go on to
form the nucleus of the postwar foreign policy elite. All were Republicans. Most had graduated from Yale (and Skull and Bones) and
Harvard Law School. All but one had worked in the law firms or
investment banks of Wall Street. "The plain fact is," Hodgson observes, "that, during a war for democracy conducted by a Democratic President . . . the War Department was directed by a tiny
clique of wealthy Republicans, and one that was almost an narrowly
based, in social and educational terms, as a traditional British Tory
Cabinet."

Hodgson does his best to portray Stimson as deeply involved in
the running of his department, but most evidence (including much of
Hodgson's own) suggests otherwise. Stimson presided magisterially
over the vast bureaucracy. He involved himself directly in broad
strategic decisions and a few particularly crucial issues. But he never
really ran the army. That was partly because Franklin Roosevelt was
himself directly involved in policy decisions, partly because Stimson's chief of staff, General George C. Marshall, moved outside the
chain of command and established direct relations with the President
(which Stimson seems not to have opposed). But it was also because
Stimson himself chose to leave most of the daily work in the hands of
subordinates. In fact, Stimson spent relatively little time in his office.
He returned home by 4:00 PM every day to ride or play golf. He spent
long weekends on his country estate and took long vacations every
summer. He combined his official travels with leisurely visits to
resorts. Stimson's detached style of management was no doubt partly
a result of his age—he was seventy-two years old when he took office

in 1940, complaining that "I am pretty nearly at the limit of my strength." William Bullitt exaggerated in 1942 when he described Stimson (to his face) as a "mere housekeeper of the War Department," but there was enough truth in the remark to irritate the secretary greatly.

Yet Stimson's personal achievements in the war department were considerable. He was one of the few, perhaps the only, official in government who could speak frankly and unfawningly with the evasive Roosevelt. ("Mr. President, I don't like you to dissemble with me," he once reportedly said.) In 1940 and 1941, his was one of the most influential voices prodding Roosevelt to move more decisively toward intervention at a time when American policy seemed mired in what Dean Acheson called an "agony of irresolution."[14] Within the war department, he was intolerant of personal rivalries and political ambitions and created an atmosphere of common purpose. His subordinates may have done most of the work, but they did it according to rigorous standards Stimson set and maintained. He was an invaluable asset to the administration in its relations with Congress, a man whose integrity helped to insulate the administration's military policies from criticism and scrutiny. When Stimson told Senator Harry Truman that a project he was investigating in 1943 was "top secret" (it was, in fact, the Manhattan Project), Truman promptly abandoned the inquiry. "I'll take you at your word," he told the secretary. That Stimson was "a great American patriot and statesman" was assurance enough that nothing was amiss.[15] Stimson's diplomatic skills and his long and close relationships with the ruling circles in Britain helped win Winston Churchill's agreement that the Normandy invasion should be placed under a single, American commander. His withering attacks on the Morgenthau Plan for the dismantling of Germany's industrial capacity after the war helped consign that radical proposal to oblivion.

Stimson's stern moral code and insular social vision made him a hard man to cross even when his policies were controversial or abhorrent. His support for the internment of Japanese-Americans in early 1942 was crucial to the success of the policy. Stimson brushed aside arguments that imprisoning American citizens without due process was both illegal and immoral, summoning what Hodgson calls "the ancient and profoundly un-American code of statecraft that is summed up in the phrase *raison d'état:* the state has its own reasons." And perhaps, too, Hodgson argues, he was receptive to the internment policy because he "never clearly dissented much from the frank belief in racial inferiority proclaimed by his closest friends, men like Elihu Root and Leonard Wood." Whatever his reasons, Stimson's reputation for probity helped to undercut the position of those within the administration who opposed the decision.

Stimson successfully defended the army's control of military contracts against the civilian agencies created to supervise the war mobilization. And he fought effectively against all efforts to increase civilian production, even in the very last days of the war. He undercut the authority of Donald Nelson, the ineffectual director of the civilian War Production Board, who complained that Stimson's goal ("complete [war department] authority over the disposition of the nation's resources") would "inevitably produce disorder, and eventually balk their own efforts by undercutting the economy in such a way that it could not meet their demands."[15] Stimson's policies also undercut efforts to assist small businesses and limit corporate profits, and they helped to bring antitrust prosecutions to a virtual halt during the war. He argued that he was simply protecting military production from delay and disruption. But he was doing so on the basis of an unquestioned assumption that production would proceed most efficiently and effectively if left in the hands of the great corporations whose interests he had served for years on Wall Street.

Certainly the most controversial event of Stimson's career was his part in the development and use of atomic weapons in the last years of the war. Stimson supported and protected the Manhattan Project, ensured that it was generously funded, and pressed its leaders to complete their work speedily. Like most other policy makers aware of the enterprise, Stimson believed (incorrectly, it later turned out) that Germany was nearing completion of an atomic weapon and that the United States must make one first. When Germany surrendered in May 1945, Stimson continued to press the project forward, although it was clear that the only potential remaining target, Japan, had no nuclear capacity. Roosevelt's death in April had placed the final decision on whether and how to use the new weapon in the hands of Harry Truman, who knew nothing of the bomb's existence until Stimson took him aside in the first moments of his presidency and told him about it. From that moment on, Truman largely deferred to Stimson's judgment. The bomb was simply another weapon, Stimson told him, and should be used to end the war. Truman adopted that position as his own and clung to it for the rest of his life.

Hodgson has little patience with the claims of revisionist historians that the United States bombed Japan in an effort to cow the Soviet Union into submitting to its proposals for the postwar world.[17] After the war, in fact, Stimson actively (and unsuccessfully) opposed using America's nuclear potential as a diplomatic tool in its emerging rivalry with the Soviet Union. Instead, he urged Truman to share the new technology with the Soviets unconditionally. "The chief lesson I have learned in a long life," he wrote in an often quoted letter to the President, "is that the only way you can make a man trustworthy is to trust him; and the surest way to make his untrustworthy is to distrust him and show your distrust." Nor does Hodgson agree with those who have seen a tinge of racism in the decision to bomb Japan (a decision, some suggest, that would never have been made had Europe been the target). Whatever racist assumptions Stimson may tacitly have embraced, they were nowhere visible in his deliberations on this issue. Stimson even overrode the wishes of military commanders and ordered that Kyoto, Japan's ancient capital and a major cultural shrine, be stricken from the list of potential targets.[18]

But Hodgson is harshly critical of the decision nonetheless. Stimson himself, he notes, lamented the "appalling lack of conscience and compassion that the war had brought about [and] the complacency, the indifference, and the silence with which we greeted the mass bombings in Europe and, above all, in Japan." But having deplored the saturation bombings of Tokyo and Dresden, Stimson raised no serious objections to the nuclear destruction of Hiroshima and Nagasaki. Instead, he opposed all proposals to give the Japanese advance warning or to drop a "demonstration" bomb on a relatively uninhabited area. The minutes of the crucial meeting on May 31, 1945, show that "the Secretary agreed that the most desirable target would be a vital war plant employing a large number of workers and closely surrounded by workers' houses" and that he recommended "that we should seek to make a profound psychological impression on as many of the inhabitants as possible." Hodgson makes his own moral revulsion from that reasoning clear in an uncharacteristically sarcastic rejoinder:

> In the brief interval before they were incinerated, or the longer and more painful interval before they died of radiation sickness, such a

course of action could certainly be relied on to produce a very profound psychological impression.

Yet Hodgson also notes that, almost alone among the principal
officials who made the decision to use the bomb, Stimson sensed the
enormity of the step the United States was now taking. He spent
much of the remainder of his life in a futile effort to limit the spread
of atomic weapons through international control and supervision.
"In this last great action of the Second World War we were given
final proof that war is death," he wrote in 1947, in *Harper's*. "Now
with the release of atomic energy, man's ability to destroy himself is
very nearly complete. The bombs dropped on Hiroshima and
Nagasaki ended a war. They also made it wholly clear that we must
never have another war."

In October, 1962, twelve years after Stimson's quiet death at age
eighty-three, a group of his protégés gathered in the White House to
shape an American response to the Cuban Missile Crisis. As the
meetings began, Robert Lovett told McGeorge Bundy, "Mac, I think
the best service we can perform for the President is to try to approach this as Colonel Stimson would." Hodgson begins his book
with this slightly shopworn anecdote to suggest the extent of Stimson's legacy. But of what does Stimson's legacy actually consist?

Stimson was never a major conceptual architect. of American
foreign or military policy. Many of the diplomatic efforts with which
he was most closely associated—in Nicaragua, the Philippines and
Japan—later turned out badly. He was an influential man, of course,
but never a genuinely powerful one—someone never capable of, and
only rarely interested in, pursuing a vision or program of his own or
in any serious way challenging the judgment of his superiors. When
his views on controlling atomic weapons were out of step with the
cold war consensus that emerged after World War II, no one in
power paid much attention to him. Stimson's legacy rests less on
specific achievements or failures than on the way he conducted
himself in public life—and on how his conduct helped to shape the
ethos of the next generation of the foreign policy elite. Stimson's
bequest included a certitude about the righteousness of American
ideals and their suitability for other nations; a conviction that diplomacy must be insulated from popular and legislative whims (and

hence from democracy); and a social and cultural elitism—born of his own rarefied station—that survived in foreign-policy circles long after it had been repudiated by the rest of American society. But Stimson also brought to public life a personal integrity, a lack of self-interest and of hypocrisy, and a commitment to the ideal of public service that compensated for many of the shortcomings of his social and political vision.

It is difficult to look at the lurching, reacting, political opportunism of recent American diplomacy without finding such qualities appealing. Whatever their flaws, Stimson and the postwar establishment he helped to shape brought to American foreign policy, at least for a time, a consistency, intelligence, and stability that their successors have conspicuously failed to match. Hodgson's sensitive account of Stimson's public career makes a convincing case for the relative advantages of an all but vanished world.

Notes

*Henry L. Stimson (1867–1950), is author of *American Policy in Nicaragua* (1927) and *On Active Service in Peace and War* with McGeorge Bundy (1948). Books about Stimson include: *Secretary Stimson: A Study in Statecraft* by Richard N. Current (1954), *Turmoil and Tradition* by Elting Morison (1960), and *The Colonel: The Life and Wars of Henry L. Stimson, 1867–1950* by Godfrey Hodgson (1990).

1. Godfrey Hodgson, *American in Our Time* (Doubleday, 1976), pp. 111–133, *The Colonel: The Life and Wars of Henry L. Stimson, 1867–1950* (Knopf, 1990).

2. Elting Morison, *Turmoil and Tradition* (Houghton Mifflin, 1960). Richard N. Current's *Secretary Stimson: A Study in Statecraft* (Rutgers University Press, 1954) is a similarly admiring account of Stimson's public life.

3. Alan Brinkley, "Minister without Portfolio," *Harper's,* February 1983, p. 46.

4. Hodgson, *America in Our Time,* p. 113.

5. David Halberstam's *The Best and the Brightest* (Random House, 1972) is perhaps the best known (if far from the most strident) attack on the establishment. Phyllis Schlafly's *A Choice Not an Echo,* 3rd edition (Pere Marquette Press, 1964) is an example of the attack from the right.

6. A recent study of the establishment that expresses general admiration for its achievement is Walter Isaacson and Evan Thomas, *The Wise Men* (Simon and Schuster, 1986). John Lewis Gaddis, *The Long Peace* (Oxford University Press, 1987) makes a case for the stability of postwar American foreign policy.

7. Henry L. Stimson and McGeorge Bundy, *On Active Service in Peace and War* (Harper and Brothers, 1948), p. xii. Only the introduction is written in the first person. Bundy was the principal writer of the body of the memoir.

8. Stimson, *On Active Service in Peace and War,* p. xiii; Evan Thomas, "The Code of the WASP Warrior," *Newsweek,* August 20, 1990, p. 33.

9. Stimson, *On Active Service,* p. 116.

10. Stimson, *On Active Service,* p. 114.

11. Stimson, *On Active Service,* pp. 114–115.

12. Larry G. Gerber makes a forceful, if at times somewhat exagger-ated, case for the importance of Stimson's capitalist convictions in *The Limits of Liberalism* (New York University Press, 1983). Stimson, he argues, "learned to believe that moral and political progress went hand in hand with economic progress and the development of a capitalist form of economic organization" (p. 30).

13. The fullest account of Stimson's involvement with the Man-churian crisis is Armin Rappaport, *Henry L. Stimson and Japan, 1931–33* (University of Chicago Press, 1963), which takes a somewhat more critical view of Stimson's role than does Hodgson: "He elected to give vent to his ire [about Japanese aggression] by brandishing the pistol, which, unhappily, was not loaded, thereby transgressing the cardinal maxim of the states-man and placing his country in jeopardy" (p. 203).

14. Dean Acheson, *Present at the Creation* (Norton, 1969), p. 21.

15. Harry S. Truman, *Memoirs,* Vol. 1, *Years of Decisions* (Double-day, 1955), pp. 10–11.

16. Donald M. Nelson, *Arsenal of Democracy* (Harcourt Brace Jovanovich, 1946), p. 359.

17. In particular, Hodgson challenges the thesis of Gar Alperovitz's *Atomic Diplomacy* (Simon and Schuster, 1965).

18. Hodgson attributes Stimson's feelings about Kyoto to a chance visit from a cousin, who had studied Japanese culture at Har-vard. But Stimson himself had visited the city several times in the 1920s and, according to Otis Cary ("The Sparing of Kyoto: Mr. Stimson's 'Pet City,'" *Japan Quarterly* 22, 1975, pp. 229–245), it was his memory of those visits that was responsible for his decision.

The Code of the WASP Warrior

Why Bush is so Willing to Stand up to Saddam

EVAN THOMAS
with
THOMAS M. DEFRANK
and
ANN McDANIEL

In June 1940, Henry Stimson, an elder statesman and soldier, laid down a challenge to an audience of privileged schoolboys at Phillips Academy in Andover, Mass. It was "a very dark hour for the civilized world," Stimson warned; Hitler's Germany was bullying smaller countries and violating "Christian principles" of "respect for justice and fair play." But Colonel Stimson said that he envied his young listeners, for they had the "opportunity" to choose between "right and wrong," to stand up for good against evil. Stimson's interventionist views were not popular at the time. Pearl Harbor was still 18 months away and many Americans were isolationist. Yet the old colonel's call to arms electrified a 16-year-old Andover boy named George Bush. When he graduated two years later, Bush couldn't wait for a college degree to go to war; he enlisted to become the youngest aviator in the U.S. Navy.

If President Bush has seemed willing, even eager to confront Saddam Hussein, he is doing no more than Colonel Stimson would expect of him. Other presidents have agonized in the most public way over putting American boys in harm's way. But last week Bush simply told the nation that he meant "to stand up for what's right and condemn what's wrong." There is a warrior ethic that runs deep in the values of the old WASP establishment. Bush is the product of a culture that prized not only good breeding and proper manners but martial virility and moral certitude. As a child Bush was taught to play fair, but he was also taught to punch the bully in the nose. The concept of a "just war" was taught, along with charity and faith, in morning chapel at Andover. To keep them from becoming soft or spoiled, the children of the American upper class were supposed to survive three "ordeals," wrote Nelson Aldrich in "Old Money," a guide to WASPdom: spartan life at boarding school, roughing it in the Great Outdoors and, if their timing was good, fighting in a war. Whether swimming off the rocks in Maine or drawing a line in the sand against Iraq, Bush likes to prove he has mastered all three.

Henry Stimson was George Bush's hero. "Bush had this special kind of respect for Stimson because he was a combination of all the things his family stood for," says a close friend. "You are self-reliant and you fight wars for your country." The president's role model was especially avid about fighting wars. A war "would be a wonderfully good thing for this country," Stimson wrote in 1896, shortly before the United States found an excuse to go to war with Spain. Stimson's own hero was Teddy Roosevelt, the ultimate WASP warrior, who had the good fortune to lead his Rough Riders up San Juan Hill. Stimson bitterly regretted missing combat as a young man, so he enlisted in the Army for World War I and fought at the age of 50.

A wealthy Wall Street lawyer who served as Franklin Roosevelt's secretary of War in World War II, Stimson was a central figure in a group of militant nationalists who believed the United States had the duty and destiny to civilize the world. The Colonel, as he preferred to be called, became a patron saint for the Best and the Brightest, whose aggressive interventionism finally came to grief in Vietnam. During the Cuban missile crisis in 1962 John Kennedy's national-security adviser McGeorge Bundy sought the advice of Robert Lovett, a former secretary of Defense and fellow Yale man. "Mac," responded Lovett, "I think the best service we can perform for the president is to approach this as Colonel Stimson would."

The tight-knit establishment of Bundy, Lovett and Stimson was the world that George Bush grew up in. His father was Lovett's business partner on Wall Street. Prescott Bush—like Stimson, Bundy and Lovett—was a member of Skull and Bones, the Yale secret society. When it was young George's turn to be tapped by Skull and Bones in the spring of 1947, he found in the society's "tomb," its brooding windowless clubhouse in New Haven, none other than Colonel Stimson, there to initiate a new class into the society's mysteries and rituals. It was naturally assumed that Bonesmen would go on to power, so the society prepared them to exercise it.

The intense fellowship of Skull and Bones taught to an exaggerated degree the virtues of loyalty and male bonding. "The only way to make a man trustworthy," Stimson preached, "is to trust him." Bush has practiced Stimson's lesson in his personal diplomacy, forging a kind of global club among the world leaders he relentlessly woos with telephone calls and personal notes. When Secretary of Defense Dick Cheney went to see Saudi Arabia's King Fahd to ask his support after the invasion of Kuwait, the Saudi king said that he trusted the United States because he had known George Bush since his days as CIA director in the mid-'70s.

Bush the Loyal Friend and Bush the War Leader effortlessly came together in the days after Saddam's invasion of Kuwait. It may be a fortuitous melding of WASP virtues, for if Bush is to successfully defy the bully of Baghdad, the American president will need all the friends he can get.

The United States and Nicaragua

*A Survey of the Relations
from 1909-1932*

The Department of State
Latin American Series, No. 6
1932

MAP OF
NICARAGUA
SCALE
1: 6,000,000
KILOMETERS
10 0 10 20 40 60 80 100
10 0 10 20 30 40 50 60
STATUTE MILES

CONTENTS

CONTENTS

INTRODUCTION

The Republic of Nicaragua is the largest in size of the Central American republics, having an estimated area of 51,000 square miles, of which Lakes Nicaragua and Managua occupy about 4,500 square miles. With the exception of Honduras, lying immediately to the north, the population, which according to the 1920 census was 638,000, is the smallest to the square mile of any of the five republics. It is composed of three distinct physiographic areas, the western plains, the central highlands, and the low-lying jungles that extend inland from the Caribbean. In the highlands, the Cordillera of Central America breaks, leaving a depression which, because of the two large lakes and the San Juan River, has afforded a natural inter-oceanic highway.

Unlike the situation in the other Central American countries, the majority of the population in Nicaragua resides on the fertile plains surrounding the lakes and not in the highlands of the interior. This is due to two reasons: one, the commerce which, during the colonial period, moved across the natural interoceanic highway; and two, the porous tufa formation of the soil, which affords natural drainage and makes living conditions more healthy than in any of the low-lying regions in that latitude. The cities which were founded in these plains in the colonial period are still the most important politically and socially.

The western section around the two lakes, which have an altitude above sea level of approximately 120 feet, contains about seven-eight ns of the total population and probably an equal percentage of the national wealth. The principal industry of this section is the production of coffee. About 44 per cent of the total crop is grown in the Departments of Carazo and Masaya off the western shores of Lake Nicaragua, and about 33 per cent comes from the more hilly region about Managua.[1]

The highland plateaus of Nicaragua, which are very rich in the natural grasses necessary for the raising of cattle, have been settled comparatively recently. The best pasture lands are situated in the Department of Chontales in the highlands to the east of Lake Nicaragua. In the mountainous section around Matagalpa, where

---

[1] Harold Playter, *Nicaragua: A Commercial and Economic Survey* (Washington, U. S. Government Printing Office, 1927), p. 25.

altitudes sometimes reach between 3,000 and 4,000 feet, considerable coffee is grown. Gold and silver mines are also located in the north central part of the Cordillera.

The eastern littoral is largely dense tropical jungle. This section was practically uninhabited by white men until the banana and mahogany trades arose, centering around the coastal ports of Bluefields and Puerto Cabezas. In the past, the revenues of the east coast went toward the improvement of communications, public works, etc., of the cities of the western section. Revolutionists have been quick to capitalize the resentment engendered by many years of this practice, so that, as a result, most revolutions have begun on the east coast. The linking of the two divisions into an organic entity is the most important administrative problem which the Republic has to face.

In Nicaragua, the Spaniards did not exterminate the Indians, as they did in Costa Rica, nor isolate them racially as in Guatemala, but fused with them into a fairly homogeneous population. This mestizo population adopted the language and religion of the Spaniards but retained the Indian ways of living and cultivating the soil. The fusion was most complete in the western part, settled by the Spaniards. East of the two lakes and within the highlands is a large Indian population that still preserves many features of primitive community life. In the low-lying plains of the Caribbean littoral are to be found some Indians and negro half-breeds. Within recent years, the banana and logging industries imported several thousand West Indian negroes. To-day, there is a fairly constant emigration, which began several years ago on the west coast and has extended to the east coast, where several logging and banana enterprises recently ceased operations.

Nicaragua has a republican form of Government, its Constitution being modeled after that of the United States. Power is highly centralized in the Federal Government. Responsible to the President is a cabinet which, besides exercising the ordinary ministerial powers, also has many duties which in many countries are exercised by the local authorities. The country is divided into 13 departments, each presided over by a *jefe político*, or chief executive, appointed by and responsible to the President. There are also six districts, all on the east coast, two of which are responsible directly to the Ministry of the Interior. The other four elect their own governors, who are responsible to the *jefe político* of the Department of Bluefields. Local self-government centers around the municipalities, administered in each instance by an elected alcalde or mayor. The alcaldes have general administrative supervision, their principal powers being the enforcement of taxation, the control over the expenditures of public funds, certain police powers, and authority to command the *jefes de cantón*, sheriffs, and the *jueces de mesta*, rural police agents. Particularly in those rural districts where there are large numbers of Indians, these latter two officials exercise an authority through intimidation far out of proportion to their actual duties as established by law.

Exports of Nicaragua are confined within a narrow range of commodities. Coffee occupies a dominating position, comprising about 40 per cent of the total exports; a decline in its value has an immediate and disturbing effect on both the balance of trade and on Government revenues. Most of the balance is included in the four items: lumber, bananas, sugar, and gold. Imports are composed principally of manufactured commodities and wheat flour. Of the total Nicaraguan exports, the United States takes approximately 53 per cent, Germany 12 per cent, and France 8 per cent; of the imports, the United States supplies approximately 63 per cent, Great Britain 11 per cent, and Germany 9 per cent.

During the 20-year period, 1909–1919, inclusive, the Nicaraguan trade balance was unfavorable only 3 times. In 4 of the 10 succeeding years, due to the heavy imports of construction material and the decline in the value of its principal exports, the trade balance was unfavorable. Even so, exports during this period averaged $10,775,900 against imports of $9,663,600, giving an average favorable balance of over $1,000,000 annually. However, Nicaragua's invisible debit items are substantial. The payments on the bonded debt, dividends on foreign investments in Nicaragua, insurance and banking charges, and the travel expenditures of Nicaraguans abroad necessitate a considerable excess of exports over imports, if the balance of payments as contrasted with the balance of trade is to be in equilibrium.

Nicaragua's bonded debt is represented by two issues: the Ethelburga Syndicate bonds of 1909, which in that year refunded all the external indebtedness, and the guaranteed customs bonds of 1918. On October 31, 1931, of the former issue there was outstanding £525,940; of the latter, $1,276,750. American participation in the Ethelburga bonds at the time of issue was negligible; at present it amounts to about 5 per cent. American participation in the guaranteed customs bonds was at the time of issue 26 per cent; it is now 33 per cent. Nicaraguan participation was 43 per cent and is now 34 per cent.[2] The reason for the increase of American and the decrease of Nicaraguan participation in this issue is to be found in the spread between the 5 per cent interest rate of the bonds and the

---

[2] *Report of the Collector General of Customs and High Commission*, 1929, p. 88.

prevailing local interest rates of from 12 to 36 per cent. Many Nicaraguans sold their bonds in order to employ the money therefrom at the more favorable rates.

In addition to the bonded indebtedness, there is a floating debt of about $800,000.[3] The total indebtedness, exclusive of claims, is about $4,632,818.[4] This compares with the total public debts of approximately $13,484,862 in Honduras,[5] $20,916,732 in Guatemala,[6] $21,-657,782 in Costa Rica,[7] and $22,094,940 in El Salvador.[8]

The civil war of 1926–27 produced claims against Nicaragua totaling $19,772,933. A Mixed Claims Commission has examined claims to a nominal value of $1,286,526 and has granted awards of $165,593, a reduction of about 88 per cent. On the same scale on which these awards were made, the total claims would be settled for about $2,740,000.

American direct investment in Nicaragua totals approximately $15,000,000, which is less than in any other of the Latin American countries except Ecuador and Paraguay. Of this amount more than seven-eighths is located in the fruit, lumbering, and mining enterprises of the Caribbean littoral. The fruit and lumber companies in some cases have their own railroads and wharves. The approximately $2,000,000 of American capital in western Nicaragua is invested in coffee and cotton plantations, mines, and the public utilities in Managua.[9]

The country is policed by a national constabulary of approximately 200 officers and 2,150 men, to whom may be added about 250 municipal police, which have been organized in 41 municipalities since January 1, 1931.

---

[3] Sept. 30, 1931.
[4] The Ethelburga debt has been changed into dollars at the rate of one pound sterling equalling $4.86.
[5] July 31, 1930.
[6] Dec. 31, 1930.
[7] Mar. 31, 1931.
[8] Feb. 19, 1931.
[9] For general economic and commercial conditions, see: (1) *Nicaragua, Report of Jeremiah W. Jenks on Commission on Public Credit, High Commission, Ferrocarril del Pacifico de Nicaragua, National Bank of Nicaragua* (New York *Evening Post* Job Printing Office, 1918); (2) U.S. Department of Commerce, *Nicaragua, A Review of Commerce and Industries, 1918–1923*, Trade Information Bulletin, No. 255 (Washington, U. S. Government Printing Office, 1924); (3) William W. Cumberland, *Nicaragua, An Economic and Financial Survey* (Washington, U.S. Government Printing Office, 1928); (4) reports of the Collector General of Customs, 1911–1931; (5) reports of the High Commission, 1918–31; and (6) Harold Playter, *Nicaragua, A Commercial and Economic Survey* (Washington, U.S. Government Printing Office, 1927).

THE SITUATION BEFORE 1912

THE POLITICAL BACKGROUND [1]

The political history of Central America can be explained largely by *localismo*, the tendency toward the national supremacy of a city, and *personalismo*, the political adherence to a leader. In Nicaragua this is especially true, because both *localismo* and *personalismo* reach their most complete development in large communities. About one-quarter of the entire population lives in six important towns on the plains surrounding the two lakes.

Granada, at the western end of Lake Nicaragua, developed early as the principal commercial center on the interoceanic route. The leading families, who controlled the trade activities, later fortified their power by developing cattle ranches. These families constitute the nucleus of a conservative aristocracy. Their numerical strength lies in the laboring and servant classes dependent upon them. The Granada aristocracy, even during the colonial period, was restive under the administrative control of the Spanish authorities at León, which was, and still is, the largest city.

León did not develop a strong creole aristocracy because Spain sent peninsular Spaniards to administer the political and social affairs of the province. Consequently the Creoles, excluded from politics, turned to intellectual and cultural activities. Moreover, in contrast to Granada, a large artisan and small landholding class grew up in León. The wide plain surrounding the city was divided into small properties, worked either by the owner or under his immediate supervision. After throwing off Spanish control, the intellectuals, the artisans, and the small landholders gave their support to the Liberal Party, which was against governmental control by the landholding aristocracy and the clerical classes.

During the early years of the Republic, Granada and León bitterly contested for the location of the capital seat. Each succeeded for a time in obtaining that privilege. Finally, however, unable to agree, they compromised on Managua, the present capital.

When the Spaniards were overthrown in 1821, the jealousy of Granada and León immediately broke forth in an armed conflict.

---

[1] See Dana G. Munro, *The Five Republics of Central America* (Oxford University Press, 1918), ch. IV, pp. 72–98.

For the next 35 years Nicaragua was kept in a turmoil by an inter-
mittent interparty warfare and by invasions from the other Central
American republics. In 1855–56 both parties united to expel the
American filibuster Walker, who, though originally invited by the
Liberals, had set himself up as President. From this alliance the
Conservatives emerged triumphant. They ruled with tolerance, so
that the next 35 years were passed in comparative peace and stability.
With considerable shrewdness their leaders ruled as a group, peace-
fully deciding among themselves the succession to the Presidency.
The Liberals even acquiesced in the rule of their former enemies,
enjoying the prosperity which arose from peace and order. How-
ever, when the dominant Conservative group split in 1893, the
Liberals quickly and successfully revolted.

Their leader was José Santos Zelaya, who ruled the country with
an iron hand for the next 17 years. Despite a progressive policy
in extending the railway and steamship service, in developing the
coffee industry, and in increasing educational opportunities, Zelaya
exploited Nicaragua to a degree theretofore unparalled. He fostered
monopolies, which brought a tribute from practically every form
of commercial activity, and he sold vast concessions of enterprises
and land to unscrupulous promoters, both native and foreign, which
were prejudicial to public interest. He inflated the currency by
emitting about 12,000,000 pesos of paper notes for which there was
no gold or silver reserve. He violated personal and private property
rights, inflicting the most brutal treatment upon his enemies.

It was his intermeddling with the other countries of Central
America that aroused concern in the United States. In order to
put an end to the continual warfare that existed from 1902 to 1907, the
United States and Mexico called a conference at Washington in
1907. At this conference the five republics of Central America
signed a series of conventions, in which they agreed as one of the
first duties in their mutual relations to avoid revolution and to remain
neutral in case of civil war in one of the other republics.[2] During
the next two years, Zelaya violated these conventions by his attempts
to force the restoration of the old Central American Union. The
Governments of Costa Rica, El Salvador, and Guatemala protested
to the United States.

THE REVOLUTION OF 1909–10

In October, 1909, a revolution against Zelaya broke out on the
east coast. It was partially financed and supplied by the other
countries of Central America and by foreigners whose interest had

---

[2] *Foreign Relations of the United States*, 1907, pt. 2, pp. 665–727.

recently been prejudiced by certain inimical concessions. The Conservative Party, which sponsored the revolution, set up a government at Bluefields under the provisional presidency of Juan J. Estrada, the Liberal Governor of the province.[3]

Although the relations between the United States and Nicaragua had been strained by a prolonged dispute over the so-called Emery Claim,[4] which had culminated in the withdrawal of the American Minister, the United States remained neutral. However, in November, 1909, the execution by President Zelaya of two American soldiers of fortune, Cannon and Groce, who held commissions in the revolutionary army, precipitated a crisis.[5] In a note of December 1, 1909, to the Nicaraguan Chargé d'Affaires, the United States broke off diplomatic relations. Its pertinent passages are as follows: [6]

SIR: Since the Washington Conventions of 1907 it is notorious that President Zelaya has almost continuously kept Central America in tension or turmoil, that he has repeatedly and flagrantly violated the provisions of the Conventions and by a baleful influence upon Honduras, whose neutrality the Conventions were to assure, has sought to discredit those sacred international obligations to the great detriment of Costa Rica, El Salvador and Guatemala, whose Governments meanwhile appear to have been able patiently to strive for the loyal support of the engagements so solemnly undertaken at Washington under the auspices of the United States and of Mexico.

It is equally a matter of common knowledge that under the régime of President Zelaya republican institutions have ceased in Nicaragua to exist except in name; that public opinion and the press have been throttled; and that prison has been the reward of any tendency to real patriotism. My consideration for you personally impels me to abstain from unnecessary discussion of the painful details of a régime which unfortunately has been a blot upon the history of Nicaragua and a discouragement to a group of republics whose aspirations need only the opportunity of free and honest government.

In view of the interests of the United States and of its relation to the Washington Conventions, appeal against this situation has long since been made to this Government by a majority of the Central American Republics. There is now added the appeal, through the revolution, of a great body of the Nicaraguan people. Two Americans who, this Government is now convinced were officers connected with the revolutionary forces and therefore entitled to be dealt with according to the enlightened practice of civilized nations, have been killed by direct order of President Zelaya. Their execution is said to have been preceded by barbarous cruelties. The Consulate at Managua is now officially reported to have been menaced. There is thus a sinister culmination of an administration also characterized

---

[3] *Ibid.*, 1909, pp. 452–453.
[4] *Ibid.*, pp. 460–467.
[5] *Ibid.*, pp. 446–451.
[6] For full note, see File No. 6369/346A; also *Foreign Relations*, 1909, pp. 455–457.

by a cruelty to its own citizens which has, until the recent outrage, found vent in the case of this country in a succession of petty annoyances and indignities which many months ago made it impossible to ask an American Minister longer to reside at Mangua. From every point of view it has evidently become difficult for the United States further to delay more active response to the appeals so long made to its duty to its citizens, to its dignity, to Central America and to civilization.

The Government of the United States is convinced that the revolution represents the ideals and the will of a majority of the Nicaraguan people more faithfully than does the Government of President Zelaya, and that its peaceable control is well-nigh as extensive as that hitherto so sternly attempted by the government at Managua.

There is now added the fact, as officially reported from more than one quarter, that there are already indications of a rising in the western provinces in favor of a presidential candidate intimately associated with the old régime. In this it is easy to see new elements tending toward a condition of anarchy which leaves, at a given time, no definite responsible source to which the Government of the United States could look for reparation for the killing of Messrs. Cannon and Groce, or, indeed, for the protection which must be assured American citizens and American interests in Nicaragua.

In these circumstances the President no longer feels for the Government of President Zelaya that respect and confidence which would make it appropriate hereafter to maintain with it regular diplomatic relations, implying the will and the ability to respect and assure what is due from one state to another.

The Government of Nicaragua which you have hitherto represented is hereby notified, as will be also the leaders of the revolution, that the Government of the United States will hold strictly accountable for the protection of American life and property the factions *de facto* in control of the eastern and western portions of the Republic of Nicaragua.

.   .   .   .   .   .

From the foregoing it will be apparent to you that your office of Chargé d'Affaires is at an end. I have the honor to enclose your passport, for use in case you desire to leave this country. I would add at the same time that, although your diplomatic quality is terminated, I shall be happy to receive you, as I shall be happy to receive the representative of the revolution, each as the unofficial channel of communication between the Government of the United States and the *de facto* authorities to whom I look for the protection of American interests pending the establishment in Nicaragua of a Government with which the United States can maintain diplomatic relations.

When his subsequent attempts to reach an understanding with the United States failed, President Zelaya resigned, depositing the Presidency in Dr. José Madriz, a distinguished Liberal of León. Despite his nonrecognition by the United States, Madriz not only managed to maintain his régime but drove the forces of General Estrada into Bluefields, where he besieged them. Toward the blockade of the city by Madriz, the United States held that "if the announced blockade . . . was effectively maintained and the requirements of international law, including warning to approaching vessels, were observed, the United States Government would not be disposed to interfere to prevent its enforcement".[7]

However, President Madriz complained that the United States naval vessels prevented the blockading activities of a Nicaraguan ship that had arrived fully armed after sailing from New Orleans under the guise of a merchantman. To this the Department of State replied:[8]

The Government of the United States has acknowledged the right of each faction to maintain blockade but has refused to permit vessels illegally and clandestinely fitted out in American waters to interfere with American commerce.

To Madriz's charge that the United States prevented a land attack, the United States replied:[9]

. . . the Government of the United States took only the customary step of prohibiting bombardment or fighting by either faction within the unfortified and ungarrisoned commercial city of Bluefields, thus protecting the preponderating American and other foreign interests . . . .

Failing to capture Bluefields, the Madriz troops were unable to maintain themselves in that region and were forced to retire. General Estrada immediately launched a successful counteroffensive. On August 21, 1910, the day after Madriz left Managua, General Estrada assumed control of the Government.

THE ADMINISTRATION OF PRESIDENT ESTRADA, 1910–11

The revolution which started at Bluefields, though led by a discontented Liberal, General Estrada, had the body of its support among the Conservatives. General Estrada had been accepted by the latter only because by his duplicity the garrison at Bluefields had been turned over to the revolutionists, a preliminary necessary to any successful uprising. General Estrada enlisted the support of another Liberal, Gen. José María Moncada, who became Minister of Government in his cabinet.

The Granada Conservatives had taken the lead in financing and organizing the revolution. During the 17 years of Zelaya's dictatorship they had been bound together by a common cause. Once Zelaya had been eliminated, the principal leaders disagreed among themselves over the control of the Government. Gen. Emiliano Chamorro enjoyed the following of the greater part of the Conserva-

[7] File No. 6369/951A; *Foreign Relations*, 1910, pp. 746–747.
[8] File No. 6369/1060B; *Foreign Relations*, 1910, p. 753.
[9] *Ibid.*

tives. His leadership was disputed by the Cuadra family, which strengthened its power by an alliance with Adolfo Diaz, one of the organizers of the revolution. However, to the displeasure of both factions, the military exploits of Gen. Luís Mena had won widespread popular favor. Before the revolution, General Mena had been a follower of General Chamorro. Because of his control of the Army he was the most powerful figure in the new Administration. Both in admiration of his military services and in fear of his popularity with the Army, which was devoted to its chief, General Estrada made him Minister of War. Due to the ambition of these popular leaders and the continual Liberal revolutionary plots, the position of General Estrada was extremely difficult and insecure.

Upon assuming control of the Government, General Estrada immediately sought the recognition of the United States. He promised to establish a constitutional government, reorganize finances, and make amends for the death of Cannon and Groce, adding that to facilitate compliance with the foregoing, he requested the Department of State to send a mission to Nicaragua.[10] Accordingly, Mr. Thomas Dawson, American Minister to Panama, was sent to represent the views of the Department of State.[11]

On October 27, 1910, General Estrada, Minister of Foreign Affairs Diaz, Minister of War Mena, and General Chamorro signed a series of pacts, commonly known as the Dawson Pacts, although Mr. Dawson was not a signatory.[12] Their provisions were the following:[13]

1. Immediate elections should be called to choose members of a constituent assembly which should choose General Estrada and Diaz as President and Vice President, respectively, for a period of two years. The assembly should also draw up a new Constitution, including the abolition of monopolies and the guarantee of the legitimate rights of foreigners, and should call general elections at the end of the 2-year provisional period. At these elections General Estrada should not be a candidate to succeed himself.

2. A mixed claims commission should be appointed to investigate and settle claims.

3. A loan to rehabilitate finances and pay claims, guaranteed by a certain per cent of the customs receipts, should be solicited through the good offices of the United States Government.

In accordance with these agreements, elections for the Constituent Assembly were held on November 27, 1910, resulting in a Conservative victory. Thirty thousand votes were cast. While the Liberal Party claimed that the elections had not been entirely free, it was felt by the Department of State that popular opinion had been fairly well expressed. On December 31, 1910, the Constituent

---

[10] *Foreign Relations*, 1910, p. 762.   [12] *Ibid.*, pp. 765–767.
[11] *Ibid.*, pp. 763–764.   [13] Appendix A, p. 125.

Assembly unanimously elected General Estrada and Adolfo Diaz President and Vice President, respectively, to which Government the United States extended recognition on the following day.

After electing the President, the Constituent Assembly proceeded to the drafting of the new Constitution. General Chamorro, who controlled the Constituent Assembly, used his power to force through a Constitution which would have made the Assembly superior to the President. President Estrada sent a message to the Constituent Assembly, stating his objections to the Constitution, and requesting a reconsideration in accordance with the announced principles of the revolution. The Chamorro majority in the Constituent Assembly ignored this message and, after the friends of President Estrada had withdrawn, adopted the Constitution. President Estrada immediately vetoed the Constitution, dissolved the Constituent Assembly, and called for new elections. [14] General Chamorro left Nicaragua a few days later, and immediately the leadership of the Conservative Party devolved upon his rival, General Mena, the Minister of War. Although under the circumstances the policy adopted by President Estrada met with the approval of the Department of State, it instructed the Minister—

to impress upon the party leaders the fact that by their agreements transmitted to Dawson they have assumed a responsibility toward this Government of working harmoniously and in a conciliatory spirit. The said agreements led to the election of President Estrada and the resulting recognition of his Government by that of the United States. The responsibility under those agreements applies especially to the approaching free elections.[15]

Through his control of the Army, General Mena succeeded in packing the new Constituent Assembly, elected on April 16, 1911, with his own adherents. Although he was the most powerful man in Nicaragua and indispensable to the maintenance of President Estrada, nevertheless he feared that the President, aided by General Moncada, the Minister of Government, was plotting against him. This fear was realized when the President suddenly arrested him, alleging his " contemplated treason." The American Minister was of the opinion at the time that this act was to have been the signal for a Liberal uprising, engineered by General Moncada.[16] The Army immediately prepared to release General Mena by force of arms. Estrada, who was incapable of defending himself, on May 9, 1911, deposited the Presidency in Adolfo Diaz. The latter immediately got in touch with General Mena who, at the request of the American Minister, had been transferred from the city jail to the

---

[14] *Foreign Relations*, 1911, pp. 657–658.
[15] *Ibid.*, p. 658.
[16] *Ibid.*, pp. 660–661.

British Consulate. They agreed that Diaz was to fill Estrada's unexpired term and that General Mena should continue as Minister of War.

THE KNOX-CASTRILLO CONVENTION OF 1911

When President Estrada assumed control in August, 1910, he found that ex-President Madriz had left a substantial sum in the Treasury. Although these funds would have been sufficient to meet the deficit in the ordinary expenses of the Government, it was paid out to Conservatives as compensation for injuries suffered under President Zelaya. Those participating in the revolution were well rewarded for their troubles, receiving either land or cash. The Zelaya and Madriz governments, in order to meet the extraordinary civil-war expenses, had resorted to currency inflation. When he had exhausted the Treasury surplus, President Estrada continued this inflationary policy, issuing 25,000,000 additional pesos of paper money. Foreign trade and exchange consequently suffered. The customs revenues in 1910 were the lowest since 1903. The internal commercial situation was equally unfavorable. Many merchants had been compelled to accept promissory notes for goods purchased by the Government, thereby freezing their capital. A great mass of claims of all descriptions had piled up. The revolution had paralyzed industry and commerce by destroying cattle and crops, dislocating the labor supply, and disorganizing the transportation system.

Although the Estrada administration continued the currency inflation, it was aware of the grave situation that threatened a default on the foreign bonded debt and even a national bankruptcy. In the so-called Dawson Pacts,[17] signed August 27, 1910, it took steps to solve the financial difficulties. The third pact reads:

In order to rehabilitate the public finances and to pay legitimate claims, both foreign as well as national, the good offices of the American Government will be solicited, with the object of negotiating a loan, which will be guaranteed by a certain per cent of the customs receipts of the Republic, collected in accordance with the terms of an agreement satisfactory to both Governments.

Upon receiving the request, the Department of State, in January, 1911, sent Mr. Ernest H. Wands, a financial expert, to make a thorough investigation of the conditions of Nicaraguan finances. Various banking corporations in the United States became interested, offering to negotiate a loan, but none of these proposals were consummated prior to the resignation of President Estrada. Shortly

---

[17] Appendix A, p. 125.

after President Diaz assumed office in May, 1911, he convoked the Nicaraguan Assembly, which had been dissolved by President Estrada. On May 6, 1911, the Assembly, by a vote of 25 to 7, authorized him to negotiate a $20,000,000 loan in the United States.

A treaty, known as the Knox-Castrillo Convention,[18] was negotiated between the United States and Nicaragua on June 6, 1911, to carry out the above agreement of the so-called Dawson Pacts. Under its terms Nicaragua obligated itself to seek a loan, subject to the approval of the United States, sufficient to refund the internal and external debt and settle claims against the Government. The customs receipts were to serve as security for the loan and were to be collected by a collector general of customs, approved and protected by the United States. The Nicaraguan Assembly ratified the Knox-Castrillo Convention on June 15, 1911,[19] by a vote of 30 to 6, and President Diaz urged the United States to hasten favorable action. A reform of the Nicaraguan Constitution was pending, and action thereon had been suspended until the loan convention should be approved. There were various American interests which complained that the loan convention as drafted did not sufficiently protect concessions and other existing rights. The Department of State held that the Nicaraguan Government would be acting within its sovereign right should it desire to set aside unconstitutional concessions or to take property by expropriation with due and proper compensation. Therefore, the Department of State refused to heed requests to include in the treaty a blanket provision that all American investments would be respected.

After long consideration of the matter, the treaty was defeated on May 9, 1912, in the Committee on Foreign Relations of the United States Senate.

The Treasury Bills Agreement of 1911

Anticipating the ratification of the Knox-Castrillo Convention, Mr. Wands, Nicaragua's Financial Adviser, opened negotiations to obtain a loan. The Department of State kept strictly aloof from these negotiations and did not commit itself to any particular bankers. In June, 1911, the banking houses of Brown Bros. & Co. and J. & W. Seligman & Co. agreed to loan Nicaragua $15,000,000, provided the treaty was ratified before the first of September, 1911. Pending ratification of the treaty, Nicaragua's lack of funds became so critical that it appealed to the bankers for cash to tide it over until the $15,000,000 contemplated loan should be issued.

---

[18] Appendix B, p. 126.   [19] *Foreign Relations*, 1912, pp. 1074, *et seq.*

By the Treasury Bills Agreement of September 1, 1911, it was agreed as follows:

1. The Nicaraguan Government was to issue $1,500,000 of Treasury bills to the bankers, obtaining in lieu thereof an identical sum of money, less the bankers' commission. The Treasury bills were to bear 6 per cent interest and to mature October 15, 1912.

2. The Treasury bills, after the payment of $430,000 annually out of customs receipts to the Ethelburga Syndicate as service on the bonds of 1909, were to be a lien and charge upon all export and import customs duties, which were to be collected by a collector general under conditions similar to those provided in the unratified Knox-Castrillo Convention. The collector general was to be nominated by the bankers, approved by the Secretary of State of the United States, and appointed by the President of Nicaragua.

3. Nicaragua agreed not to alter the import and export duties, so long as any of the Treasury bills remained outstanding, without the agreement of the bankers.

4. A National Bank, with an authorized capital stock of $5,000,000, was to be established. Its initial capital, to be entirely subscribed by Nicaragua, was to be $100,000. The stock of the National Bank was pledged as security for the Treasury bills. The bankers were given an option of 51 per cent at par of the shares of the National Bank.

5. A study was to be made of the currency conditions and requirements of Nicaragua and a plan prepared for introducing and maintaining a stable currency system. At that time currency circulation totaled about 32,000,000 paper pesos.

6. The bankers were authorized as agents of Nicaragua to confer with the Ethelburga Syndicate in order to settle various differences that had arisen between the Ethelburga Syndicate and Nicaragua.

At the same time, Nicaragua and the bankers signed a bond-purchase contract under which the bankers agreed to purchase $12,000,000 of bonds, bearing 5 per cent interest and maturing in 37 years, their purchase conditional upon the ratification of the Knox-Castrillo Convention. The agreement also provided for an additional $3,000,000 of bonds to be used to pay awards of the Mixed Claims Commission [20] and to inaugurate construction on the projected railway to the Atlantic coast. On October 9, 1911, the Constituent Assembly approved the Treasury Bills Agreement and bond-purchase contract by a vote of 26 to 6.

The bankers nominated for Collector General of Customs Mr. Clifford D. Ham, an American citizen with the Philippine Customs Service. In approving the selection of Mr. Ham by the bankers, the Secretary of State said: [21]

. . . my approval of the person selected for the post of Collector-General of Customs of Nicaragua must not in any wise be understood as indicating that the Government of the United States will

---

[20] See p. 15.   [21] File No. 817.51/256; *Foreign Relations*, 1912, p. 1080.

lend any other or further good offices in the protection of the American citizens parties to this contract than it would accord to any legitimate American enterprise abroad, nor that this approval places the bankers in any better position in regard to seeking this protection than if I took no part whatever in the approval of a Collector-General of Customs.

The President of Nicaragua appointed Mr. Ham to office on November 23, 1911, and the latter assumed his duties on December 16, 1911. Mr. Ham served as Collector General of Customs from that time until June, 1928, when he resigned. His successor, Mr. Irving A. Lindberg, had been Deputy Collector General since 1912.

The Mixed Claims Commission

The so-called Dawson Pacts of 1910 provided for an impartial commission to adjudicate without appeal the unliquidated claims against the Nicaraguan Government, especially those originating out of the cancellation of concessions, monopolies, and contracts of former governments. President Zelaya had plastered the country with concessions, which President Estrada abolished as unconstitutional, illegal, and burdensome monopolies. The decree approved by the Assembly on May 17, 1911,[22] and amended by the Assembly on October 14, 1911,[23] provided that the Mixed Claims Commission be composed of three members: a Nicaraguan appointed by the Nicaraguan Government, another member appointed by the Nicaraguan Government on the recommendation of the Department of State, and an umpire designated by the Department of State. Under the terms of this decree, a Nicaraguan and two Americans were appointed. The majority of the claimants were Nicaraguan, but the sums claimed by American citizens amounted to more than the claims of all other persons together. Although certain European countries protested that the preponderance of two Americans on the Mixed Claims Commission would prejudice findings in favor of American claimants, the latter received a much smaller sum in proportion to the amount claimed than other foreigners or Nicaraguans. The reason for this was that most of the American claims were based upon the cancellation by the Government of concessions that were illegal and the claims included large items for estimated future profits which the Mixed Claims Commission would not allow. The Mixed Claims Commission passed upon 7,908 claims against Nicaragua, all of which were decided by unanimous vote. Of a total of $13,808,161 demanded, the awards totaled only $1,840,432. On 66 American claims, totaling $7,576,564, but $538,749 was allowed.

---

[22] *Foreign Relations*, 1911, pp. 631–632.   [23] *Ibid.*, pp. 640–642.

The failure of the United States to ratify the Knox-Castrillo Convention, and as a result the failure of the loan of $15,000,000 to Nicaragua, left the Government without funds to satisfy the awards. During the early part of 1914, the Mixed Claims Commission was assigned $158,548, with which it paid 4,618 small claims, mostly of Nicaraguans for losses of live stock and similar property during the civil war of 1909–10 and the revolt of 1912. The payment of the remaining awards vexed the Nicaraguan Treasury for the next three years.[24]

---

[24] *Report of Nicaraguan Mixed Claims Commission*, 1915; *American Journal of International Law*, vol. 9, No. 4, Oct., 1915, pp. 858–869.

POLITICAL AND FINANCIAL DEVELOPMENTS
1912–1925

The Supplementary Loan Contract of March, 1912

Under the Treasury Bills Agreement of 1911, the bankers sent two currency experts, Messrs. Harrison (English) and Conant (American) to Nicaragua to prepare a plan for introducing and maintaining a stable currency system. They found that between March, 1911, when Mr. Wands had investigated finances, and the time of their arrival in November, the Nicaraguan Government had issued additional paper currency to the amount of 16,000,000 pesos. The outstanding paper currency had thereby increased from 32,000,000 pesos to 48,000,000 pesos. The currency experts reported that the $1,500,000 borrowed under the Treasury Bills Agreement was therefore insufficient to retire the depreciated paper currency. In addition, the Government, for lack of funds, faced immediate bankruptcy.[1] The bankers thus found themselves faced with a situation which required an additional loan or else envisaged the failure of the plan outlined under the Treasury Bills Agreement.[2]

On March 20, 1912, the Assembly, by a vote of 23 to 2, enacted a monetary law in accordance with the reports of the two experts, definitely legalizing the financial reforms provided for in the Treasury Bills Agreement, and also a law providing for a supplementary loan from the bankers. Upon the passage of these two laws, the bankers on March 26, 1912, signed a supplementary loan contract with Nicaragua by which they agreed to extend a short-term loan. The terms were:

1. A loan of $755,000 at 6 per cent, maturing October 15, 1913. The bankers' commission was to be 1 per cent on all drafts drawn by Nicaragua.
2. $500,000 was to be set aside for retiring paper currency. Nicaragua guaranteed that not more than 48,000,000 pesos of paper currency was then outstanding.[3]
3. $255,000 was to be applied to current expenses of the Nicaraguan Government.
4. The loan was secured by a third lien on the customs duties, subject to the prior liens of the bonds of 1909 and the Treasury bills of 1911, by the entire capital stock of the Pacific Railway when

---

[1] *Foreign Relations*, 1912, p. 1093.
[2] See letter to the Department of State from Brown Bros. & Co. and J. & W. Seligman & Co., Feb. 21, 1912, *Ibid.*, pp. 1096–1097.
[3] More than 49,000,000 pesos of this currency was finally redeemed.

reorganized, by the currency redeemed with the $500,000 previously mentioned, and by any funds resulting from a settlement of the dispute between Nicaragua and the bondholders of the 1909 loan.[4]

5. The bankers agreed to extend until October 15, 1913, the maturity of the Treasury bills of 1911.

6. Nicaragua agreed to reduce its budget along lines suggested by Messrs. Harrison and Conant.

7. The Pacific Railway, together with its steamship lines, was to be reorganized and incorporated in the United States.

8. The bankers obtained an option to purchase 51 per cent of the stock of the railway for $1,000,000 agreeing at the same time, should they exercise their option, to issue an additional $500,000 of first mortgage 6 per cent bonds for railway improvements and extensions. During the continuance of this option, the railway and steamship lines were to be managed by the bankers.

THE AGREEMENT WITH THE BONDHOLDERS OF THE 1909 ETHELBURGA SYNDICATE LOAN

Nicaragua's financial plight [5] was further alleviated by an agreement reached on May 25, 1912, by the bankers with the Council of Foreign Bondholders representing the holders of the Ethelburga bonds of 1909. Nicaragua had defaulted on July 1, 1911, on the sinking-fund service and on January 1, 1912, on the interest charges of these bonds, in spite of the fact that £371,730 was on deposit with the Ethelburga Syndicate, legitimately belonging to Nicaragua but withheld from it on the ground that the fund was dedicated to the building of a railroad to the Atlantic coast, the concession for which Nicaragua had declared invalid. A settlement was negotiated in December, 1911, with the Ethelburga Syndicate, which, however, the bondholders declined to carry out. The new agreement provided as follows:

1. Of the £371,730 held by the Ethelburga Syndicate, £140,000 was to be reserved for the payment of coupons up to and including January 1, 1913, arrears of sinking fund on the 1909 bonds, and expenses of the Council of Foreign Bondholders. From the balance, sufficient was to be used to liquidate the supplementary $500,000 loan of March 26, 1912.

2. The interest rate on the 1909 bonds was to be reduced from 6 to 5 per cent. Nicaragua was given an option whereby it could retire the bonds at 93 per cent of par within one year, at 94 per cent within two years, at 95 per cent within three years, and thereafter at par.

3. The bonds of 1909 were to be given a first lien upon the customs receipts and, so long as any such bonds should remain unpaid, the customs revenues of the Republic were to continue to be collected by the Collector General of Customs, in this respect carrying out the provision of the Treasury Bills Agreement.

[4] See *infra.*
[5] *Foreign Relations*, 1912, pp. 1092–1100.

4. The bankers were given a maximum commission of 1 per cent for handling the amortization of the bonds, including all expenses of bondholders' committees, etc.

The English bondholders accepted this settlement on June 20; the French bondholders, on June 26.

THE NATIONAL BANK

The National Bank, which was provided for by the Treasury Bills Agreement of September, 1911, and also by the Monetary Law of March, 1912, was incorporated under the laws of Connecticut as the Banco Nacional de Nicaragua, and opened for business in August, 1912. Its authorized capital stock was $5,000,000, but its paid-in capital was only $100,000, all subscribed by the Nicaraguan Government. Its management was under the supervision of the bankers.

The National Bank has the exclusive right to issue notes which are legal tender. It is the fiscal and disbursing agent of the Government and the depository of Government funds. It manages the currency system, including the purchase and sale of drafts on the exchange fund in New York.

THE REVOLT OF GENERAL MENA, JULY–SEPTEMBER, 1912

Although Diaz was the nominal head of the Government, General Mena was the real power. He had the complete support of the Army and controlled the Constituent Assembly. Shortly after Diaz became President in May, 1911, the two leaders signed an agreement by which Mena pledged his assistance to Diaz during the present Administration and Diaz in turn promised to put no obstacles in the way of the election of General Mena for the succeeding constitutional term.[6] However, during the succeeding months it became increasingly clear that General Mena was restless. He proposed that the Constituent Assembly elect him President for the 4-year term beginning January 1, 1913, in contravention of the so-called Dawson Pacts, which provided for a popular election. President Diaz, who favored this plan, believing that free elections were hopelessly impracticable for several years in Nicaragua, asked that the situation be submitted to the Department of State. The Department of State replied that "of the Nicaraguan matters under consideration by the Department the ratification of the pending loan contract and the amendment of the decree establishing a Claims Commission are of the first importance and should be disposed of before attention is directed to other subjects."[7] Finally, however, General Mena had the Constituent Assembly in October, 1911, elect him President for

[6] *Foreign Relations*, 1911, pp. 663–664.
[7] File No. 817.00/1696; *Foreign Relations*, 1911, p. 667.

the term beginning January 1, 1913. This action was distinctly distasteful to the Granada Conservatives, who hoped to elect one of their own members to the Presidency. General Chamorro returned from El Salvador and immediately threatened a revolution if the so-called Dawson Pacts were not strictly adhered to. Encouraged by the popular protests against the Treasury Bills Agreement and the $15,000,000 bond-purchase contract of September 1, 1911, General Mena forced through the Constituent Assembly a Constitution which would have made difficult the rehabilitation of Nicaraguan finances under the terms of the Knox-Castrillo Convention. It also made constitutional the election to the Presidency of General Mena. Despite the request of the Department of State that promulgation of the Constitution be delayed until after the arrival in Managua of the American Minister,[8] and directly against the wishes of President Diaz, the Constitution was irregularly promulgated by the Constituent Assembly on January 12, 1912.

During the spring, the political situation became more acute. The Constituent Assembly was determined that General Mena should be President and opposed the efforts of General Chamorro for financial reform. In July, President Diaz learned of General Mena's preparations for a revolt. On July 29, 1912, he curtailed the powers of General Mena, appointing Chamorro the General in Chief of the Army. General Mena immediately took up arms. After an unsuccessful attempt to capture the Loma Fortress, he accepted the Government's offer of amnesty for himself and his adherents in exchange for his resignation as Minister of War. That same evening, General Mena broke his pledge and, after cutting the electric-light wires in Managua, fled in open revolt to Masaya. The revolution was joined by a large body of Liberals under the leadership of General Zeledón, formerly Minister of War under Zelaya. The Liberals of León revolted and took over the city, which became a focal point for the revolution.

In December, 1911, President Diaz had proposed to the United States the insertion of a clause in the Constitution then under discussion which would permit intervention by the United States in order to maintain peace and the existence of a lawful government. The Department of State refrained from expressing an opinion in regard to this proposal.[9] Shortly after the outbreak of the revolution led by General Mena, American and other foreign property was seized by the revolutionists and the lives of American citizens threatened. The Department of State immediately asked President Diaz for protection. President Diaz replied that his Government

---

[8] *Foreign Relations*, 1912, p. 994.
[9] *Ibid.*, 1911, pp. 670–671.

was unable to comply with this request, adding " in consequence my Government desires that the Government of the United States guarantee with its forces security for the property of American citizens in Nicaragua and that it extend its protection to all the inhabitants of the Republic." [10] The Department of State replied as follows: [11]

The policy of the Government of the United States in the present Nicaraguan disturbances is to take the necessary measures for an adequate Legation guard at Managua, to keep open communications and to protect American life and property.

In discountenancing Zelaya, whose régime of barbarity and corruption was ended by the Nicaraguan nation after a bloody war, the Government of the United States opposed not only the individual but the system and this Government could not countenance any movement to restore the same destructive régime. The Government of the United States will, therefore, discountenance any revival of Zelayaism and will lend its strong moral support to the cause of legally constituted good government for the benefit of the people of Nicaragua, whom it has long sought to aid in their just aspiration toward peace and prosperity under constitutional and orderly government.

. . . .

The revolt of General Mena in flagrant violation of his solemn promises to his own Government and to the American Minister, and of the Dawson agreement by which he was solemnly bound, and his attempt to overturn the Government of his country for purely selfish purposes and without even the pretense of contending for a principle, make the present rebellion in origin the most inexcusable in the annals of Central America. The nature and methods of the present disturbances, indeed, place them in the category of anarchy rather than ordinary revolution. The reported character of those who promptly joined Mena, together with his uncivilized and savage action in breaking armistices, maltreating messengers, violating his word of honor, torturing peaceable citizens to exact contributions, and above all, in the ruthless bombardment of the city of Managua, with the deliberate destruction of innocent life and property and the killing of women and children and the sick in hospitals, and the cruel and barbarous slaughter of hundreds reported at Leon, give to the Mena revolt the attributes of the abhorrent and intolerable Zelaya régime.

In conformity with this pronouncement, 360 United States marines were sent to open the railway communciations from Corinto to Managua. A Legation guard at Managua of 100 men had been landed on August 4. The pronouncement sounded the end of the revolution. General Mena, who had fallen ill after the outbreak, soon surrendered. Zeledón, who had taken up a position in the

---

[10] File No. 817.00/1822; *Foreign Relations*, 1912, p. 1032.
[11] File No. 817.00/1940b; *Foreign Relations*, 1912, pp. 1043 and 1044.

Barranca Fort overlooking Masaya, refused to surrender. United
States marines stormed and captured the fort. Shortly afterwards,
with the surrender of León, the revolution came to an end. It had
cost the Nicaraguan Government about $2,000,000 to suppress the
revolution which once again imperiled the Republic's financial position. In suppressing the revolution, seven American marines and
bluejackets lost their lives.[12] Thenceforth the United States
retained at Managua a Legation guard of approximately 130 men.

The Election of Adolfo Diaz, 1912

The revolt of General Mena crushed, the farmers and merchants
wanted the Government to hold presidential elections at once in
order to remove one of the principal causes of unrest and agitation.
The Conservative Party was divided. The Granada aristocracy and
the Army wanted General Chamorro. The great majority of Conservatives, however, preferred either the continuation of Diaz or the
nomination of some other civilian. Although Diaz wanted to retire,
he finally accepted the nomination when the Conservatives could
agree on no other candidate. Moreover, because of his leniency
toward them, the moderate Liberals supported Diaz. They feared
the military rule of General Chamorro, even though he had resigned
as Commander in Chief to show them he was no longer a military
man. The Liberals did not nominate candidates; they were unable
to agree among themselves and also preferred to be in a position
afterwards to declare the elections fraudulent. The elections passed
off quietly, resulting in a Conservative landslide. After his election,
Diaz appointed General Chamorro Minister at Washington.

The Short-Term Loan of November, 1912

The revolutionary disturbance which broke out in July, 1912,
depleted the Government's resources and precipitated another crisis.
For the three months prior to the revolution, customs receipts had
produced an average of $138,579 per month. In August, customs
receipts fell to $56,372.64, and in September, to $30,890.75. Although receipts regained their former level with the defeat of
General Mena, the loss of revenues during August and September,
together with the cost of suppressing the revolution, had placed a
terrific burden on the Nicaraguan Treasury.

In August, the Government obtained a $100,000 short-term ad-
vance from the National Bank. Since under the Treasury Bills
Agreement of 1911 the entire stock of the National Bank was

---

[12] *Annual Reports of the Navy Department: For the Fiscal Year 1912* (Washington, Government Printing Office, 1913), p. 13.

pledged as security to the bankers, the latter wrote the Department of State of their intention to file with the Department of State a copy of their letter regarding the loan " in order that the loan may receive the same measure of protection which the United States Government will doubtless extend to the loans heretofore made by us." [13] The Department of State replied that—

this Government always exercises every proper effort to protect legitimate interests abroad insofar as the particular facts and circumstances of the given case may warrant. However, you will of course appreciate that this Department could not undertake in any way to guarantee investments of American capital in foreign countries. [14]

The loan from the National Bank was only a stop-gap. President Diaz appealed to the bankers to exercise their option to purchase 51 per cent of the stock of the Pacific Railway. While not recommending that this option be exercised, the Department of State nevertheless informed the bankers that whatever financial relief they might be prepared to give Nicaragua, if it were to be effective, should be given immediately. On November 4, 1912, Nicaragua and the bankers entered into another loan agreement. Its pertinent provisions were:

1. The bankers agreed to turn over to Nicaragua $100,000 out of the customs collections pledged as service on the Treasury bills of 1911 and to the supplementary loan of March, 1912.
2. The bankers agreed to modify the settlement of May 25, 1912, with the Council of Foreign Bondholders to the extent of setting aside to the credit of Nicaragua $400,000 out of the $500,000 due them to liquidate the supplementary loan of March 26, 1912. This money was to be held as a separate fund, payable in installments at such times and in such amounts as might be agreed upon between the President of Nicaragua and the bankers.
3. The bankers were given a preferential right to purchase for $1,000,000 the 49 per cent of the Pacific Railway stock. Under the supplementary loan contract of March, 1912, they had already received a purchase option on 51 per cent of the capital stock.
4. All of the internal taxes, including liquor and tobacco taxes, were to be collected by the National Bank.

MONETARY REFORM

The Monetary Law of 1912 provided for a new monetary unit, the " cordoba," equal in value to one dollar United States currency. The fiduciary issues of the cordoba, which were to form the greater part of the new circulating medium, were to be kept at par through the operations of a gold-exchange fund, maintained in New York

---

[13] File No. 817.51/487; *Foreign Relations*, 1912, p. 1103.
[14] *Ibid.*, pp. 1103–1104.

by the Republic with its own money but managed by the National Bank. The bank notes could be redeemed by drafts on the gold-exchange fund in New York and were thus at a parity with gold. In order to insure the permanent maintenance of this fund, it was provided in the 1913 loan agreements [15] that whenever it was depleted below $100,000, one-fourth of the customs revenues were to be applied to it month by month until it was again replenished. This system enabled Nicaragua to reduce to a minimum the reserve necessary to redeem its fiduciary currency.

In order to establish the cordoba as the currency medium, it was necessary to retire the old and depreciated paper pesos. Of the Treasury bills loan of 1911, $780,000 was allotted for this purpose and of the supplementary loan of March, 1912, an additional $500,-000. The new cordoba was to be exchanged for the old peso at a rate to be fixed by agreement between the President of Nicaragua and the bankers, but in no case to be higher when finally stabilized than 15 pesos for one cordoba. The Government did not immediately announce the fixed rate but purchased at the open market rates. A certain amount was secured at 18 to 1; a larger amount, at 16 to 1. As the purchase continued, the rate gradually decreased to 15; in October, 1912, to 14; and in December of the same year, to 13. Finally in January, 1913, a public announcement fixed the conversion rate at 12½ to 1, and that all currency then outstanding would be redeemed at that rate. By not announcing the fixed rate until it had an opportunity to purchase a large quantity at a more favorable rate, the Government saved a considerable sum in carrying out the conversion. The paper pesos ceased to be legal tender after November 1, 1915.

The selection of the conversion rate was a matter of considerable local interest. The merchants and business men expressed themselves as favoring a rate of 10 to 1. The rate of 12½ to 1 was selected in part to restore to laborers a portion of the purchasing power lost by the lag in the adjustment of wages to advancing prices. Moreover, the higher rate had the advantage for the Government of requiring a smaller outlay for the redemption of the paper currency.

The Diaz Administration, 1913–1917

Although there were several abortive attempts at revolution during the four years of his Administration, President Diaz gave the country comparative peace. He observed the civil liberties guar-

---

[15] See p. 25.

anteed by the Constitution, thereby appeasing the Liberals. His Administration, however, did not enjoy complete popularity. His support of the two interoceanic canal treaties aroused the opposition of the Liberals and of the other Central American countries. The financial condition of the country did not improve. Larger revenues were surpassed by greater expenditures. Moreover, the collection of internal revenues by the National Bank caused so much criticism by taxpayers, who had been accustomed to securing various sorts of rebates, that it was given up after one year's trial.

Early in 1913 the discontented Liberals circulated the rumor that the new Administration which would assume power in Washington on March 4 would withdraw recognition from the Diaz government and actively assist the Zelayistas in regaining power.[16] The failure of the new Administration to carry out this predicted policy eventually led many of Diaz' opponents to drop their machinations.

In July, 1914, two Americans, aided by several negro laborers, attempted to seize the barracks at Bluefields in order to set up an independent republic on the eastern coast. The plot, which was immediately frustrated, brought forth the following cable from the Department of State to the American Consul at Bluefields: [17]

Please warn all Americans that this Government will not countenance insurrection and that Americans interfering with the Government do so at their own peril.

For a short time a small detachment of marines was landed to prevent disorder.

THE 1913 LOAN AGREEMENTS

Despite the loan of November, 1912, Nicaragua early in the following spring was again critically in need of funds.[18] Although Nicaragua and the bankers were unable to come to any understanding as to the terms under which the bankers would exercise their preferential right to purchase 51 per cent of the Pacific Railway stock, the bankers consented to the release of all customs revenues in excess of fixed charges (the service on the Treasury bills of 1911 and the supplementary loan of March, 1912) and also advanced to Nicaragua $150,000. Nevertheless, Government salaries continued in arrears, the adjudicated claims and recently contracted governmental debts remained unpaid, and the Treasury bills were due on October 15, 1913.

---

[16] *Foreign Relations,* 1913, pp. 1035–1036.
[17] File No. 817.00/2364; *Foreign Relations,* 1914, p. 944.
[18] *Foreign Relations,* 1913, pp. 1037–1052, *passim.*

After negotiations lasting eight months, Nicaragua and the bankers signed a new set of loan agreements on October 8, 1913. The salient features were:[19]

1. The Government agreed to issue $1,060,000 of Treasury bills at 6 per cent interest, maturing October 1, 1914. The bankers agreed to purchase this entire issue for $1,000,000.

2. The loan paid off in full the Treasury bills of 1911 still outstanding and the supplementary loan of March, 1912, increased the gold-exchange fund by $350,000, and provided $100,000 to pay awards of the Mixed Claims Commission.

3. The loan was secured by a third lien on the customs duties, by a new first lien on 49 per cent of the stock of the Pacific Railway and on 49 per cent of the stock of the National Bank.

4. The bankers exercised their option to purchase 51 per cent of the Pacific Railway stock for $1,000,000. They also agreed to loan $500,000 for railway extensions and improvements.

5. The bankers agreed to purchase 51 per cent of the stock of the National Bank at par for $153,000. Nicaragua added this amount, together with an additional $47,000, to the capital of the National Bank, bringing the total capitalization up to $300,000.

6. The bankers obtained a preferential right to purchase the 49 per cent of the National Bank and Pacific Railway stock given in security of the loan.

7. The option held by the bankers under the loan agreement of March 26, 1912, for a railway concession to the Atlantic coast was canceled.

8. The collection of internal revenues which had been undertaken by the National Bank under the loan agreement of November 4, 1912, was to be resumed by the Nicaraguan Government.

9. The National Bank and Pacific Railway were each to have nine directors. The bankers were to name six, Nicaragua, two, and the Secretary of State of the United States, one. The latter was to serve also as the examiner of the National Bank and Pacific Railway. This arrangement was to cease with respect to that corporation in which the Republic should fail to own 49 per cent of the stock.

THE PACIFIC RAILWAY OF NICARAGUA

Under the terms of the supplementary loan contract of March, 1912, the railway, under the name of Ferrocarril del Pacifico de Nicaragua, was incorporated in Maine in June, 1912. Construction on the Pacific Railway had been begun in 1878. By 1903 an all-rail route from Corinto to Granada, a distance of 127 miles, had been completed. In 1930 the railway's total length was 146 miles.

From 1905 to 1909 the railway was leased to a private syndicate, but in 1909 the Government again took over operation of the road.

Under the terms of the 1913 loan agreements, the bankers purchased the railway for $1,000,000. The railway was exempted from

---

[19] *Foreign Relations*, 1913, pp. 1034, *et seq.*

all taxes and from customs duties on importations for a period of 20 years. The Government, on the other hand, had the right to ship its freight at one-half the published rates and to receive free transportation for various of its officials and employees. The bankers appointed the J. G. White Co. as operating manager of the railway.

There are several other short railways engaged in lumbering or agriculture which are operated by private companies. They are the Cuyamel Fruit Co. Railway, the Bragman's Bluff Lumber Co. line, and the Nicaraguan Sugar Estates Railroad, all located in the eastern littoral, except the last named. The total mileage of these lines is 157 miles, of which the Bragman's Bluff Lumber Co. line owns 83.

FINANCES, 1914–1917

An attempt was made by President Diaz in January, 1914, to obtain the consent of the bankers to an increase of from $250,000 to $500,000 in the amount of the October, 1913, loan,[20] but the bankers took the attitude that business prudence prevented them from making additional loans at that time. Before the 1913 Treasury bills fell due, a series of circumstances put an end to all hope of the immediate financial rehabilitation of the Republic. Droughts and a plague of grasshoppers practically ruined the coffee crop. For instance, in the Department of Matagalpa, production amounted to only 20 per cent of that of the previous year. The Government, despite the 1913 loan, still owed large sums to merchants for supplies purchased or requisitioned, to its employees for salaries, and to property owners whose claims, rising out of the two previous revolutions, had been adjudicated but not paid. Internal commerce had fallen, due to the rise of brigandage and crime. Therefore, the outbreak of war in Europe and the immediate cancellation of commercial credits by European firms precipitated a crisis. To meet the situation, President Diaz contemplated both a new bond issue and inflation of the currency. Congress passed two bills, the first declaring a moratorium on the internal debt service, the second, on the external. Though signing the first of these bills, President Diaz postponed signature of the second, pending efforts to reach some agreement with the external creditors. In September and October, by agreement with the three classes of creditors who had liens on the customs revenues to guarantee their loans,[21] such liens were suspended, so that all of the customs receipts could be paid to the

---

[20] *Foreign Relations*, 1914, pp. 944–945.
[21] The bondholders of the 1909 loan, the bankers under the 1913 agreement, and the National Bank of Nicaragua, which, during 1914, made several short-term advances to the Government.

Government for its current expenses. This temporary relief was confirmed in a contract of December 2, 1914.

The war put a severe strain upon the new currency system. The National Bank, unable to replenish its reserve fund, suspended the sale of foreign exchange in September, 1914, by which the par value of its notes had been maintained. Moreover, due to the closing of foreign money markets, the coffee growers appealed to the Government for financing the movement of their crop. The tight money situation was alleviated by another agreement of December 2, 1914, between Nicaragua and the National Bank, which reaffirmed the decree suspending the sale of foreign exchange. It also provided for a new issue of cordobas, 1,000,000 cordobas to be used exclusively for loans on products for exportation, and 500,000 cordobas [22] guaranteed by a first charge on the proceeds from a new capital tax for the payment of salaries and other budgetary obligations of the Government. At the same time, the agreement authorized the National Bank to pay its depositors with its own notes secured by mortgages and other securities; the option previously given in the 1913 loan agreements to resell 51 per cent of the railway shares to the Nicaraguan Government at the original purchase price of $1,000,000 plus 6 per cent interest was extended four months; and the bankers were released from their obligation to loan $500,000 for railway improvements. Although the suspension of the sale of foreign exchange and the new issues of paper currency caused a temporary abandonment of the gold standard, in the latter part of 1915 the National Bank unofficially resumed the sale of foreign exchange, which raised its notes again to their par value.

During 1915 and the early part of 1916, the contracts suspending the interest and sinking-fund payments were renewed. By the terms of the last renewal it was provided, should the suspended payments on the bonds of 1909 and on the Treasury bills and National Bank loans not be made by July 1, 1916, and by January 1, 1917, respectively, that their liens on the customs revenues should become operative. The Republic hoped to meet these payments out of the proceeds of the Canal Treaty which had been negotiated. In as much as the ratifications of the Canal Treaty were not exchanged until June 22, 1916, and the $3,000,000, although appropriated some months later, was not available for payment to Nicaragua until July 1, 1917, the provisions regarding the customs liens automatically became operative. After January 1, 1917, all of the customs revenues were retained by the Collector General of Customs who, because of the condition of foreign exchange, was unable to remit the funds abroad.

---

[22] This loan was paid off in 1921.

The Bryan-Chamorro Canal Treaty

The chronic instability of Nicaraguan finances after 1913 was increased by the uncertainty regarding the ultimate outcome of the interoceanic canal negotiations.[23] In the early negotiations between Nicaragua and the American bankers, clauses had been inserted in the agreements giving the bankers an option on a Nicaraguan canal route. This feature of the agreements was eventually eliminated, and negotiations were reopened directly between the Nicaraguan and the United States Governments for the conclusion of a treaty granting to the United States an option to construct an interoceanic canal across Nicaragua. On February 8, 1913, a treaty (Weitzel-Chamorro) was concluded, which gave the United States an option on a canal route in return for a cash payment of $3,000,000. The United States Senate refused to ratify this treaty when the Administration sought at the suggestion of President Diaz [24] the inclusion of provisions similar to those commonly called the Platt Amendment in the treaty between the United States and Cuba [25] of May 22, 1903.

Thereupon, a new treaty (Bryan-Chamorro) was negotiated on August 5, 1914,[26] which omitted the objectionable features. By this treaty Nicaragua granted in perpetuity to the United States the right to construct an interoceanic canal, leased for 99 years Great and Little Corn Islands, and granted for 99 years the right to construct a naval base on Fonseca Bay, in exchange for which the United States agreed to pay Nicaragua $3,000,000. This payment, according to article III of the treaty, was " to be applied by Nicaragua upon its indebtedness or other public purposes for the advancement of the welfare of Nicaragua in a manner to be determined by the two High Contracting Parties." Immediately upon its terms becoming known, Costa Rica and El Salvador protested that the treaty impaired their existing rights. The United States Senate ratified the treaty on February 18, 1916, adding a proviso that its consent was given with the understanding that " nothing in said convention is intended to affect any existing right " of Costa Rica, El Salvador, or Honduras. Nicaragua ratified the treaty on April 12, 1916. In the Senate, the treaty was approved by a unanimous vote, and in the Chamber of Deputies, by a vote of 28 to 7.

During the negotiation of the treaty, Costa Rica lodged a protest with the United States based upon the following grounds: (1) by

---

[23] Six different treaties were negotiated during the 19th century between the United States and Nicaragua regarding an interoceanic canal.

[24] *Foreign Relations*, 1914, p. 953.

[25] Malloy, *Treaties, Conventions, International Acts, Protocols and Agreements between the United States and Other Powers, 1776–1909*, vol. 1, pp. 362–364.

[26] Appendix C, p. 128.

the Treaty of Limits of 1858 between Costa Rica and Nicaragua, the latter agreed not to enter into any arrangement for " canalization or transit . . . without first hearing the opinion of the Government of Costa Rica ";[27] and (2) on the award of President Cleveland rendered March 22, 1888, in a boundary dispute between Nicaragua and Costa Rica which stated that " The Republic of Nicaragua remains bound not to make any grants for canal purposes across her territory without first asking the opinion of the Republic of Costa Rica " [28] as provided in the Treaty of Limits of 1858. The award also stated that " in cases where the construction of the canal will involve an injury to the natural rights of Costa Rica her opinion or advice . . . should be more than ' advisory ' or ' consultative.' It would seem in such cases that her consent is necessary . . . ." [29]

To this protest the Department of State replied that " It is not perceived that Nicaragua, by the proposed treaty with the United States, has done or contemplates doing anything that can be regarded as a violation of the Treaty of 1858." [30] The consultative right of Costa Rica was to exist only, according to the award by President Cleveland in 1888 " where the territory belonging to the Republic of Costa Rica is occupied or flooded; where there is an encroachment upon either of the said harbors injurious to Costa Rica; or where there is such an obstruction or deviation of the River San Juan as to destroy or seriously impair the navigation of the said River or any of its branches at any point where Costa Rica is entitled to navigate the same." [31] The Department of State held that " The claim that an interoceanic canal, when constructed through Nicaragua, might eventually affect some of the territory or rights of Costa Rica is too speculative and conjectural to serve as a basis of a present protest against the grant of the option secured by the treaty with Nicaragua." [32]

After the signing of the treaty, Costa Rica protested again, declaring that the Senate's proviso " could not in any way free that agreement [Bryan-Chamorro Treaty] from the fundamental defect which invalidates it, Nicaragua's incomplete capacity to conduct the business." [33] The Secretary of State replied that in the light of

---

[27] Art. VIII of the Treaty of Limits of 1858. See *Argument on the Question of the Validity of the Treaty of Limits between Costa Rica and Nicaragua filed on behalf of the Government of Costa Rica* (Washington, 1887), pp. 188–189.
[28] *Arbitration by the President: Costa Rica and Nicaragua*, 1887–88, p. 271; *Foreign Relations*, 1888, pt. 1, p. 458.
[29] *Arbitration by the President*, p. 272; *Foreign Relations*, 1888, pt. 1, p. 459.
[30] File No. 817.812/76; *Foreign Relations*, 1914, p. 964.
[31] *Arbitration by the President*, pp. 271–272; *Foreign Relations*, 1888, pt. 1, p. 458.
[32] File No. 817.812/76; *Foreign Relations*, 1914, p. 965.
[33] File No. 817.812/153; *Foreign Relations*, 1916, p. 818.

previous declarations of the Department of State " and of the afore-said explicit declaration by Congress, I am unable to perceive any ground for protest on the part of your Government." [34]

Costa Rica then brought suit against Nicaragua before the Central American Court of Justice, which had been established by the Washington Treaties of 1907. In a circular telegram to the diplomatic missions of the United States in the five Central American republics, the Secretary of State made the following statement: [35]

Convention of Central American Governments for establishment of Central American Court of Justice concluded at Washington December 20, 1907, was long subsequent to the binding agreements of Nicaragua and Costa Rica, respectively, to enter into necessary arrangements with United States for construction of Nicaraguan Canal as embodied in the protocols signed by each of said Governments December 1, 1900. The Department does not consider that any of the treaties or conventions between Central American Governments concluded at Washington in 1907 affect, or were intended to affect, the international relations of any of those Governments with the United States. Manifestly it was not contemplated that Central American Court for settlement of controversies between the signatory Governments would attempt jurisdiction of any matter of diplomatic relation between the United States and any of those countries.

In view of repeated declarations by Department and of proviso adopted by United States Senate, that the treaty with Nicaragua was not intended to affect injuriously any right of Costa Rica involved, attempt by Costa Rica to interfere with freedom of action of Nicaragua in this matter cannot but be viewed by the United States as an unjustifiable effort to prevent Nicaragua from fulfilling her contractual obligations.

Nicaragua denied the competence of the Court to recognize the suit. Moreover, it informed the Court that the treaty was not a contract for the sale of canal rights but merely an option granting the United States the right to conclude a treaty or contract at the proper time. On September 30, 1916, the Court rendered a decision holding that Costa Rica's rights had not been respected by Nicaragua. The Court held that since it had no jurisdiction over the United States, it could not declare the treaty null and void.[36]

El Salvador, too, protested the treaty, both before and after its signing. Its protestations were based on the claim that the Gulf of Fonseca, on the Nicaraguan part of which the United States had been given the right to establish a naval base, was jointly owned by El Salvador, Honduras, and Nicaragua. Both the United States and

---

[34] *Ibid.*, p. 820.
[35] File No. 817.812/184a ; *Foreign Relations*, 1916, pp. 831–832.
[36] For full decision, see *Foreign Relations*, 1916, pp. 862–886.

Nicaragua denied that there was any sort of a condominium of the waters of the Gulf of Fonseca, and Honduras joined them in declaring in a note to El Salvador that it " does not recognize and has not recognized, any state of co-domination with Salvador, nor with any other Republic, in the waters of Fonseca Bay which correspond to Honduras."[37] The United States and Nicaragua also denied El Salvador's protests that the treaty impaired the neutrality of Honduras, guaranteed by the Washington Treaty of 1907, and that it would interfere with the reestablishment of a Central American union.

El Salvador also filed suit with the Central American Court against Nicaragua. On March 9, 1917, the Court handed down a decision favorable to El Salvador's contentions, and in this case, as in the other, the Court declined to declare the treaty null and void.[38]

In 1923 the United States and Costa Rica signed a protocol[39] under the terms of which they agreed—

that when the President of the United States is authorized by law to acquire control of the rights which Costa Rica possesses in the San Juan River, or in Salinas Bay, and such portion of the territory now belonging to Costa Rica as may be desirable and necessary on which to construct and protect a canal . . . they mutually engage to enter into negotiations with each other to settle the plan and the agreements, in detail, found necessary to accomplish the construction and to provide for the ownership and control of the proposed canal.

This protocol has not been ratified by either country.

The Elections of 1916

The electoral situation in 1916 was complicated by a split in the Conservative Party and by the decision of the Liberals to present a candidate. During the Diaz administration, the Cuadra family had built up a powerful organization. Eulogio Cuadra was Minister of Finance. Later he acquired, in addition, the Ministries of Public Works and War. He employed these positions both to influence President Diaz in his favor and to build up a party machinery. The President gave the support of his Administration first to Pedro Rafael Cuadra, Nicaraguan Financial Agent in the United States, and later to Carlos Cuadra Pasos, member of the Mixed Claims Commission. Under ordinary circumstances, the support of the Administration, which controlled the electoral machinery, would have insured election. However, General Chamorro, who had stepped aside in favor of Diaz in 1912 on the understanding that the President would support his candidacy in 1916, was indig-

---

[37] *Foreign Relations*, 1916, p. 891.
[38] For full decision, see *Foreign Relations*, 1917, pp. 1101–1104.
[39] Appendix D, p. 130.

nant at the President's attitude. He returned to Nicaragua, where a faction of the Conservative Party nominated him.

The Liberals, profiting by the dissension within the Conservative ranks, were in a strong position to regain power. Since their party had numerically about the same strength as the Conservative, the Liberals were anxious for electoral supervision by the United States in order to secure a fair election. The United States offer of assistance was declined by President Diaz, who agreed to afford Nicaraguans free and full exercise of the suffrage. However, the Liberals lost their opportunity by nominating Julián Irías, Zelaya's most trusted minister.

Two weeks before the elections the two Conservative factions compromised their differences. Carlos Cuadra Pasos withdrew his candidacy in favor of General Chamorro, who agreed in case of his election to appoint Cuadra Pasos as Minister at Washington. A few days later, discouraged by his failure to make an alliance with the Cuadra faction, Irías withdrew, counselling the Liberals not to participate in the elections. General Chamorro, who as a result became the only candidate, received 51,810 votes and took office on January 1, 1917.

The Loan Agreements and Financial Plan of 1917

In the latter part of 1916, even before the $3,000,000 due Nicaragua under the terms of the Bryan-Chamorro Treaty had been appropriated by the United States Congress, a discussion arose between Nicaragua, the Department of State, and the bankers, as to its disposition.[40] The bankers maintained that the deferred interest and sinking-fund payments should be met before all other debts; the Department of State, on the other hand, declared that the bankers did not have a preferential right to payment from the treaty fund, that holders of claims antedating the entrance of American bankers into Nicaraguan financial affairs had not been paid, and that it was the spirit and intent of the Canal Treaty that the $3,000,000 be distributed among all creditors, of whom only the bankers were secured by liens on other revenues.

When General Chamorro assumed the Presidency on January 1, 1917, he found that a large deficit had accumulated, amounting in salaries alone to over $500,000. He vigorously continued the negotiations initiated under President Diaz to secure the release of the embargoed customs revenues [41] and the treaty fund. The Ethelburga Syndicate and the bankers, under their various contracts with Nicaragua, insisted upon preferential treatment for their debts. Although Nicaragua was in favor of employing whatever was necessary

---

[40] *Foreign Relations,* 1916, pp. 898–917.
[41] See p. 28.

to liquidate these obligations [42] the Department of State maintained that any settlement should take into consideration Nicaragua's entire indebtedness. When the Department of State learned that Nicaragua by contract had agreed to pay the bankers specified amounts out of the treaty funds, it informed Nicaragua that, if Nicaragua considered itself bound by this contract, it " would appear to have placed itself in a position in which it will be unable to cooperate with the Government of the United States in carrying out the stipulations in Article III " [43] of the Canal Treaty. Nicaragua replied agreeing to give " faithful compliance with the stipulations contained in the treaty " and expressed the desire that the interests of the bankers be conciliated with those of other creditors. [44]

Once this matter had been settled, [45] the Department of State called a conference at Washington with representatives of Nicaragua and the bankers. As a result of the conference, the bases of the settlement were outlined. Upon Nicaragua's agreement to the appointment of a commission to investigate all foreign and domestic claims and the nomination of the members of the commission, and upon Nicaragua's consent to the appointment of a financial adviser, the United States Government turned over $250,000 out of the Canal Treaty funds for the specific purpose of Nicaragua's meeting pressing Government indebtedness and paying the back salaries of Government employees. [46]

An important part of the program to rehabilitate Nicaragua's finances was the Financial Plan. It was because of the inclusion within the Financial Plan of a financial adviser having certain advisory and supervisory powers over Nicaragua's finances that the Department of State secured the cooperation of the bankers. [47] General Chamorro, when he became President, opposed the creation of this office, wishing to conduct the finances of Nicaragua as theretofore. [48] The Department of State reiterated its view that the finances could not be effectively administered under the existing contracts with the bankers and that the moment was opportune for carrying out a thorough reform. Upon General Chamorro's continued opposition, the Department of State approached the bankers, who consented to the appointment of a commission of three to have advisory functions regarding general expenditures, to act as the arbitrator of any difficulties between Nicaragua and the

---

[42] *Foreign Relations*, 1916, pp. 898–902.
[43] File No. 817.51/821 ; *Foreign Relations*, 1916, p. 908.
[44] File No. 817.51/846 ; *Foreign Relations*, 1916, p. 911.
[45] *Ibid.*, pp. 911–915.
[46] *Foreign Relations*, 1917, pp. 1116–1117.
[47] *Ibid.*, p. 1121.
[48] *Ibid.*, pp. 1120 and 1123.

bankers, and to disburse certain surplus funds over and above the regular budget. General Chamorro agreed to this arrangement. However, so protracted were the negotiations that after unsuccessful efforts to obtain surplus customs revenue and the declaration of a railway dividend, he threatened to seize the customhouses. The bankers immediately stated their intention of withdrawing from further negotiations should he take this step. President Chamorro withheld action awaiting an indication from the United States regarding his attitude. The Department of State informed President Chamorro that the seizure of the customhouses would be considered by the United States as a breach of faith on the part of Nicaragua.

After weeks of negotiations, the bases of the Financial Plan and of the settlement with Nicaragua's creditors were agreed upon.[49] The Nicaraguan Congress on August 29, 1917, authorized the President to sign the necessary contracts with the interested parties. These contracts were signed on October 20, 1917, and approved by the Nicaraguan Congress without amendment on November 14.

The agreements with Nicaragua's creditors regarding the release of the embargoed customs revenues and the disposition of the treaty funds were a compromise:[50]

1. The Ethelburga Syndicate, the bankers, and the holders of the Emery Claim received approximately $2,025,000 representing deferred interest and sinking-fund payments, and in the case of the Treasury bills of 1913, one-half of the principal ($530,000).

2. The loan of $100,000 from the National Bank was liquidated.

3. Nicaragua received $500,000 for back salaries and other expenses, and $334,840 for the settlement of internal and floating debts and claims.

4. The Ethelburga Syndicate agreed to postpone certain interest payments during the next three years. Nicaragua paid off these postponed payments on June 30, 1920, out of customs revenues and 25 per cent of the surplus revenues.

5. The balance of the principal of the Treasury bills of 1913 with interest was paid off from 25 per cent of the surplus revenues. This balance was liquidated on June 30, 1919.

6. The holders of the Emery Claim agreed to take deferred Treasury bills for the remainder of the principal and interest due them not paid off from the treaty fund. This debt was liquidated on June 30, 1920.

The principal features of the Financial Plan were as follows:

1. A High Commission of two members was established, composed of a Nicaraguan appointed by the President of Nicaragua and an American appointed by the Secretary of State of the United States.

[49] *Ibid.*, pp. 1138–1141.
[50] *Ibid.*, pp. 1149–1150; *Report of the Collector General of Customs, 1921,* pp. 15–16.

In case of disagreement between the two members, the disputed point was to be decided by an arbiter appointed by the Secretary of State. The decisions of the High Commission were to be final. One of its principal functions became the supervision of payment on the guaranteed customs bonds, which the agreement contemplated in part payment of claims.

2. If any question should arise between Nicaragua and the Collector General of Customs, or under any agreements between Nicaragua and the Council of Foreign Bondholders or the bankers, such question was to be referred to the High Commission, whose decision was to be final and binding.

3. The office of Collector General of Customs was reaffirmed and its duties clarified. The customs collections were also pledged to the service of the internal bond issue whenever it should be floated. Nicaragua agreed not to alter the import or export duties unless such changes were first approved by the High Commission.

4. All internal taxes except forestry and school taxes were to be collected by Nicaragua, and the receipts deposited with the National Bank. Should the total amount of such revenues fall below $180,000 during any three consecutive collections, a collection was to be undertaken by the Collector General of Customs.

5. All the general revenues (i. e. internal revenues and the balance of the customs not already pledged) were to be deposited in the National Bank. Payments against these funds were to be made by check, signed either by the Minister of Finance or such deputy as he might appoint for that purpose.

6. Fifty per cent of the surplus revenues was to be available for the service of the guaranteed customs bonds and for public works. The remaining 50 per cent was pledged to the service on the bonded and short-term indebtedness.

7. A definite budget of $95,000 per month was fixed. Additional expenditures of $26,666 per month were authorized upon the approval of the High Commission.

The Guaranteed Customs Bonds of 1918

As a preliminary to payment from the Canal Treaty fund, the Department of State suggested that Nicaragua appoint a Commission on Public Credit,[51] consisting of a Nicaraguan member, an American member, and an umpire to be named by agreement between the two Governments, to review the claims adjudicated by the Mixed Claims Commission and other outstanding· debts against the Republic. This was done in February, 1917.[52] Since the sittings of the first Mixed Claims Commission, the Nicaraguan Government had again accumulated huge claims against it for goods and services. Moreover, many of the claims adjudicated by the Mixed Claims Commission had been sold to speculators for a fraction of their values. The total of both claims and debts was about $13,500,000,

---

[51] *Foreign Relations*, 1916, pp. 915, 916, and 917.
[52] *Ibid.*, 1917, pp. 1113–1120.

which was far beyond Nicaragua's capacity to pay. In view of the necessities of the situation, every creditor was impressed with the idea that if his credit were a good one, i.e. for cash advances, for merchandise sold, or for services rendered, the Commission would ask him to voluntarily rebate, if his credit were not of this kind, the Commission would make its own revision. The response made was extremely gratifying, as practically all the large claimants offered some concessions, either a reduction of principal, a waiving of interest, or a reduction of interest.[53] The Commission scaled down the unpaid awards and other debts to $5,304,386. Adjudicated claims in the hands of the original holders were not reduced, whereas claims in the hands of third parties and speculators were decreased to 50 and 30 per cent, respectively, of their original values. Cash payments were made in 1918 of $1,427,536, of which $1,092,695 was embargoed customs revenues released by the 1917 agreements, and the balance came from the canal fund.

In December, 1917, the Nicaraguan Congress approved a bond issue of $4,000,000, to be used in paying the balance of the adjudicated debts; [54] $3,744,150 of 5 per cent bonds were issued. The principal security of these bonds is a 12½ per cent surcharge on the customs import duties, which had been provided for in the 1917 agreements. Of these bonds, Nicaraguan citizens received 43 per cent, Americans 23 per cent, English 10 per cent, Italians 9 per cent, and Germans 3 per cent. Their issue terminated the problem of claims and internal debts which had vexed Nicaragua since 1909.

THE LOAN AGREEMENTS AND FINANCIAL PLAN OF 1920

The Financial Plan of 1917 was highly successful in settling financial difficulties of the Republic. Instead of the five years expected and allowed for the payment of the deferred interest and sinking-fund charges, the Republic in July, 1919, foresaw liquidation of the debt within a year's time. The demand for raw materials during the World War and postwar period increased Nicaragua's foreign trade by 100 per cent during the 4-year period 1917–1920. Because of the consequent increase in the customs and internal revenues, Nicaragua had had a large surplus in its Treasury at the end of each year since 1917. By the terms of the Financial Plan of 1917, 50 per cent of this surplus was to be available for the service of the guaranteed customs bonds and for public works. This amount was not sufficient to begin the construction of a railway from the Atlantic coast to Lake Nicaragua, a project that had been included in the unratified

---

[53] *Preliminary Report of the Commission on Public Credit* (Managua, 1919), pp. 16–17.
[54] *Foreign Relations*, 1918, pp. 828–831.

Knox-Castrillo Convention. Therefore, in September, 1919, Nicaragua sent the Minister of Finance to the United States, primarily to secure a loan for the construction of the railway and secondarily to refund the existing bonded debts. Although he found sympathy for the project, he discovered that the competitive demand for money following the close of the World War had raised interest rates to a high figure. It took a year to work out the details of an arrangement with the bankers which, though failing to provide for the immediate construction of the Atlantic Railway, did contemplate a bond issue in the future. On June 30, 1920, Nicaragua paid off the last of the deferred service charges on the bonds of 1909 and the Treasury bills of 1913. The surplus Treasury balance on that date amounted to well over a million dollars. The Department of State at this time impressed the Nicaraguan Government with the advisability of using its surplus revenues for constructive purposes, such as railway or highway development.

The agreements which were signed on October 5, 1920, provided as follows:

1. Nicaragua agreed to purchase 51 per cent of the stock of the Pacific Railway from the bankers for $1,750,000. It will be recalled that the bankers had purchased 51 per cent of the stock of the Pacific Railway in 1913 for $1,000,000. During the control by the bankers approximately $700,000 was spent on improvements. A new railway company was to be incorporated with an authorized capital of $3,300,000.

2. For the railway, Nicaragua paid $300,000 in cash and Treasury bills series A to the amount of $1,450,000 at 9 per cent interest. The Republic agreed to set aside 75 per cent of its surplus revenues and dividends from the Pacific Railway to meet the service of these bills. Moreover, it pledged the entire capital stock of the railway as security.

3. In order to start immediate construction on the Atlantic Railway, a flotation of Treasury bills series B of $2,650,000 was proposed to be issued in anticipation of surplus revenues. These Treasury bills were to mature before the bond flotation next described. A survey for the proposed Atlantic Railway was to be made at once by engineers approved by the bankers and appointed by Nicaragua.

4. In order to complete the construction of the Atlantic Railway, to retire the outstanding bonds of 1909, and to retire the Treasury bills series A, a 15-year bond issue of $9,000,000 bearing 7 per cent interest was proposed. The bankers, although not promising to purchase the issue, were given a prior right to purchase upon terms agreeable to both parties. If no agreement should be reached with the bankers, Nicaragua was then at liberty to dispose of the bonds elsewhere, provided the price was not less than that offered by the bankers.

In connection with the proposed loan, there was a slight revision of the Financial Plan of 1917. Those features which had become obsolete, such as that recording the settlement of claims, were dropped. The High Commission and Collectorship of Customs were reaffirmed. The Nicaraguan budget was raised from $95,000 per month to $105,000 per month, with a provision similar to that of the Financial Plan of 1917 for the expenditure of an additional $26,666 per month with the approval of the High Commission. Moreover, any surplus remaining after budgetary and debt charges were paid was to go partly to finance the construction of the Atlantic Railway and partly for public improvements.

The economic crisis of 1921 drastically affected Nicaragua's national income. The surplus upon which was predicated the issue of the Treasury bills series B and the bonds for the construction of the Atlantic Railway fell from $610,000 on January 1, 1921, to nil on July 1, 1922. During the latter part of 1921 and 1922, Nicaragua negotiated with the bankers for a loan to be used partly to retire outstanding indebtedness [55] and partly for such purposes designated by the Nicaraguan Government and approved by the High Commission, including the Atlantic Railway project. The negotiations were not consummated during 1922 and, with return of better business conditions in 1923, were dropped.

THE ELECTIONS OF 1920

During the four years following the 1916 elections, the Liberals criticized the Department of State for its support of an electoral machinery that tended to perpetuate the power of the Conservatives who controlled it. The Liberals claimed that since the elections were manipulated to their disadvantage and since the United States would not countenance revolution, it was impossible for them ever to secure control of the Government. Early in 1920 the Department of State, anxious that the approaching presidential elections should express the will of the people, suggested that the Nicaraguan Government invite someone to make a study of the electoral system and suggest possible revisions therein. President Chamorro replied that it was inopportune to make any changes, since the existing electoral law amply provided for free elections and the proximity of the elections would not permit a thorough study. In view of President Chamorro's attitude, the Department of State informed him that, although it still felt that a revision of the electoral law was necessary in order to satisfy public opinion in Nicaragua, it was gratified

---

[55] Besides its unpaid bills, the Government had borrowed $60,000 from the National Bank.

to have the President's assurance that fair and free elections would be held. To clarify its position to the Nicaraguan people, the Department of State authorized the American Minister to issue the following statement on July 1, 1920: [56]

Repeated inquiries have been made at the Department of State at Washington by representatives of different political parties of Nicaragua inquiring whether certain named persons would be agreeable to the Government at Washington as candidates for the presidency. In order to avoid any misapprehension with reference to the situation, my Government authorizes me to state that the question of candidates for the presidency of Nicaragua is a matter to be decided by the people of Nicaragua in the full and free expression of public opinion. The exceptionally close relations existing between Nicaragua and the United States creates in both the Government and the people of the United States a deep and abiding interest that presidential elections in Nicaragua shall be conducted on the highest plane, assuring to every qualified voter not only the free expression of opinion but also the accurate registration of that opinion in the final result.

The Government of the United States has expressed no opinion with reference to the persons who have been mentioned as candidates for the presidency. Its sole interest is that the forthcoming elections be characterized by the utmost fairness and freedom; that an accurate count of the votes cast be made, and that the candidate receiving the largest number of popular votes be declared president-elect of Nicaragua.

In December, 1919, President Chamorro hinted that he might be a candidate to succeed himself. The Department of State immediately expressed surprise at this proposal, since the provisions of the Constitution forbade his candidacy.[57] Thereupon General Chamorro withdrew but through his control of the party machinery secured the Conservative nomination for his uncle, Diego Chamorro, the Nicaraguan Minister at Washington. At a later date, Bartolomé Martínez, of Matagalpa, was nominated for the Vice Presidency. Diego Chamorro's nomination was not popular either with the party or the country at large. Doctor Urtecho, the Minister for Foreign Affairs, resigned from the cabinet and announced his own candidacy on an independent ticket.

The Liberals, who attracted various dissatisfied elements, led a formidable opposition to the Conservatives under the name of the Coalition Party. Their candidate was José Esteban González, a rich coffee planter and well-known business man. With the dis-

---

[56] File No. 817.00/2648.
[57] NICARAGUAN CONSTITUTION, ART. 104: " The term of office of the President and Vice President of the Republic shall be four years, and shall begin on the first of January. No citizen who holds the office of President, either as the duly elected incumbent or accidentally, shall be eligible to the office of President or Vice President for the next term." (File No. 817.011/17.)

affection in the Conservative ranks, the likelihood of the Coalition- ists winning the elections became a real possibility if fair and free elections were held.

The preelection period was a turbulent one. The Coalitionists demanded that all eligible voters should have the right of casting the ballots regardless of whether or not they were inscribed on the official catalogues. At the suggestion of the Department of State, President Chamorro granted two additional days for registration, although even then all eligible Coalitionists were not able to register. In view of the importance which both Conservatives and Coalition- ists attached to the elections, and of their conflicting claims, the Department of State designated as special electoral observer Maj. Jesse I. Miller, who was thoroughly cognizant with electoral pro- cedure.

During the registrations, disturbances took place in many cities. In Managua, one civilian and one policeman were killed. Thou- sands were unable to register. The Government imprisoned many of the Coalition leaders. The Minister was instructed to deliver verbally the following statement to President Chamorro: [58]

The Department of State has received with the deepest concern reports showing that disturbances have arisen throughout Nicaragua incident to the registration of voters. Information has reached the Department that very many voters have been deprived of the right to register, and it appears that several persons have been killed in the disturbances which have ensued. Furthermore, the Department has been advised that certain political leaders have been arrested and imprisoned by the Government authorities.

While the Department does not presume to form any judgment as to the reasons for the disturbances which arose, it cannot but view with the gravest apprehension the imprisonment of the leaders of one of the political parties. The Department recently had occasion to make its position very plain by stating publicly that the Govern- ment of the United States favored no candidate in the coming elec- tions in Nicaragua, and that its only interest, because of the close relations which exist between Nicaragua and the United States, was that the election should be conducted in such a way that every quali- fied voter in Nicaragua should be enabled to register with complete liberty and to express freely his opinion in the subsequent elections. The action taken by the Government in arresting and imprisoning the leaders of one of the political parties is bound to produce the most unfortunate impression upon the people of the United States.

The Department of State trusts that the reports which have reached it regarding alleged acts of violence on the part of the gov- ernmental authorities during the registration period are incorrect or have been exaggerated. It hopes that the Government of Nica- ragua will realize that elections cannot be held in such a manner as to permit a candidate for the Presidency to be chosen by the full and

---

[58] File No. 817.00/2674.

free expression of public opinion if acts of intimidation are now undertaken by the authorities under the control of the Government. It therefore feels confident that the Government of Nicaragua will take steps immediately to dispel the impression created by the arrest of these political leaders and will take no further action which will cause this Government to feel that the people of Nicaragua will not be able to vote freely, without constraint or hindrance of any kind, in the coming elections.

An unfounded rumor spread that the United States would intervene to supervise the elections. To quash this rumor, the American Minister issued a statement to the effect that the attitude of the Department of State " has been in no way modified since the publication of its official statement " of July 1, 1920. Just before the elections, President Chamorro decreed -that all citizens should be allowed to cast a ballot whether inscribed or not, and that when the votes were counted there should be rejected the ballots of all citizens whose names did not appear on the official catalogues, not only of that of 1920 but of all prior years.

The elections resulted in a victory for Diego Chamorro, who received 62,000 votes, to 32,000 for González and 762 for Doctor Urtecho. Immediately there were charges by the Coalitionists and Doctor Urtecho that the Administration had conscripted soldiers in contradiction to the law, had arrested persons immediately prior to the elections, thereby making them ineligible to vote, had eliminated names from the official catalogues, and padded the same with the names of Conservatives. There was definite evidence that the vote for Doctor Urtecho had not been fairly counted. Major Miller reported to the Department of State that the strength of the two parties was nearly the same, that no violence or intimidation took place during the election period, and that while fraud undoubtedly did take place in the registration and the counting of the votes by the Administration authorities, a fair election could not have been held under any circumstances under the existing election law. The Department of State believed that unless very radical measures were adopted at once with a view to satisfying the aspirations of a large part of the Nicaraguan people for immediate reform in the electoral system, disturbances were liable to occur. It instructed the Minister to inform General Chamorro of this belief and to impress upon him the desirability of immediately adopting a law safeguarding the rights of voters. Shortly before the completion of his term, General Chamorro agreed to a revision and requested the Department of State to send an expert to draft the law.

In January, 1922, the Department of State, in accordance with the agreement reached with ex-President Emiliano Chamorro, recommended Dr. Harold W. Dodds to investigate the Nicaraguan electoral situation. Doctor Dodds, who was the Secretary of the National Municipal League, had been studying for many years electoral laws and their reform. After painstaking inquiries into the Nicaraguan electoral situation during the spring and summer of 1922, he drew up and presented a draft of a new electoral law. This draft, with minor changes, was enacted into a law on March 16, 1923. The new law provided an administrative organization adequate to the task of conducting an election on a national scale, gave the minority party in each department a share in each step of the electoral process, and legalized and regularized appeals from the arbitrary conduct of the majority. Abuses in registration, balloting, and counting the votes were eliminated.

REVOLUTIONARY ACTIVITIES, 1921–22

During the latter part of 1921, disgruntled opponents of President Diego Chamorro carried on a series of revolutionary raids along the Nicaraguan-Honduran boundary. President Chamorro declared martial law throughout the country, and sent a well-equipped force to police the frontier. Although none of these revolutionary incursions assumed serious proportions, they caused a heavy drain on the Treasury and created political unrest.

In May, 1922, the Loma Fortress, which dominates the city of Managua, was seized by a band of dissatisfied Conservatives. The American Minister informed the revolutionists that firing upon the American Legation guard barracked in the Campo de Marte or upon the city would result in the immediate intervention of American forces. At a conference in the American Legation, the revolutionists agreed to surrender the fortress in return for complete amnesty for civil and mild punishment for military participants.

A little later, Liberals attacked León and Chinandega. Martial law was again declared. The Department of State ordered the Legation guard not to interfere in any internal disturbances except in an emergency which actually threatened the safety of the Legation or the lives of members of the Legation guard.

THE POLICY OF THE UNITED STATES REGARDING RECOGNITION OF CENTRAL AMERICAN GOVERNMENTS

The early years of the twentieth century were ones of continuous warfare in Central America. The ambitions of Zelaya to force a union upon the other republics, his control of Honduras, and the tactics of the other countries in opposing his influence kept Central America in constant turmoil. In view of the imminent danger of war in the summer of 1907, the Presidents of the United States and Mexico jointly offered their mediation. This was accepted by all of the Central American governments, it being agreed that a conference should be held in Washington to settle all outstanding difficulties and to establish the basis for peaceful relations between the Central American republics.

The Conference adopted eight treaties. The United States and Mexico, though their delegates were present at the Conference, did not sign the treaties. To the first treaty, the General Treaty of Peace and Amity, was added an annex upon which has subsequently been based the recognition policy of the United States toward Central America. Its principal provisions are the following:

ARTICLE I. The Governments of the High Contracting Parties shall not recognize any other Government which may come into power in any of the five Republics as a consequence of a *coup d'etat*, or of a revolution against the recognized Government, so long as the freely elected representatives of the people thereof, have not constitutionally reorganized the country.

ARTICLE II. No Government of Central America shall in case of civil war intervene in favor of or against the Government of the country where the struggle takes place.

ARTICLE III. The Governments of Central America, in the first place, are recommended to endeavor to bring about, by the means at their command, a constitutional reform in the sense of prohibiting the reelection of the President of a Republic, where such prohibition does not exist, secondly to adopt all measures necessary to effect a complete guarantee of the principle of alternation in power.

The provision of the first article may have been suggested by a letter of March 15, 1907, by Dr. Carlos Tobar, former Minister of Foreign Affairs of Ecuador, to the Bolivian Consul at Brussels. Writing in regard to the revolutions from which Latin America suffered, Doctor Tobar said: [59]

The American Republics, for their good renown and credit, if not for other humanitarian and " altruistic " considerations, should intervene indirectly in the internal dissensions of the republics of that continent. This intervention might consist at least in a refusal to recognize the *de facto* governments resulting from revolutions against the Constitution.

Since this proposal provoked considerable discussion at the time, it was doubtlessly well known to the delegates of the Conference.

At the 14th session of the 1907 Conference, one of the Honduran delegates presented a project which later became article I of the annex to the General Treaty of Peace and Amity. The next session adopted the project, after receiving a favorable report from the committee to which it had been referred.[60]

---

[59] *Revue Générale de Droit International Public,* vol. XXI, 1914, p. 483.
[60] *The Central American Peace Conference: Acts and Documents,* p. 77.

The beneficial effects of the treaties did not show themselves until after the resignation of Zelaya. From 1910 to 1921 the combined effects of the treaties and the prosperity caused by the World War eliminated international wars in Central America. In 1922, to avert impending trouble, the Presidents of Nicaragua, Honduras, and El Salvador met on board the *Tacoma*, a war vessel of the United States, and signed an agreement reaffirming and strengthening the 1907 treaties. Article V of the "Tacoma Agreement" [61] provided for another conference to which all the Central American countries would be invited, and at the suggestion of the three signatory nations, the invitations for this conference were issued by the United States. The conference, which met in Washington, in article II of the General Treaty of Peace and Amity signed February 7, 1923, not only reiterated the provisions of the 1907 treaty regarding the nonrecognition of Governments coming into power through a *coup d'état* or revolution but also strengthened it. This article reads as follows:[62]

Desiring to make secure in the Republics of Central America the benefits which are derived from the maintenance of free institutions and to contribute at the same time toward strengthening their stability, and the prestige with which they should be surrounded, they declare that every act, disposition or measure which alters the constitutional organization in any of them is to be deemed a menace to the peace of said Republics, whether it proceed from any public power or from the private citizens.

Consequently, the Governments of the Contracting Parties will not recognize any other Government which may come into power in any of the five Republics through a *coup d'etat* or a revolution against a recognized Government, so long as the freely elected representatives of the people thereof have not constitutionally reorganized the country. And even in such a case they obligate themselves not to acknowledge the recognition if any of the persons elected as President, Vice-President or Chief of State designate should fall under any of the following heads:

(1) If he should be the leader or one of the leaders of a *coup d'etat* or revolution, or through blood relationship or marriage, be an ascendent or descendent or brother of such leader or leaders.

(2) If he should have been a Secretary of State or should have held some high military command during the accomplishment of the *coup d'etat*, the revolution, or while the election was being carried on, or if he should have held this office or command within the six months preceding the *coup d'etat*, revolution, or the election.

Furthermore, in no case shall recognition be accorded to a government which arises from election to power of a citizen expressly

---

[51] *Diario Oficial* of El Salvador, vol. 93, No. 187, Aug. 22, 1922.
[62] *Conference on Central American Affairs* (Washington, Government Printing Office, 1923), pp. 288–289.

and unquestionably disqualified by the Constitution of his country as eligible to election as President, Vice-President or Chief of State designate.

While the United States is not a party to the treaty, it has never-theless given its moral support to that declaration by the five Central American republics of their consensus as to the best means of dis-couraging revolutions in their countries, and in June, 1923, at a time of turbulent political conditions in Honduras, this Government publicly announced that in the future it would be guided by the principles set forth in that treaty in recognizing new governments in Central America.

NICARAGUA'S REPURCHASE OF THE NATIONAL BANK, 1924

On August 1, 1924, Nicaragua liquidated the balance of the Treasury bills of 1920, series A, issued in part payment of the Pa-cific Railway. At the same time and in conformity with a policy of regaining control of all national enterprises, it began negotia-tions for the repurchase of the 51 per cent of the stock of the Na-tional Bank, which had been bought by the bankers for $153,000 under the agreement of October 8, 1913. In 1924 the net assets of the National Bank were $615,542. As a condition of the bank-stock sale, the New York owners required the Nicaraguan Government to purchase the property and assets of the Compañia Mercantil de Ultramar, a commercial company formerly engaged in the coffee trade and at this time in process of liquidation. In September, 1924, the Government purchased the National Bank stock for $300,000 and the Compañia Mercantil de Ultramar for an additional $300,000.

At the time of the purchase of the National Bank stock there was a rumor that the Government intended to inflate the currency with which it would pay the holders of the guaranteed customs bonds. The stock-market quotation for the guarantee customs bonds fell from 65 to 50. In order to allay the rumor, President Martínez, who succeeded President Chamorro after his death in October, 1923, made a public declaration that " the dogma or the permanent sub-stantial basis will be the immovable stability of the cordoba at par with the American dollar." [63] Shortly after his inauguration on Jan-uary 1, 1925, President Solórzano made a similar declaration.[64] These two vigorous declarations put an end to the fears which existed regarding the possible depreciation of the cordoba.

In the case of both the National Bank and the Pacific Railway, Nicaragua requested the continuance not only of the American man-agement but also of a representation of the bankers on the Boards of Directors.

---

[63] *La Gaceta*, No. 212, Sept. 18, 1924.   [64] *La Gaceta*, No. 25, Jan. 31, 1925.

THE ELECTIONS OF 1924

After 1920 the policy of the Department of State was directed to the withdrawal of the Legation guard, which had remained after the 1912 revolution as a moral support of the constituted authorities. The Department of State considered that this withdrawal could be effected with safety only after a strong government backed by the majority of the people had been established. Since the 1920 elections had been accompanied by patent frauds, the opposition to the Administration withheld its support and, in 1921 and 1922, carried on revolutionary activities. Therefore, in order to withdraw the Legation guard without throwing the country open to revolution, the Department of State based its policy on the following program: (1) passage of a new electoral law and the assistance of an American electoral mission in putting into effect this law both during registration and election; and (2) the reorganization of the Army by converting it into an efficient constabulary under American instruction. This program was communicated to the Nicaraguan Government in a note from the American Minister to Nicaragua on November 14, 1923:[65]

I have the honor to inform Your Excellency that my Government desires that the Legation Guard, which has remained in Nicaragua since Your Excellency's Government requested the assistance of the Government of the United States in 1912, in the maintenance of constitutional order, should be withdrawn as soon as practicable. My Government, however, does not desire to make any sudden radical change which would inject a new element into the situation in Central America that might perhaps be a cause for unrest and disturbance.

In this connection I am instructed to state that my Government has noted with gratification and with sympathetic appreciation the steps which have already been taken by the Nicaraguan Government to assure freedom and fairness in the approaching elections. The enactment of the electoral law, drafted by an expert employed by the Nicaraguan Government for this purpose, may be regarded as the first step toward assuring the people of Nicaragua that complete freedom will exist during the electoral period, and my Government is confident that this step will be followed by such effective measures during the electoral period as will assure a free expression of the will of the people and convince all parties that the Government which may result from the elections will have the support of the majority of the people of Nicaragua. Therefore, my Government instructs me to inform Your Excellency that upon the installation in January, 1925, of the government coming into office as the result of the elections to be held in October, 1924, it will feel that there is no further reason to maintain a Legation Guard at Managua and the American Marines will accordingly be withdrawn at that time.

---

[65] File No. 817.1051/26.

I am further instructed by my Government to state that the American Marines will be retained in Managua during the approaching electoral period only if the Nicaraguan Government considers that their presence will assist the constituted authorities in assuring complete freedom in the presidential elections, and that they remain specifically for the purpose of helping to maintain tranquillity and order during the electoral period.

The electoral law recently voted is as yet unfamiliar alike to the officials charged with its carrying out and enforcement, as to the Nicaraguan electorate which will exercise its rights according to its provisions. Therefore, in order to assist the Nicaraguan Government in the installation of this new electoral system with the least possible amount of confusion, my Government will be glad, should the Nicaraguan Government so desire, to ask Mr. Dodds, the author of the law, or some other qualified technical experts, to come to Nicaragua a few months in advance of the next election in order that he may, by his counsel and advice, assist the Nicaraguan authorities in putting the law into effect. My Government will also be glad to assist the Nicaraguan Government to obtain the services of such additional assistants as may be required to travel throughout Nicaragua to help the local authorities in the installation of the new system and in its proper enforcement, and to report to the authorities at Managua any difficulties that may be encountered throughout the country in the proper enforcement of the law in order that those difficulties may be promptly overcome.

As another evidence of its desire to assist Nicaragua in the orderly and undisturbed conduct of its normal existence, my Government would be glad to assist the Nicaraguan Government in the organization and training of an efficient constabulary which would assure the maintenance of order after the Marines are withdrawn. In establishing a force of this nature the Nicaraguan Government would be carrying out the terms of Article II of the Convention for the Limitation of Armaments, signed at the recent Conference on Central American Affairs. If the Nicaraguan Government desires, my Government will be glad to suggest the names of persons suitable to act as instructors in the new constabulary, in order that their experience may be made available to Nicaragua.

My Government feels that with the aid of Mr. Dodds and the other assistants in the efficient installation of the new electoral system, free and fair suffrage should be possible in the coming elections so that the government resulting therefrom should have the support of the majority of the Nicaraguan people and would, therefore, need no other assistance in maintaining order than that of the Nicaraguan constabulary, which my Government is ready to assist in training, and that, therefore, upon the installation of that government the Marines may be withdrawn without any noticeable effect upon the normal course of affairs in Nicaragua.

The new government should be in a very strong position indeed, and it is hoped that long before its entry into office the General Treaty of Peace and Amity, signed at Washington on February 7, 1923, by the representatives of the five Central American powers, will have been ratified and put into effect so that any individual or group of individuals who might endeavor to overthrow the constituted authorities will know full well in advance that the other four Central American Governments will not, on account of Article II of that Treaty, recognize any government coming into power contrary to the provisions of that Treaty. In any case, the position and policy of the United States Government with regard to such recognition is and will continue to be that announced by the American Minister to Honduras under instructions from the Department of State of June 30, 1923, which is in complete consonance and accord with the stipulations of Article II of the General Treaty of Peace and Amity, as signed by the delegates of the five Central American Republics at Washington on February 7, last.

With the enactment of the electoral law on March 16, 1923, the Nicaraguan Government provided a law which, if impartially and rigidly applied, would provide a free and fair election. Moreover, at the Government's request, Doctor Dodds, with two American civilians and four marine aides, assisted at the first application of the new electoral law in the registration of voters in March, 1924. Shortly afterwards a series of unforeseen political developments prevented Doctor Dodds from assisting at the elections in October.

President Diego Chamorro died on October 12, 1923. His successor, Bartolomé Martínez, although selected as Vice President by the Chamorro-dominated Conservative convention of 1920, was ambitious to continue his control of the Administration. His plans ran counter to those of Gen. Emiliano Chamorro and the Granada Conservatives, who wanted to regain the leadership lost through the death of President Diego Chamorro. The attempts of the Conservative leaders to agree to a national party in which the Liberals would participate were unsuccessful. The Conservative convention, which was again dominated by General Chamorro, nominated him for the Presidency.

The Liberal Party, which met shortly afterwards, likewise split into two factions. The larger, under the party name of Liberal Nationalists, nominated Juan B. Sacasa, a noted physician and citizen of León; the smaller, under the party name of Liberal Republican, nominated Luís Corea.

In the meantime President Martínez had developed a new party, ostensibly in order that it might defeat General Chamorro and elect one of its own leaders but, in reality, for the purpose of bringing about his own nomination. Coincidentally with the carrying out of this maneuver, the President had been conducting unsuccessful negotiations with the Liberal Nationalists for the creation of a national government with himself as presidential candidate. After securing his nomination, President Martínez requested the views of the Department of State on the political situation in Nicaragua. The American Chargé d'Affaires in Nicaragua, acting on the instructions of the Department of State, addressed the following letter to the President on June 13 : [66]

In response to Your Excellency's request for an expression of my Government's views with regard to the existing political situation in Nicaragua, I have the honor to inform Your Excellency that the Government of the United States has no desire to intervene in the internal affairs of Nicaragua and has no preference whatsoever as between political parties or candidates who may take part in the forthcoming elections. It desires only that the new President of Nicaragua should be freely and constitutionally elected by the people of that country.

On January 1, 1925, however, the Government of the United States in the natural course of events will be confronted by the necessity of deciding whether it can consistently recognize the incoming administration in Nicaragua as the constitutional government of that country. My Government would be precluded by the policy which it has already publicly announced with regard to the recognition of new governments in Central America from recognizing a government arising from the election to the presidency of a citizen expressly and unquestionably disqualified by the constitution of his country.

My Government desires very much that there should be no question in January, 1925, of the eligibility of the person who shall have been chosen as President of Nicaragua, because it desires to be in a position to extend the fullest and most sympathetic cooperation to the new Government. After a careful consideration of the matter my Government has felt constrained to express the opinion that the election to the presidency of a person who had held office during the next preceding term would be contrary to the Nicaraguan constitution. Your Excellency will appreciate that this expression by the United States Government is due solely to the requirements of its general policy in the recognition of new governments, and has no relation whatsoever to any personal considerations affecting the present President of· Nicaragua, for whom my Government entertains the highest regard.

I feel sure that Your Excellency will appreciate the fact that the Government of the United States has been led to express its opinion on this matter at this time solely out of friendship to Your Excellency's Government and to the people of Nicaragua. and that its purpose is to avoid the embarrassment which might be caused to both Governments should its position not be clearly understood. My Government earnestly hopes that the new President of Nicaragua may be constitutionally chosen by elections in which the will of the Nicaraguan people may be given the fullest and freest expression, and it has no doubt that the very gratifying success which has already been realized in conducting the registration of the voters will be followed by an election which, in accordance with the public declarations already made by Your Excellency, will be conducted with the utmost freedom and impartiality.

---

[66] File No. 817.00/3081.

Upon the receipt of this letter, President Martínez renounced his candidacy and entered into a union with the Liberal Nationalists, which called itself the Transaction. By the terms of the agreement, Carlos Solórzano, a Conservative follower of Martínez, was selected as presidential candidate, and Doctor Sacasa, who previously had been given the presidential nomination by the Liberal Nationalists, accepted renomination as the vice presidential candidate. Furthermore, the agreement provided that at least two cabinet posts should be given to the Liberals as well as five *jefaturas políticas*, and that the Supreme Court and the lesser courts should be as evenly divided as possible. This coalition united the larger of the Liberal factions with the smaller of the Conservative. In answer to President Martínez's request that the Department of State give its views on the coalition, the American Chargé d'Affaires was instructed to reply as follows:[67]

My Government has received Your Excellency's telegram stating that prominent Conservatives and Liberals agreed on Señor Carlos Solorzano as candidate for President for the next constitutional term and Señor Juan Bautista Sacasa for Vice President and you inquire whether the Department of State will look with favor on the alliance for the organization of a National Government.

In reply I am instructed by my Government to state that it has no preferences whatever regarding candidates for the high office of President of Nicaragua. My Government supports no candidate and is hostile to no candidate; it desires only that free and fair elections may be held in order that the will of the people may be expressed without hindrance at the polls. My Government feels that the transference of the center of political activity of Nicaragua to Washington would be detrimental to that Government's interests and this Government therefore cannot express its views regarding any ticket.

My Government desires that no candidate for the Presidency, not prohibited from holding such office by Article II of the Treaty of Peace and Amity, signed at Washington on February 7, 1923, may be impeded from presenting his candidacy to the electors of Nicaragua and any person who gains the office of President through free and fair elections in accordance with the electoral law and the Constitution and who is not comprised within the classes above mentioned will be accorded the recognition of the United States Government and my Government will be glad to carry on with him the friendly relations that have always existed between the United States and Nicaragua and will be glad to lend him its advice and counsel.

Because of Martínez's alliance with the Liberal Nationalists among whom were several Zelayistas, many of the dissenting Conservatives returned to the genuine Conservative Party.

---

[67] File No. 817.00/3101.

Although the Conservatives controlled the electoral machinery, Congress, and the Supreme Court, the Transactionists had the full support of the Administration, which in the past had meant the election of the Administration candidate. Therefore, when the United States suggested as a part of its program the assistance of Doctor Dodds at the elections, President Martínez declined. Less than a week before the elections, President Martínez inquired whether the United States would not designate marines to observe the elections and examine the election returns. The Department of State replied that it was unable to grant this request since the time before election was too short to instruct the marines in the provisions of the electoral law and their participation would attach a responsibility on the part of the United States to the outcome of the election, over which it had exercised no supervision.

Except for one clash the elections passed off quietly. Of a total of 115,000 registered, 84,096 voted. Of the votes cast, Solórzano received 48,072, General Chamorro, 28,760, and Corea, 7,264.

The elections were reported to be marked by sustained governmental pressure and intimidation of the Conservative and Liberal Republican Parties and support of the Transactionist Party. The refusal of electoral privileges, the misuse of the Government-owned telegraph service and liquor supply, the alteration of ballots, and the unwarranted state of siege were only a few of the practices to which the Administration apparently resorted to throw its influence to the Transactionist Party. However, after giving consideration to the advisability both of a new election and the appointment of a coalition cabinet headed by a designate chosen by Congress, the Department of State decided to accord recognition to Solórzano when he assumed the Presidency on January 1, 1925. Prior to his inauguration, Solórzano made the following statements to the American Chargé d'Affaires: [68]

One. I make definite assurance that the 1928 elections will be carried out in full freedom and fairness for all parties and strictly in accordance with the provisions of the Dodds electoral law and that the latter will not be modified except in strict accordance with the advice of Dr. Dodds or another suitable electoral expert in accord with the Department of State.

Two. I give definite formal engagement that immediately upon assuming office I will form a constabulary in order to provide a suitable means to maintain order upon the withdrawal of the American marines for which I will request the assistance of the government of the United States in its training and organization according to the convention for the limitation of armaments signed at Washington February 7th, 1923.

---

[68] File No. 817.00/3242.

Three. I give formal definite engagement that I will undertake adequate and satisfactory measures with which the government of the United States could cooperate for the solution of the economic problems of Nicaragua, and,

Four. I shall consider the expediency of obtaining the cooperation of as many political elements in Nicaragua as possible in forming my government.

THE CONSTABULARY

In order that the withdrawal of the Legation guard should not be a signal for disorder, the United States, in its note of November 14, 1923, to the Nicaraguan Government, offered its assistance in the organization of a constabulary. Although in December, 1923, President Martínez accepted this offer in principle, he made no effort during his Administration to bring about the reorganization of the Army. Among the statements which President Solórzano made to the American Chargé d'Affaires prior to his inauguration was a promise to establish a constabulary and to request the assistance of the United States in doing so.

In the meantime arrangements had been made to withdraw the Legation guard in the latter part of January, 1925. On January 7, however, President Solórzano stated that his Government was not only obligated to create but greatly desired to establish a national constabulary. He enumerated various undesirable results which it was felt would follow the immediate withdrawal of the marines and expressed his desire that they should not be withdrawn until the constabulary was actually established under the guidance of American instructors. In conclusion, he expressed the hope, whatever might have been the circumstances responsible for the decision to withdraw the marines, that reconsideration would be given to the order for withdrawal, in behalf of peace, order, well-being, and the benefit of Nicaragua.

The Department of State replied by referring to the Legation's note of November 14, 1923. The attention of the Nicaraguan Government was called to the fact that 14 months' advance notification had been given of the intention to withdraw the Legation guard, in order to allow ample time for that Government to take such steps as might be deemed advisable. Under these conditions the responsibility for any unfortunate developments resulting from the failure to meet the situation created by the withdrawal of the marines clearly rested upon the Nicaraguan Government. The United States felt that it would be entirely justified in withdrawing the Legation guard in accordance with its announced plan. However, desiring to cooperate in promoting the peaceful development and prosperity of Nicaragua, the United States was prepared, in view of the representations of the Nicaraguan Government, to permit the Legation guard to remain for such time as was absolutely necessary for the organization of the new constabulary. This would only be done, however, upon the definite understanding that the organization of the constabulary would be undertaken immediately and energetically.

In March, 1925, the Department of State found it necessary to inform the Nicaraguan Government that, if the constabulary was not established at once, the Legation guard would be withdrawn. In May, an act providing for the constabulary was passed by the Nicaraguan Congress and approved by the President. The Nicaraguan Government requested the Department of State to suggest to it persons competent to organize the constabulary. At that time no legislation existed in the United States whereby the active Army, Navy, and Marine forces of the United States could be detailed for such purpose.[69] Therefore, the Department of State recommended several persons, none of whom was in active service in the armed forces of the United States. In July, the American instructors arrived and began the organization of the constabulary. The Legation guard left Managua on August 1 and sailed from Corinto on August 4, 1925.

---

[69] An act of May 19, 1926, gave the President this right:

The President of the United States be, and hereby is, authorized, upon application from the foreign governments concerned, and whenever in his discretion the public interests render such a course advisable, to detail officers and enlisted men of the United States Army, Navy, and Marine Corps to assist the governments of the Republics of North America, Central America, and South America and of the Republics of Cuba, Haiti, and Santo Domingo, in military and naval matters: *Provided*, That the officers and enlisted men so detailed be, and they are hereby, authorized to accept from the government to which detailed offices and such compensation and emoluments thereunto appertaining as may be first approved by the Secretary of War or by the Secretary of the Navy, as the case may be: *Provided further*, That while so detailed such officers and enlisted men shall receive, in addition to the compensation and emoluments allowed them by such governments, the pay and allowances whereto entitled in the United States Army, Navy, and Marine Corps and shall be allowed the same credit for longevity, retirement, and for all other purposes that they would receive if they were serving with the forces of the United States. (May 19, 1926, ch. 334, 44 U. S. Stat. L., pt. 2, 565.)

THE CIVIL WAR, 1926–27

THE COUP D'ÉTAT OF GENERAL CHAMORRO, 1925

President Solórzano was inaugurated on January 1, 1925, under inauspicious circumstances. The genuine Conservatives refused to admit the legality of his Administration, and their opposition heightened when the Conservative Senators and Deputies, whose elections had been conceded by the National Board of Elections, were expelled by the Martínez-controlled Congress and Transactionists seated in their stead.

The Liberal Nationalists, with the prospect of acquiring complete control of the Administration for the first time since 1911, used every means of influencing President Solórzano and of discrediting the genuine Conservatives. They secured the appointment of ex-President Martínez as Minister of Government, thereby continuing the tutelage exercised by the former President.

Under these circumstances the lack of strong leadership of President Solórzano and his vacillation between the support of the Conservatives and of the Liberals proved his undoing. Less than four weeks after the withdrawal of the Legation guard, a band of nondescript Government troops, under a Conservative officer, arrested at a social function at the International Club, the Minister of Finance, General Moncada, and various other Liberal leaders, avowing their intention of liberating the President from the alleged domination of the Liberal element. As a result, the Liberal Minister of Finance was replaced by a Conservative and the Ministry of War annexed to the Presidency. However, disturbances increased throughout the country, martial law was declared, the operation of the railway was temporarily suspended, and, on September 10, 1925, the United States found it again desirable to send cruisers to Corinto and Bluefields. The moral effect of their presence was immediately noted, and conditions remained temporarily quiet throughout the country. The cruisers were withdrawn on September 21.

On October 25, 1925, supporters of General Chamorro seized the Loma Fortress and by noon of the same day dominated the city, President Solórzano having refused sufficient ammunition to the newly organized constabulary to quell the disturbance. General

Chamorro compelled President Solórzano to sign a pact in which the latter agreed:

1. That the Transaction pacts be broken and be considered as of no value henceforth;
2. That the Cabinet be composed entirely of Conservatives;
3. That full amnesty be granted to all partisans in the recent outbreak;
4. That the Government pay General Chamorro $10,000 for the expenses of the uprising, in addition to paying the troops involved;
5. That General Chamorro be named Commander in Chief of the Army.

The American Minister at once informed General Chamorro that he would not recognize any government assuming power by force. The Department of State had told General Chamorro prior to President Solórzano's inauguration that any revolutionary movement would meet with the American Government's decided disapproval and would have the effect of throwing the moral support of the United States to the side of the constituted Nicaraguan Government.

The Liberals immediately protested the violation of the Transactionists' pact and requested the United States to appeal to the signatories of the 1923 treaties signed at Washington to cooperate in the reestablishment of constitutional order. The Liberal leaders were informed that the Department of State could not act as a channel of communication between a political party and other foreign governments or lend itself in any way to further internal activities which were in the nature of a protest against the recognized constitutional Government of Nicaragua.

After the capture of the Loma Fortress, Doctor Sacasa, the Vice President, had returned to León, there remaining in hiding. Early in November, General Chamorro sent 1,200 men to León, stating that they would be held there until Doctor Sacasa should resign. Shortly afterwards he intimated that if milder means could not produce Doctor Sacasa's resignation, sterner measures might be adopted toward relatives and friends of the Vice President. Doctor Sacasa immediately fled the country.

Unable to secure Doctor Sacasa's resignation, General Chamorro took steps to ascend the Presidency by means which would secure recognition of the United States. First of all, he caused the expulsion from Congress of the Liberal and Conservative Republican Congressmen, whom he claimed had been forcibly and therefore illegally seated the previous year. The Department of State indicated that it would consider as illegal proposals to call a Constitutional Assembly to revise the Constitution in order to permit General Chamorro's assumption of the Presidency or to declare the last election null and void and proceed to hold new ones under Conservative control.

Finally, General Chamorro proceeded on quasi-constitutional grounds:

Article 101 of the Constitution [1] provides that—

The executive power shall be held by a citizen called the President of the Republic, in his default by the Vice President, and in the default of the latter by one of the Designates according to their order.

Article 106 of the Constitution provides that—

In case of the absolute or temporary default of the President of the Republic, the executive power shall devolve upon the Vice President, and in default of the latter upon one of the Designates in the order of their election. In the latter case, should Congress be in session, it shall be its duty to authorize the entrustment of the office to the representative whom it may designate who must fulfill the requirements for President of the Republic.

On January 3, 1925, General Chamorro was elected without opposition Senator from Managua, the vacancy having been created by means of the resignation of one of his friends. On January 12, Congress, which had previously ordered Vice President Sacasa to appear and answer charges of conspiracy, declared the Vice Presidency vacant when Doctor Sacasa did not heed the order and banished him from Nicaragua for a period of two years. Congress then elected General Chamorro First Designate for the Presidency.

On January 16, Congress granted Solórzano an indefinite leave of absence, and General Chamorro, as First Designate, assumed executive power, thereby relegating President Solórzano to a titular position. Congress did not act on President Solórzano's resignation, which had been presented on January 14, 1926. General Chamorro kept President Solórzano under surveillance so that he could not leave the country and thereby disturb the technical constitutional status of the Government.

The Department of State, when it learned of General Chamorro's scheme, indicated to him that in view of his seizing the Loma Fortress and dominating the constitutional Government by armed force, it considered that the manipulation of the laws to give him the Presidency was merely a subterfuge to obtain recognition by the United States in spite of the provisions of the Washington Treaty of 1923. In the opinion of the Department of State, such a Government would be founded on a *coup d'état*. Regardless of this advice, General Chamorro proceeded to the execution of his plan, thinking that the Department of State, faced with the *fait accompli* of his control, after an interval of time would recognize him.

---

[1] File No. 817.011/17.

The policy of the United States toward General Chamorro was clearly set forth on January 22, 1926, in a letter addressed by the Secretary of State to the Nicaraguan representative in Washington. The letter read as follows:[2]

DEAR DOCTOR CASTRILLO: In your communication of the 19th instant addressed to the Secretary of State you advise that President Solorzano having resigned his office General Emiliano Chamorro took charge of the executive power on January 17.

The hope expressed in your letter that the relations which have been close and cordial for so many years between Nicaragua and the United States will continue and grow stronger has been noted with pleasure. The Government and people of the United States have feelings of sincerest friendship for Nicaragua and the people of Nicaragua, and the Government of the United States will of course continue to maintain the most friendly relations with the people of Nicaragua. This Government has felt privileged to be able to be of assistance in the past at their request not only to Nicaragua but to all the countries of Central America more especially during the Conference on Central American Affairs which resulted in the signing of a General Treaty of Peace and Amity on February 7, 1923, between the five Republics of Central America. The object of the Central American countries, with which the United States was heartily in accord, was to promote constitutional government and orderly procedure in Central America and those Governments agreed upon a joint course of action with regard to the non-recognition of governments coming into office through *coup d'etat* or revolution. The United States has adopted the principles of that Treaty as its policy in the future recognition of Central American Governments as it feels that by so doing it can best show its friendly disposition towards and its desire to be helpful to the Republics of Central America.

It is therefore with regret that I have to inform you that the Government of the United States has not recognized and will not recognize as the Government of Nicaragua the régime now headed by General Chamorro, as the latter was duly advised on several occasions by the American Minister after General Chamorro had taken charge of the citadel at Managua on October 25th last. This action is, I am happy to learn, in accord with that taken by all the Governments that signed with Nicaragua the Treaty of 1923.

The other Central American republics also refused to recognize the régime of General Chamorro.

THE RÉGIME OF GENERAL CHAMORRO, 1926

Notwithstanding the refusal of the United States and the Central American governments to recognize his régime, General Chamorro proceeded in the apparent expectation that by maintaining an orderly and peaceful Government he could eventually compel recog-

---

[2] File No. 817.00/3416.

nition. General Chamorro was aided by unusual prosperity. The foreign-trade movement, the customs revenues, and the total revenues of the country were greater than those of any other previous year except 1920. The excellent situation was due almost entirely to the large coffee crop and its high price, coffee representing more than 60 per cent of the total exports of the year. General Chamorro's attitude during the spring of 1926 delayed any serious efforts toward effecting a settlement of Nicaraguan difficulties. On April 13, 1926, continuing his policy of eliminating the Liberal elements from the Government, he had the National Congress discharge four Liberal Supreme Court justices.

Doctor Sacasa, after he fled Nicaragua, went to Washington to seek the intercession of the United States. The Department of State informed him that it would never recognize the *de facto* Chamorro régime. At the same time, it pointed out that in the 1923 treaties signed at Washington, to which the United States gave its moral support, there was no provision compelling the signatories to intervene to depose the *de facto* authorities in favor of the *de jure;* and that the United States would not look with sympathy on the resort to arms to bring about a constitutional régime.

Revolutionary activities broke out on the east coast early in May, 1926. Within a short time the Liberals controlled the entire east coast except Cabo Gracias a Dios and San Juan del Norte. The U. S. S. *Cleveland* was ordered to Bluefields where marines were landed and the city declared a neutral zone. The Navy Department ordered American naval forces to maintain the strictest neutrality between the contending factions, and forbade them to hinder the forces either of General Chamorro or of the Liberals, except in so far as was necessary to protect American lives and property. The better-equipped Conservative troops quelled the outbreak in the latter part of May.

During their brief control of Bluefields, the Liberals ousted the American Collector of Customs. He was reinstated when it was pointed out to the Liberal leaders that only the Collector General of Customs had the authority to remove from office any of his subordinates. The Department of State did not accord protection to the Nicaraguan customhouse or customs revenues any more than it did to other property belonging to the Nicaraguan Government or Nicaraguan citizens. The Department of State reiterated its policy established the previous year of looking to whichever régime was functioning for the carrying out of the Financial Plan and for meeting the external obligations of Nicaragua.

Notwithstanding the apparent healthy conditions of commerce within the country, there was general dissatisfaction. Merchants

complained of requisition of goods and cattle owners of their live-
stock. Both planters and ranchers were unable to secure sufficient
labor because of the conscription of workers for the Army. The
mahogany and banana companies suffered from military operations
in the east coast. General Chamorro had established martial law
and a rigid censorship of cables and newspapers. He arrested hundreds of Liberals for alleged political offenses and forbade the return of those who had emigrated.

Many of the prominent Conservatives opposed the arbitrary measure of General Chamorro and of the military clique that surrounded
him. They desired a return to constitutional government and the
peaceful elimination of General Chamorro. Due to the strict press
censorship, the position of the Department of State toward the
Chamorro régime had been consistently misrepresented to the Nicaraguan people, many of whom continued to believe that recognition
would ultimately be accorded. In order to clarify this position, on
June 15, 1926, the American Chargé d'Affaires called a meeting of
the Conservative leaders at the American Legation. General Chamorro protested against this action, stating that it represented an interference in the domestic problems of the country and was an in-
stigation to violence. However, at this meeting the Chargé d'Affaires did not discuss the internal political situation with the Conservative leaders but only made clear the policy of the United States
toward the Chamorro régime, reiterating the hope that a constitutional solution might be achieved through peaceful negotiations.
Shortly afterwards, the Chargé d'Affaires held a similar meeting
with the Liberal leaders.

In August, the revolutionary movement better organized and
equipped broke out again, this time on both the west and east coasts.
Although their activities were checked in the former area, the Liberals were soon in possession of several ports on the east coast. In
order to protect the lives and property of Americans, United States
naval vessels were dispatched to Bluefields and Corinto. On August
28, 1926, a force of 204 bluejackets landed at Bluefields after the
Jefe Político of Bluefields had informed noncombatants of his inability to guarantee protection in the event of a battle. Bluefields
was declared a neutral zone.

Although General Chamorro spent $507,147 out of a 6-months'
budget surplus of $761,346 in combating the revolution, he was
forced to draw upon the surplus of the National Bank. The bank's
reserves were thereby depleted to a point where the directors, in order
to protect the national currency, refused to declare further dividends. The action of the bank in this matter was looked upon with

approval by the Department of State, since the maintenance of a stable cordoba was a thing which had been successfully striven for from the time of the first financing of the Nicaraguan Government in 1911. It is likewise a matter closely allied to the protection of the interests of the large number of persons holding the guaranteed customs bonds of 1918, since these bonds were issued in Nicaraguan currency.

The Corinto Conference, September, 1926

During the summer the situation had reached a deadlock. General Chamorro controlled the Administration but could not dislodge the Liberals from the east coast. The Liberals, although occupying certain east-coast ports, had no governmental machinery and at that time were not sufficiently well organized to invade the west coast.

On August 27, 1926, the Department of State delivered through the Chargé d'Affaires the following letter to General Chamorro: [3]

The Government of the United States has viewed with grave apprehension the situation existing in Nicaragua brought about by the unconstitutional usurpation of the executive power by a military leader. That General Chamorro, who was one of the delegates to the Central American Conference of 1923 and, as the representative of his country, signed a treaty which has as its basic principle the prevention of revolution and the seizure of the Government through a *coup d' etat*, could have permitted himself to have brought disaster upon his country through the usurpation of the executive power is almost unbelievable. The Government of the United States reaffirms its statement that it will not recognize General Chamorro as President of the Republic of Nicaragua.

Since the assumption of power by General Chamorro last January two revolutionary movements have already broken out in Nicaragua, and reports which have reached the Department show a state of unrest in that country which cannot but cause serious concern. Should events in Nicaragua continue their present course which can only result in ultimate civil war and economic chaos and imperil the lives and property of Americans and other foreigners in Nicaragua, the United States Government will be compelled to take such measures as it may deem necessary for their adequate protection.

While anxious and desirous to avoid interference in the purely domestic affairs of Nicaragua the Department of State cannot but point out that actions on the part of those in control of the Government of Nicaragua which, according to present advices received by the Department are tending to prevent the free operation of the Financial Plans of 1917 and 1920, entered into between the Nicaraguan Government and its foreign creditors under the good offices of the Department of State, are being viewed with considerable anxiety by the United States Government.

---

[3] File No. 817.00/3738a.

126702—32——5

It would now appear that the only way by which further bloodshed and serious disorders, which can only bring about the ruin of the country, may be avoided is by the withdrawal of General Chamorro from the position which he now holds and a prompt return to constitutional government. It is believed that as a first step towards this consummation a conference could be held attended by the political leaders of importance of all parties in Nicaragua, with a view to deciding upon a feasible plan.

After discussion with the Conservative leaders, General Chamorro requested the good offices of the United States to reestablish peace and constitutional government. The Department of State in accepting this request instructed its Chargé d'Affaires to make clear to both parties that the United States would not be a party to any agreement. The Liberal leaders, after consultation with Doctor Sacasa, who had gone from Washington to Guatemala, accepted the invitation to a conference.

As a preliminary, an armistice of 15 days was arranged, which was extended for an additional 15 days during the conference. The United States offered the Nicaraguan Liberals in Guatemala transportation on board the U.S.S. *Tulsa*, since at that time no regular commercial transportation was available. Doctor Sacasa did not personally attend the conference but sent delegates instead.

The conference was held at Corinto from October 16 to 24, 1926. Both parties asked that American marines be landed and maintained there during the conference as a means of guaranteeing the security of the delegates. A neutral zone was established on October 10. At the request of the delegates, the sessions were held on board the U.S.S. *Denver*, and the American Chargé d'Affaires acted as chairman at the meetings.

After two days of discussion the conference decided that its program should be " to reestablish peace on the basis of constitutionality and the treaties of Washington."[4] From the beginning the conference was deadlocked over the method of carrying out this program. Both parties demanded the office of Chief Executive, and on this basis neither was willing to grant concessions to the other. The Liberal delegation proposed that the following question be submitted to arbitration by representatives of the Central American governments and by the Secretary of State of the United States: " Whether the reestablishment of the Government on the basis of constitutionality and the Treaties of Washington of 1923 must be made with the Vice President of the Republic, Dr. Juan Bautista Sacasa as Chief of the Government or if it is legally possible to constitute the

---

[4] File No. 817.00/4094.

Government without taking account of the said Vice President, Dr. Sacasa. In the last mentioned case it shall be decided by the arbitration what settlement must be adopted."[5]

The American Chargé d'Affaires informally explained to the Liberal delegation that the United States did not consider internal political problems justiciable or the proper subject of international arbitration as were the disputes between nations. He stated that the people of Nicaragua must decide what political party or parties, what officials, and what form of régime should constitute the Government of Nicaragua. The United States would then decide, in view of the 1923 treaties of Washington, whether *de jure* recognition could be extended to that régime. The form of régime must be the responsibility of the Nicaraguan people.

The Liberals threatened immediate withdrawal when the Conservatives failed to accept their proposal, but were persuaded to remain to seek a solution. However, the successor to General Chamorro proved to be an *impasse* to the conference. The Liberals would not accept a Conservative even though they should receive cabinet positions, diplomatic posts, and other positions, and the restoration of the expelled members of Congress and of the Supreme Court magistrates. The Conservatives rejected the Liberals' counter-proposal for a third-party provisional president, stating that the disastrous Solórzano régime occurred because of a minor party executive. Unable to agree, the conference came to an end on October 24, 1926. Hostilities were resumed on October 30.

The Election of Adolfo Diaz, November, 1926

On October 30, 1926, in accordance with article 106 of the Constitution,[6] General Chamorro deposited the Presidency in the Second Designate, Senator Sebastián Uriza, the First Designate being absent in the United States. The same day, Senator Uriza appointed General Chamorro as Commander in Chief of the Army. The Department of State did not accord any form of moral support to the Uriza régime, feeling that it had no more of a constitutional basis than that of General Chamorro, but was merely a transition between the Chamorro régime and a government which could be recognized.

In the midst of renewed revolutionary activities Uriza convoked Congress in extraordinary session. The Senators and Deputies who had been expelled by General Chamorro from the previous Congress were invited to return and resume their seats. The Liberal Nationalists illegally seated by the Martínez-controlled Congress of

---

[5] *Ibid.*   [6] See p. 57.

1925 were to be replaced by the Conservatives who had been declared elected by the National Board of Elections.

On November 11, 1926, Congress in joint session designated Señor Adolfo Diaz for the Presidency. At this session 51 members were present out of a total membership of 67, of whom 44 voted for Diaz and 2 for Solórzano.[7] Five Liberals refrained from voting, claiming infractions of the rules of procedure which prevented the complete attendance of their representatives. On November 14 Señor Diaz took office. The American Chargé d'Affaires attended the inauguration, although formal recognition by the United States was not accorded until November 17. In announcing that formal recognition had been made, the Secretary of State added:[8]

I am much gratified that a solution has been found for the Nicaraguan political problems which is in accordance with the Constitution of that country and in harmony with the Central American treaty of 1923. When General Chamorro seized the power a year ago, it was of course impossible to accord recognition to his government, since it originated in a *coup d'état*. When General Chamorro withdrew from power, this left the way open for the election by Congress of one of its own members to assume the executive power as provided for by the Nicaraguan Constitution under certain circumstances. The members of the Congress which was chosen at a popular election in 1924 were called to meet in an extraordinary session for this purpose and elected Señor Adolfo Diaz. Changes which had been made in the membership of this Congress during the régime of General Chamorro were nullified, and members who had been expelled were invited to resume their seats, thus restoring the Congress to its original complexion. The entire Congress in joint session has a membership of 64. Fifty-three members voted in the election of Diaz, and he received 45 votes, or an absolute majority of the total membership of Congress. The last constitutional President of Nicaragua, Carlos Solórzano, resigned in January, 1926, and the Vice President elected with him has been out of the country since November, 1925. In the absence of these two, the duty devolved upon Congress of naming a designate from one of its own members to fill out the unexpired term of President Solórzano. The Department has been informed that President Diaz intends to make overtures of peace and general amnesty to his political opponents and that he will offer the Liberal Party participation in the new government, including certain cabinet posts. I sincerely hope that this offer, if made, will be accepted by the Liberals, since only by cooperation between all factions can peace and tranquillity be restored to that country now so unhappily torn by revolution, a condition which has invited interference from outside sources; a state of affairs which must cause concern to every friend of stability in Central America. It must be in the best interests, not only of Nicaragua but of Central America as a whole and all countries interested in its welfare, that normal conditions should soon be restored per-

---

[7] *La Gaceta*, No. 270, Nov. 30, 1926.   [8] Press release of Nov. 17, 1926.

mitting a return to that prosperity and economic development which have been so marked in Nicaragua during the last decade and a half.

Honduras and El Salvador immediately recognized President Diaz, Guatemala established relations which were later withdrawn, and Costa Rica failed to recognize him.

The elimination of General Chamorro did not occur until December, 1926. President Diaz, shortly after taking office, requested the President of the United States to lift the arms embargo laid against both General Chamorro and the Liberals on September 15, 1926, in so far as it applied to the recently recognized Government. President Diaz was informed that the United States would not comply with his request so long as General Chamorro was Commander in Chief of the Army. General Chamorro, yielding to the pressure exerted upon him by the Conservative Party and even members of his own family, submitted his resignation on December 8. He was appointed Minister to Great Britain, France, Italy, Spain, and the Vatican. He turned over the Army on December 15 and left Nicaragua on December 20.

The congressional elections which were postponed awaiting the outcome of the Corinto Conference were held late in November except in the Departments of León, Chinandega, and Esteli, where the unsettled conditions made elections impossible.

ATTEMPTS AT RECONCILIATION

The Liberals did not accept the election of Diaz to the Presidency but made plans to set up a rival government. On December 1, 1926, Doctor Sacasa, accompanied by 45 followers, landed at Puerto Cabezas, where he proclaimed himself " Constitutional President of Nicaragua." He named a cabinet, which included General Moncada as Minister of War and Navy. On December 2 he formally asked recognition by the United States, on which request the Department of State took no action. Although Doctor Sacasa immediately solicited recognition from the other Latin American countries, Mexico alone accorded it.

As he had promised in his inaugural address, President Diaz attempted a *rapprochement* with the Liberals. His proposals, which included participation of the Liberals in the cabinet and in the Government, a cash payment to the Liberal troops and complete amnesty and full guarantees, were declined. Doctor Sacasa insisted upon the joint mediation of the Central American republics and the United States, the same proposal made at the Corinto Conference, and accepted an offer of mediation by Costa Rica. President Diaz would not consider mediation as a basis of negotiation, believing that because of the complexion of Central American politics no mediation, least of all that of Costa Rica, which had not recognized him, would be impartial.

In a public statement in the latter part of January, 1927, Doctor Sacasa announced that while he declined to accept the peace proposals of President Diaz, nevertheless he favored American supervision of the elections in 1928, and suggested that representatives of all of the republics which were signatory to the Washington treaties of 1923 be included to aid in the supervision. President Diaz was agreeable to this suggestion. He did not accept, however, Doctor Sacasa's additional proposal of the designation of some impartial person to the Presidency until 1928, since he felt no really impartial and strong person was available.

During the informal conversations carried on by the representatives of the two parties, the United States took the opportunity of informing Doctor Sacasa that he could not look forward to eventual recognition by the United States.

The Protection of American Life and Property

Following the resumption of hostilities on October 30, 1926, the Liberals required the American mahogany companies operating on the east coast to pay to them the tax on logs exported from ports under their control. This tax was again collected by the customs officials of the Diaz government. The companies complained of this double taxation to the Department of State, which replied that this tax should not be paid to the revolutionists unless compelled, and then only under protest. The Department of State took the position that the customs revenues in Nicaragua had been pledged to the service of the outstanding bond issues. The Diaz government decided not to insist upon the second payment of the tax, if the mahogany companies could show receipts of payments to the Liberals.

In a note of November 15, 1926, to the American Chargé d'Affaires,[9] President Diaz requested the assistance of the United States Government in protecting American and foreign lives and property. During the following weeks it became evident that President Diaz appeared to rely upon the United States to protect the Government by physical means against the activities of the revolutionists. On December 8, 1926, the Department authorized the American Chargé d'Affaires to inform President Diaz that the fact that the United States Government had accorded him recognition did not put upon the United States any obligation to protect his Government by physical means; that the United States Government was prepared to lend to him such moral encouragement and support as are ordina-

---

[9] File No. 817.00/4197; *Congressional Record*, 69th Congress, 2d session, vol. 68, pt. 2, p. 1325.

rily due constitutional governments with which the United States maintains friendly relations, when those governments are threatened by revolutionary movements, but that further than this the United States Government was not prepared to go.

On December 14, the Nicaraguan Minister for Foreign Affairs addressed a note to the American Minister in which he authorized " the Government of the United States to employ all measures appropriate for the protection of the lives and property of American citizens,"[10] adding that " my Government will consider as a friendly aid whatever steps the Government of the United States may take for the reestablishment of peace and order in this country. These acts will be viewed by my Government as demonstrations of the friendship of your Government made in the best interests of Nicaragua."

In his message to Congress on January 10, 1927, President Coolidge set forth the policy of the United States Government toward Nicaragua:[11]

For many years numerous Americans have been living in Nicaragua, developing its industries and carrying on business. At the present time there are large investments in lumbering, mining, coffee growing, banana culture, shipping, and also in general mercantile and other collateral business. All these people and these industries have been encouraged by the Nicaraguan Government. That Government has at all times owed them protection, but the United States has occasionally been obliged to send naval forces for their proper protection. In the present crisis such forces are requested by the Nicaraguan Government, which protests to the United States its inability to protect these interests and states that any measures which the United States deems appropriate for their protection will be satisfactory to the Nicaraguan Government.

In addition to these industries now in existence, the Government of Nicaragua, by a treaty entered into on the 5th day of August, 1914, granted in perpetuity to the United States the exclusive proprietary rights necessary and convenient for the construction, operation, and maintenance of an oceanic canal. . . .

. . . .

. . . The proprietary rights of the United States in the Nicaraguan canal route, with the necessary implications growing out of it affecting the Panama Canal, together with the obligations flowing from the investments of all classes of our citizens in Nicaragua, place us in a position of peculiar responsibility. I am sure it is not the desire of the United States to intervene in the internal affairs of Nicaragua or of any other Central American Republic. Nevertheless it must be said that we have a very definite and special interest in the maintenance of order and good government in Nicaragua at the present time, and that the stability, prosperity, and independ-

---

[10] File No. 817.00/4357.
[11] *Congressional Record*, 69th Congress, 2d session, vol. 68, pt. 2, Jan. 10, 1927, pp. 1325, 1326.

ence of all Central American Countries can never be a matter of indifference to us. The United States can not, therefore, fail to view
with deep concern any serious threat to stability and constitutional
government in Nicaragua tending toward anarchy and jeopardizing
American interests, especially if such state of affairs is contributed
to or brought about by outside influences or by any foreign power.
It has always been and remains the policy of the United States in
such circumstances to take the steps that may be necessary for the
preservation and protection of the lives, the property, and the interests of its citizens and of this Government itself. In this respect
I propose to follow the path of my predecessors.

Consequently, I have deemed it my duty to use the powers committed to me to insure the adequate protection of all American interests in Nicaragua, whether they be endangered by internal strife
or by outside interference in the affairs of that Republic.

The President also referred to the connections of Mexico with the
Nicaraguan civil war.[12]

In the latter part of December, 1926, after repeated requests from
American firms for protection, neutral zones were established at
Rio Grande and Puerto Cabezas. In January, American lumber
companies and other interests complained that their operations were
being interfered with through the seizure of boats, the enforced recruiting of laborers on the plantations, and fighting near their properties. American forces thereupon established neutral zones at Pearl
Lagoon, Prinzapolca, and Rama. In addition, after the British and
Italian envoys at Managua pointed out the imminent peril to their
subjects unless outside protection was extended, a Legation guard
of 175 men was again established on January 8. The Belgian, British, Chinese, and Italian Governments also formally requested the
Department of State to afford protection to their nationals in
Nicaragua.

President Diaz proposed on February 20, 1927, that an offensive
and defensive treaty be negotiated between the United States and
Nicaragua for the purpose of securing the territorial integrity and
peace of Nicaragua and guaranteeing to the United States its canal
rights. The Nicaraguan Congress in joint session upheld President
Diaz in this proposal by a vote of 45 to 10. It was reported that
many of the Liberal leaders were agreeable to such a treaty. The
Department of State immediately instructed the American Legation
at Managua that the Nicaraguan Government should not be encouraged in its proposition.

THE ARMS EMBARGO AND THE SALE OF ARMS TO NICARAGUA BY THE UNITED STATES GOVERNMENT

On September 15, 1926, when negotiations leading up to the
Corinto Conference were initiated, the President of the United

---

[12] *Ibid.*, p. 1325.

States placed an embargo on the export of arms or munitions of war to Nicaragua.[13] The President acted under the authority given him by a joint resolution of Congress, approved January 31, 1922.[14] The Department of State notified the other Central American republics of this embargo, and the latter assured the Department of State that they would cooperate in this measure. President Diaz, on December 2, 1926, issued a decree prohibiting the importation of arms and ammunition into Nicaragua for the period of a year. After General Chamorro relinquished leadership of the Army, the Department of State relaxed the arms embargo to permit the shipment of arms by private firms to the Nicaraguan Government.

In February, 1927, the Nicaraguan Government inquired whether the United States Government itself would sell certain arms and ammunition from its surplus stocks. On February 25, 1927, the United States Government and Nicaragua entered into a contract for the sale of 3,000 rifles, 200 machine guns, 3,000,000 rounds of ammunition, and other accessories. A long-term credit was extended for the payment of this material. In selling this equipment, the United States Government acted under the authority of an act of Congress of June 5, 1920,[15] as follows:

. . . That the Secretary of War be, and he is hereby, authorized, in his discretion, to sell to any State or foreign Government with which the United States is at peace at the time of the passage of this Act, upon such terms as he may deem expedient, any matériel, supplies, or equipment pertaining to the Military Establishment, except foodstuffs, as, or may hereafter be found to be surplus, which are not needed for military purposes and for which there is no adequate domestic market.

NICARAGUAN FINANCES, 1926-27

The Diaz administration came into power with a Treasury greatly depleted because of the military activities of the Chamorro régime. President Diaz, therefore, indicated his desire to obtain loans in the United States for the suppression of the revolution and for the current governmental expenses. The Department of State indicated its disapproval of loans from individual Americans to the Diaz régime under the present circumstances. On November 25, 1926, the Government-owned National Bank extended a short-term credit of $300,000 to the Government, secured by the stock of the Pacific Railway.

On January 1, 1927, President Diaz received a budgetary surplus of $215,844 of which he used $150,201 for military purposes. Never-

---

[13] 44 U.S. Stat. L. (pt. 3) 2625.
[14] Senate Joint Resolution 124, entitled a " Joint Resolution To pohibit the exportation of arms or munitions of war from the United States to certain countries, and for other purposes ", 42 U.S. Stat. L. (pt. 1), 361–362.
[15] 41 U.S. Stat. L. 949.

theless, the extraordinary expenses incurred in combating the continued revolutionary activities were so heavy that despite the budgetary surplus and the National Bank loan, together with dividends declared by the National Bank and the Pacific Railway and the diversion of funds from Public Instruction, Forestry, Land Sales, and Port Fees, the Government, in March, 1927, was without funds.

On March 25, 1927, the Government secured a short-term loan of $1,000,000, from the Guaranty Trust Co. and J. & W. Seligman & Co. Although the Department of State realized that the Nicaraguan Government, in order to maintain order, needed immediate funds, it did not suggest or recommend this loan and assumed no responsibility in connection with the transaction. It had previously indicated the undesirability of the sale of the Pacific Railway or of the National Bank, or of an inflation of currency as a means of securing the temporary funds necessary to meet military expenditures. Under the terms of the contract, the money was advanced as needed, the Government paying 6 per cent interest on the amounts actually outstanding. The banker's commission was 1 per cent. The total stock of the Pacific Railway and the National Bank was pledged as security for the loan, which was repaid from 50 per cent of the surplus revenues of the Republic, from the dividends of the Pacific Railway and the National Bank and from that part of the revenue arising from certain additional taxes placed in effect during the early part of 1927, these being subject to the prior lien of the Ethelburga loan. The loan of $300,000 extended by the National Bank in November, 1926, was repaid from the new loan. At the request of the bankers, all disbursements from the loan were subject to approval by a commission consisting of the Minister of Finance, the Resident High Commissioner, and the manager of the National Bank, this authorization in turn being subject to the approval of the President of Nicaragua.

This loan was paid off in installments, the final payment being made on April 21, 1928. The stock of the Pacific Railway and the National Bank, which was pledged as security to the loan, reverted to the National Government, and since that time has not been employed as collateral.

THE STIMSON MISSION, 1927

Events Leading Up to the Stimson Mission

By the defeat of the Government forces in the sanguinary battle of Pearl Lagoon in late December, 1926, the Liberals consolidated their position on the east coast. They were in control of all the military strongholds except Bluefields, El Bluff, and Rama, which were declared neutral zones by the American naval forces. In January, 1927, General Moncada led the revolutionist troops over land to attack the cities of the west coast. As he approached, small bands of Liberals revolted and roamed the countryside, committing depredations on the ranches and plantations of Conservatives.

In February, 1927, a band of Liberals attacked and captured the city of Chinandega. During the successful counter-attack of the Government troops, two American aviators in the constabulary, who, incidentally, had not been recommended by the United States Government, dropped bombs on the revolutionists. When this action was reported, the Department of State informed the aviators that if they actively participated in hostilities between the Government forces and the revolutionists they could not call upon the United States Government for protection while thus engaged.

Because of the fighting at Chinandega, the railway service between Corinto and Managua was interrupted. As a means of insuring the maintenance of communications between the Legation and the Legation guard at Managua and the seacoast, United States naval forces declared neutral the zone along the Pacific Railway, including the cities through which the railway passed, and prohibited fighting in that zone. At the request of President Diaz, the American forces in Managua occupied the Loma Fortress. Two weeks later the British Embassy in Washington informed the Department of State that a man-of-war had been dispatched to Corinto in order that it might serve as a base of refuge for British subjects. Forces were not landed. The vessel remained in Nicaraguan waters only for a few days.

Early in March, 1927, the United States naval forces extended their protection of the Pacific Railway as far as Granada. After an attack by unknown parties on the American Consular Agent at Matagalpa, that city was declared a neutral zone and American marines stationed there. By March 15 a total of 2,000 naval and military forces had been landed in Nicaragua to maintain the neutral zones and protect American and other foreign lives and property.

General Moncada, during February, had advanced over land from the east coast and, after a sharp encounter with the Government forces, occupied Muy Muy in the Department of Matagalpa. There he was joined by other Liberal generals in command of small bands. In March he prepared to advance upon the city of Matagalpa, an important center of the coffee industry. The expected attack never took place. There was only sporadic fighting during March, neither side apparently desiring to risk a decisive engagement. General Moncada offered little encouragement of an early settlement to a commission of Liberals from Managua who conferred with him.

PRELIMINARY NEGOTIATIONS

In view of the continued hostilities and the increasingly difficult situation within Nicaragua, and as it became more and more evident that some early solution must be found if the country were to be saved from complete financial ruin and conditions approaching anarchy, President Coolidge decided to send Mr. Henry L. Stimson as a personal representative to carry the President's own views to the American Minister at Managua and to Admiral Latimer, who commanded the United States naval forces, to discuss the situation with those officials, and to convey to the President the first-hand information thus obtained.

Mr. Stimson sailed from New York on April 9, arriving at Managua on April 17, where, after conferring with the American Minister and Admiral Latimer, he immediately held conferences with President Diaz and other Government officials, as well as with various leaders of the Liberal Party. In these conferences the policy of the United States was plainly set forth, and ideas on the situation and possible remedies were freely exchanged.

Mr. Stimson reported that, without exception, every one with whom he conferred stressed the absolute necessity for supervision of the elections of 1928 by the United States. In the past, the party in power in Nicaragua, whether Liberal or Conservative, had made use of its dominant position to control and manipulate elections, with the result that the opposition, feeling that it could not have a fair chance, had at times resorted to violence. Revolutions thus became inevitable and chronic. Therefore, it was felt that whichever party controlled the electoral machinery in 1928 would determine the result of the election at that time in its own favor, unless a free election could be assured through American supervision. Furthermore, Mr. Stimson reported that the Washington Treaty of 1923 had made the electoral question the very heart of the Nicaraguan problem. Unless fair elections were assured, the treaty tended to perpetual control of the governmental machinery by the party in power. Free and fair elections every four years were, therefore, a first necessity.

President Diaz proposed the creation by Nicaraguan law of an electoral commission to be controlled by Americans nominated by the President of the United States, and offered to turn over to this board the entire police power of the state. The organization of a nonpartisan constabulary under the instruction and command of American officers was further suggested by President Diaz, who, in this connection, asked for the continuance in Nicaragua of a sufficient portion of the American naval force to insure order pending the organization of the constabulary.

On April 22 President Diaz proposed the following peace terms to the revolutionists:

1. Immediate general peace and delivery of arms simultaneously by both parties into American custody;
2. General amnesty and return of exiles and return of confiscated property;
3. Participation in the Diaz cabinet by representative Liberals;
4. The organization of a Nicaraguan constabulary on a nonpartisan basis, to be commanded by American officers;
5. Supervision of 1928 and subsequent elections by Americans who would have ample police power to make effective such supervision;
6. A temporary continuance of a sufficient force of American marines to secure the enforcement of peace terms.

The Liberal leaders in Managua transmitted the above proposal to Doctor Sacasa. At the same time they informed him that Mr. Stimson would be glad to confer in Managua with Doctor Sacasa or his authorized representatives. Thereupon, Doctor Sacasa, while declining to proceed to Managua himself, appointed representatives. The United States destroyer *Preston* was placed at their disposal, and they left Puerto Cabezas on April 27, arriving at Managua, via Panama, two days later. In the meantime, Mr. Stimson visited León, where he conferred with various prominent Liberals and arranged for them to confer with Doctor Sacasa's representatives.

Doctor Sacasa's representatives announced their acquiescence in all of the propositions discussed in their conference with Mr. Stimson, except that for the continuance of Diaz as President during the remainder of his term. Mr. Stimson, though appreciating the desire of the Liberal representatives for a new President acceptable to both parties, was unable to agree to their proposal. For, as a practical matter, it was not possible under the existing circumstances to find any government which would be supported by both sides. On this subject, Mr. Stimson reported to the Department of State:[1]

. . . I am quite clear that in the present crisis no neutral or impartial Nicaraguan exists. . . . Moreover, any attempt by the Nicaraguan Congress to elect a substitute for Diaz under the forms of Nicaraguan law would almost certainly in the present situation become the occasion of further bitter factional strife.

The Liberal representatives reserved making any commitments until after they had communicated with Doctor Sacasa and General Moncada.

Admiral Latimer thereupon arranged for General Moncada to attend a conference with Mr. Stimson and the other Liberal representatives. A truce was declared during the conversations which took place at Tipitapa, May 4.

THE FIRST TIPITAPA CONFERENCE, MAY 4, 1927

Mr. Stimson found General Moncada's attitude frank and earnest. The latter admitted that while he believed he could defeat the Government forces, neither he nor any Nicaraguan could, without American help, pacify and tranquilize the country, and with every week that passed the condition of anarchy was growing worse. He admitted that the country was becoming filled with groups of armed men responsible neither to himself nor to the Diaz government. He warmly approved of the plan of supervision of the 1928 elections as the best method to save the country, but like Doctor Sacasa he urged the immediate substitution for Diaz of some other man, chiefly as a point of honor to pacify his Army. He also told Mr. Stimson frankly that he would not oppose the United States troops if the United States had determined to insist on the Diaz issue. Mr. Stimson then told General Moncada that the United States Government intended to accept the request of the Nicaraguan Government to supervise the elections of 1928; that the retention of President Diaz during the remainder of his term was regarded as essential to that plan and would be insisted upon; that a general disarmament was also necessary for the proper conduct of such an election; and that American forces would be authorized to accept the custody of the arms of the Government and those others willing to lay them down, and to disarm the rest. Mr. Stimson then confirmed this conversation in a written communication to General Moncada.[2]

The Sacasa delegates were then called into the conference, and Mr. Stimson made the same statements to them as to General Mon-

---

[1] File No. 817.00/4759.
[2] Henry L. Stimson, *American Policy in Nicaragua* (New York, C. Scribner's Sons, 1927), pp. 76–79.

cada. They announced that they would recommend to Doctor Sacasa that no resistance be offered to the American forces.

Events Subsequent to the First Tipitapa Conference

The advent of the rainy season, which made communications with Doctor Sacasa and the other Liberal generals difficult and slow, delayed the acceptance of disarmament for eight days. During that time a truce was declared between the Government and the Liberal forces. Upon withdrawal of the Government Army from the Tipitapa River, American marines were stationed between opposing troops and in a position where the arms of both sides could be received if an agreement were reached.

On May 5, President Diaz issued a proclamation of general amnesty to political exiles and prisoners. He also announced that the freedom of the press would be restored as soon as actual disarmament occurred. On May 6, President Diaz took steps looking toward the restoration of the legal Constitution of the Supreme Court as it stood prior to the illegal changes made by Chamorro. He further agreed, at the suggestion of General Moncada, to appoint Liberal *jefes políticos* in six Liberal provinces.

While it was anticipated that General Moncada would be successful in persuading his forces to disarm, it was necessary to consider that certain sections of the country outside of the district controlled by American forces or by the Diaz troops, or by General Moncada, had been in a state of anarchy for some time and at the mercy of marauding bands. General Moncada's presence had had a restraining influence over the leaders of these bands, but with this influence removed it was apparent that it might become necessary for American forces to occupy certain parts of the country rapidly in order to prevent a reign of terror. Mr. Stimson was warned by General Moncada himself that such a situation would probably arise after disarmament. Therefore, in order to insure the rapid and effective tranquilization of the country, and at the request of both the Diaz government and General Moncada, 800 additional marines were ordered to proceed from the United States to Nicaragua.

The Second Tipitapa Conference, May 11, 1927

At the second conference at Tipitapa on May 11, General Moncada informed Mr. Stimson that his army had voted confidence in the proposition advanced by Mr. Stimson at the previous conference. In response to General Moncada's request for a statement of the steps

President Diaz would take to restore the *status quo ante*, Mr. Stimson gave him the following letter: [3]

TIPITAPA, NICARAGUA, *May 11, 1927.*

GENERAL JOSÉ MARÍA MONCADA,

DEAR GENERAL MONCADA: I am glad to learn of the authority that has been placed in you by your army to arrange for a general disarmament. I am also glad to make clear to you and to your army the attitude of the President of the United States as to this matter. In seeking to terminate this war, President Coolidge is actuated only by a desire to benefit the people of Nicaragua and to secure for them a free, fair and impartial election. He believes that only by such free and fair elections can permanent peace be secured for Nicaragua. To insure this in 1928 he has consented to the request that American representatives selected by him shall supervise the election. He has also consented to assign American officers to train and command a non-partisan national constabulary for Nicaragua which will have the duty of securing such a fair election and of preventing any fraud or intimidation of voters. He is willing also to leave in Nicaragua until after the election a sufficient force of marines to support the work of the constabulary and insure peace and freedom at the election.

As further evidence of the good faith of the American Government and of the present Nicaraguan Government in this matter, I am glad to tell you what has already been done. It will answer the questions contained in the letter of your soldiers which you have shown me. General amnesty has already been granted by the President of Nicaragua. I have recommended to President Diaz that the Supreme Court be reconstituted by the elimination of the illegal judges placed in that court under Sr. Chamorro. President Diaz has already called upon those judges for their resignations and I believe that these resignations will be obtained. I have already advised that the Congress be reconstituted by holding of special elections in those Liberal districts where elections were not held in 1926 under conditions which will insure that the Liberal voters will be amply protected in their rights. I have also recommended that members of the Congress illegally expelled by Sr. Chamorro whose terms have not yet expired be reinstated. I have been assured that this will be done.

I have recommended that Liberal *Jefes Politicos* be appointed in the six Liberal districts of Bluefields, Jinotega, Nueva Segovia, Esteli, Chinandega, and Leon. I have been assured that this will be done.

In short, I have recommended that steps be taken so far as possible to restore the political condition as it existed in Nicaragua before the Chamorro *coup d'etat* and I believe that so far as possible it will be done.

I hope that these steps will assure you and your army of the fairness of the United States Government and its desire to see peace, justice and freedom re-established in Nicaragua without any unfair-

---

[3] File No. 817.00/4866.

ness or favoritism towards any party but being regardful of the rights of Liberals and Conservatives alike.

Very respectfully yours, HENRY L. STIMSON

General Moncada thereupon dictated the following statement: [4]

. . . The Liberals cannot believe that the United States Government through the personal representative of President Coolidge will give a promise which it will not fulfill. Once again the Liberals place their confidence in the United States. The leaders of the army will try to convince their men that this promise of fair elections will be fulfilled. The central point which the army wishes to be assured of is that the United States will do its best to give Nicaragua a fair election in 1928.

DISARMAMENT

In order to carry out the disarming of the Government and revolutionary forces, the following notice was given wide publicity throughout the Republic on May 11: [5]

The Government of the United States, having accepted the request of the Government of Nicaragua to supervise the election in the latter country in 1928, believes a general disarmament of the country necessary for the proper and successful conduct of such election and has directed me to accept the custody of the arms and ammunition of those willing to place them in my custody, including the arms and ammunition of the forces of the Government, and to disarm forcibly those who do not peaceably deliver their arms.

The Government of Nicaragua has expressed its willingness to deliver the arms under its control and I have directed that such arms of the Government be accepted for custody in the same proportion that arms are delivered by the forces opposing the Government.

The Nicaraguan Government has granted general amnesty to all political and armed opponents. To facilitate the return to peaceful occupations of those who have heretofore opposed it that Government will pay 10 cordobas to each and every individual delivering a serviceable rifle or machine gun to the custody of the United States forces. Amnesty and protection are assured to such individuals by the Nicaraguan Government and by the forces under my command.

To avoid the regrettable and useless shedding of blood all individuals and leaders of groups, now having in their possession or in hiding serviceable rifles, machine guns or ammunition or who know of the location of such munitions as may be hidden, should immediately deliver them to the custody of the nearest detachment of the American forces. Upon such delivery payment of 10 Cordobas will be made, in the presence of a Commission of United States officers, for each serviceable rifle or machine gun so delivered. . . .

J. L. LATIMER,
Rear Admiral, U. S. Navy,
Commander Special Service Squadron,
Commanding United States Forces in Nicaragua.

---

[4] File No. 817.00/4781.   [5] File No. 817.00/4866.

126702—32——6

On May 12 Mr. Stimson received the following telegram [6] signed by General Moncada and 11 of his generals, including all his prominent chiefs except Sandino:

The military chiefs of the Constitutionalist army assembled in session today have agreed to accept the terms of the declaration made by General Henry L. Stimson, personal representative of President Coolidge of the United States and consequently have resolved to lay down their arms. They hope that there will be immediately sent to receive these arms sufficient forces to guarantee order, liberty and property.

General Moncada having recommended to his troops that they yield, a general disarmament of both sides began, resulting by May 26 in the delivery to the American forces of 11,600 rifles, 303 machine guns, and 5,500,000 cartridges.

Minor conflicts occurred at León and Chinandega between American forces and revolutionary forces or leaders, resulting in the death of 2 marines and 10 revolutionists at León, and of General Cabulla, a revolutionary leader, at Chinandega.

THE REQUEST FOR ELECTORAL SUPERVISION

On May 15, 1927, President Diaz, in a letter addressed to the President of the United States, formally requested the assistance and good offices of the United States in insuring a free, fair, and impartial election. His letter reads as follows: [7]

EXCELLENCY: In order that the elections which under the constitution of Nicaragua are to be held in October, 1928, for the purpose of electing a President of the Republic and members of its National Congress shall be free, fair, and impartial and not open to fraud or intimidation practiced by any of the parties contending at such election upon each other, the Government of Nicaragua requests the President of the United States to lend to it its assistance and good offices in insuring such an election. To this end, the Government of Nicaragua requests the friendly assistance of the President of the United States in preparing a proper election law in Nicaragua, in securing supervision by impartial Americans over the actual conduct of the elections, in securing American assistance to train and direct an impartial and non-partisan force of constabulary to secure law and order and prevent intimidation of voters and to in other ways secure American assistance in tranquillizing the sorely disturbed condition of the country so that such election can be fairly held.

I have the honor to submit a memorandum showing the steps which my Government suggests may be desirable or appropriate to be taken in order that the President of the United States may be able adequately to perform this great service to the Republic of Nicaragua, should he be willing to do so. The Government of Nicaragua

---

[6] File No. 817.00/4775.   [7] File No. 817.00/4902.

will gladly consider the taking of any other steps on its part which may be suggested by the President of the United States as essential or desirable for the accomplishment of that purpose.
Believe me [etc.]

ADOLFO DIAZ
President

[Enclosure]

Memorandum as to suggested steps to be taken looking towards the holding of a free, fair, and impartial election in Nicaragua in October, 1928, with the assistance of the President of the United States and under the supervision of American officials suggested by him.

I. *Enactment of an Adequate Election Law.*

(1). The President of the United States may select an expert in matters of election law to advise him as well as the Nicaraguan Congress as to a proper electoral law to be enacted by said Congress in order to provide the means and method by which the assistance of impartial American advice and supervision can be rendered for holding Nicaraguan elections. The salary and expenses of this expert shall be borne by the Nicaraguan Government.

(2). While reserving to the President of the United States, through this expert or otherwise, to suggest modifications and changes in the electoral plan to be prescribed by this law, the following outline of the electoral system is suggested as appropriate:

(A). Under the electoral law there shall be created a National Electoral Commission which shall have full and general power to supervise the election and to prescribe regulations having the force of law for the registration of voters, the casting of their ballots, and all other matters pertaining to the election that are not covered by the electoral law. Among other powers, the National Electoral Commission shall have the exclusive right to canvass the number of votes cast at the election and to determine all questions and contests as to the regularity and legality of such votes, and their determination as to the number and legality of the votes cast shall be final and shall be reported directly to Congress for its certification and declaration of the result of the election.

(B). This Commission shall consist of three members to be suggested by the President of the United States, one such member being a Conservative, one a Liberal, recommended by the respective party organizations to which they belong, and the third, the Chairman, being an American. A majority of the Commission shall be (sufficient) to constitute a quorum and to take action on any matter but no such action or resolution of the Commission shall be valid or effective unless concurred in by the American Chairman.

(C). There shall be in each Department a Departmental Election Commission composed of three members, one Conservative, one Liberal, and the Chairman, the latter being an American. These members shall be appointed by the National Electoral Commission, the Liberal and Conservative members being appointed after consultation with the local organizations of the respective parties.

(D). In each polling place, there shall be a Local Election Board composed of three members, one Conservative, one Liberal, and the Chairman, the latter being an American. These members shall be appointed by the National Electoral Commission, the Liberal and Conservative members being appointed after consultation with the local organizations of the respective parties.

(E). In the Departmental Commissions and Local Boards, a majority of the members shall be sufficient to constitute a quorum and to take action by resolution or otherwise but no such action or resolution shall be valid or effective unless concurred in by the American Chairman.

II. *Preservation of Law and Order for the Purpose of the Conduct of the Election.*

(1). The National Army shall be disbanded and mustered out of service contemporaneously with the disbandment of the opposing forces and the function of preserving law and order throughout the country shall be assumed by a National Constabulary to be organized under the instruction and, so far as possible, the direction and command of American officers now in active service and detailed to this duty by the President of the United States.

(2). The National Electoral Commission, through its Chairman, shall have the right to command the services of the National Constabulary and to issue orders thereto for the purpose of preventing intimidation and fraud in the election and of preserving law and order during the various acts of registration and voting. It shall also have the right by regulation to prescribe the method under which the Departmental Election Commissions and the Local Election Boards shall each have the right to command the services of members of the National Constabulary located within their jurisdiction for the similar purpose of preventing intimidation and fraud and preserving law and order for the election.

(3). In view of the disturbed condition of the country after the recent civil war and of the fact that a very considerable time will be required for the organization, instruction, and discipline of the National Constabulary, the Government of Nicaragua requests that the President of the United States will permit a sufficient force of American marines to remain in the country pending the organization and instruction of the Constabulary and during the election to reinforce the work of the Constabulary in securing an absolutely impartial election between both parties.

A[DOLFO] D[IAZ]

President Coolidge replied on June 10, 1927:

EXCELLENCY: I have received Your Excellency's letter dated May 15, 1927, requesting the friendly assistance of the President of the United States in preparing a proper election law in Nicaragua, in securing supervision by impartial Americans of the actual conduct of the elections, in securing American assistance to train and direct an impartial and nonpartisan force of constabulary to secure law and order and prevent intimidation of voters, and in other ways to secure American assistance in tranquillizing the sorely disturbed condition of the country so that elections can be fairly held. Your Excellency submitted with this letter a memorandum showing the steps which your Government suggests may be desirable or appropriate to be taken in order that the President of the United States may be able adequately to perform this great service to the Republic of Nicaragua. Your Excellency adds that the Government of Nicaragua will gladly consider the taking of any other steps on its part which may be suggested by the President of the United States as essential or desirable for the accomplishment of that purpose.

In reply I am pleased to inform Your Excellency that I shall welcome the opportunity to assist the Government of Nicaragua to hold free and fair elections at the time appointed by the Constitution. I have been much gratified at the recent settlement of the difficulties in Nicaragua brought about through the good offices of my personal representative, Colonel Stimson, and the wisdom and patriotism shown by the Nicaraguan Government and the Nicaraguan people of all factions. It is my earnest desire that the peace which has now been arranged may be a permanent one, and to this end it is my desire to be of all possible assistance in the future. I am instructing the American Minister at Managua to discuss with Your Excellency the manner in which the aid and assistance of the United States can be best extended both for supervising the elections in Nicaragua and for maintaining order in the country until that time. Mr. Eberhardt has my entire confidence and will, I know, welcome this opportunity to be of service to the Nicaraguan people.

Accept [etc.] CALVIN COOLIDGE

THE DEPARTURE OF DOCTOR SACASA AND THE STIMSON MISSION, MAY, 1927

Doctor Sacasa refused to accept for his party any cabinet positions under President Diaz. However, he indicated that his party would cooperate in congressional by-elections in certain districts during 1927 and that they would accept those positions necessary for holding elections in 1928 or for the future reconstruction of the country. Doctor Sacasa and his supporters left Nicaragua on May 20 for Costa Rica.

Mr. Stimson returned to the United States on May 22, where he immediately reported to President Coolidge the results of his mission, which was considered entirely successful.

RECONSTITUTION OF THE SUPREME COURT, JULY, 1927

On July 18, 1927, the Nicaraguan Congress in special session accepted the resignation of the four judges of the Supreme Court who had been appointed during the Chamorro régime. The Congress thereupon reelected the four Liberal judges who had been deposed by Chamorro to make room for his appointees.

THE ELECTIONS OF 1928

NOMINATION OF THE CHAIRMAN OF THE NATIONAL BOARD OF ELECTIONS

The following statement was made public at the White House on July 2, 1927:[1]

In order to carry out the promise made to the Nicaraguan Government and to the Liberal Party in Nicaragua that the United States would supervise the Nicaraguan Presidential elections in 1928, to insure that all Nicaraguans may freely express their preference at the polls, it will be necessary to establish a commission to supervise the elections. It has been agreed that the Chairman of this Commission should be an American nominated by the President of the United States and appointed by the President of Nicaragua. The President will nominate for this position General Frank R. McCoy.

It will be necessary for General McCoy to visit Nicaragua before the Presidential elections in order to study conditions and to make recommendations, and he will probably leave for Nicaragua in August as the President's representative for this preliminary work.

General McCoy arrived in Managua August 24 on a preliminary trip of investigation. He was accompanied by Dr. Harold W. Dodds, who had drawn up the 1923 electoral laws. After a study of the local situation, General McCoy and Doctor Dodds returned to the United States.

CONGRESSIONAL AND MUNICIPAL ELECTIONS OF 1927

American marines acted as unofficial observers in various departments where elections were held at the end of August, 1927, to select Senators and Deputies in those districts where elections were not held in 1926 because of revolutionary disturbances, but there was no American supervision of these elections. The Conservatives did not contest in the principal Liberal departments. Municipal elections were held throughout the Republic on November 6 in an orderly manner. There were few disputes and few cases of fraud reported. An analysis of the vote indicated a fairly even division between the Liberal and Conservative parties.

---

[1] File Nos. 817.00/4921a and 4960.

THE ELIGIBILITY OF GENERAL CHAMORRO FOR THE PRESIDENCY

General Emiliano Chamorro, having resigned his diplomatic positions in Europe, came to the United States on his way to Nicaragua. On October 22, 1927, he sought an interview with the Secretary of State during which he was handed the following statement:[2]

On January 1, 1929, the Government of the United States will be confronted by the necessity of deciding whether it can consistently recognize the incoming administration in Nicaragua as the constitutional government of that country. While the United States is not supporting or opposing any political candidate it is most desirous that there should be no question at that time as to the eligibility under the Constitution of the person who may have prevailed at the presidential elections, since it wishes to extend the fullest and most sympathetic cooperation to the new government.

In these circumstances and in view of the reports that General Chamorro contemplates becoming a candidate for the Presidency of Nicaragua in the 1928 elections, the Government of the United States has no choice but to point out that it regards General Chamorro as ineligible under the provisions of the Nicaraguan constitution to the office of President of Nicaragua during any part of the term commencing January 1, 1929.

Article 104 of the Nicaraguan constitution provides that

" No citizen who holds the office of President either as the duly elected incumbent or accidentally, shall be eligible to the office of President or Vice President for the next term."

General Chamorro unquestionably held the office of President *de facto* from January 17 to October 30, 1926, thus bringing himself within the prohibition of Article 104 of the Constitution and Article II of the General Treaty of Peace and Amity of February 7, 1923, thus making it impossible for the Government of the United States to regard him as eligible to the office of President of Nicaragua for the term beginning January 1, 1929, or to recognize him as the Constitutional President of Nicaragua if he should claim or attempt to occupy the office during any part of said term.

General Chamorro returned to Nicaragua the latter part of November. He specifically indicated his intention not to be a candidate in the forthcoming presidential elections but to lend his support instead to the candidate selected by the Conservative Party.

THE ELIGIBILITY OF GENERAL MONCADA

General Moncada, the Liberal leader with whom Mr. Stimson arranged the terms of peace in May, 1927, also came to the United

---

[2] File No. 817.00/5096.

States, after having carried on a political campaign in favor of his candidacy for the Nicaraguan Presidency, and, having sought an interview with the Secretary of State, was informed by the latter substantially as follows: [3]

As I have said before, the United States is not going to select any candidate for President of Nicaragua either conservative or liberal. Neither is the United States going to back or use its influence for the election of any particular person. The United States is going to do its best to see that there is a fair, open and free election where everybody who is entitled to vote has an opportunity to do so. This has been made perfectly plain. Of course following the Constitution of Nicaragua and the Treaty the United States cannot recognize anybody who is not qualified under the Constitution to hold the office.

Neutral Policy of the United States in the Presidential Elections

On November 8, 1927, the Nicaraguan Minister at Washington addressed the Secretary of State with regard to press reports which the Minister considered might be interpreted as the official expression of the attitude of this Government indicating a tendency in favor of one of the political parties in Nicaragua. The reply of the Secretary of State setting forth the policy of the Government of the United States, read in part as follows: [4]

On October 26, 1927, in answer to an inquiry by press correspondents, I stated that this Government is not going to select any candidate for President of Nicaragua, either Conservative or Liberal, nor is the United States going to back or use its influence for the election of any particular person. This country is going to do its best to see that there is a fair, open and free election where everybody who is entitled to vote has an opportunity to do so. Of course following the Constitution of Nicaragua and the Central American Treaty of 1923, the United States will not recognize anybody who is not qualified under the Constitution to hold the office.

.   .   .   .

In the above statement you will find an exact expression of the attitude of the United States Government toward individual candidates for the Nicaraguan Presidency, whoever they may be and with whatever party they may be affiliated. It would be a source of deep regret if the policy of this Government should be considered in any other light, whether as a result of interpretations placed upon the unofficial acts or utterances of private individuals in the United States, or perchance through articles appearing in the press, over which, as I have already said, this Government exercises no control. It would be unfortunate indeed if a misunderstanding of the true motives of the United States should result in disadvantage to any particular candidate in the forthcoming election; whether

---

[3] File No. 817.00/5099a.   [4] File No. 817.00/5127.

this disadvantage arose through unconscious forces of public opinion, or from the conscious dissemination of unwarranted propaganda in favor of any one candidate. This could not occur if the stated policy of this Government, which has been so clearly expressed, were constantly kept in mind.

On February 23, 1928, the Secretary of State issued the following statement to the press: [5]

In view of numerous tendentious rumors and newspaper articles evidently of a propagandist nature which have come to my attention I desire once more to state with the utmost emphasis that the United States is maintaining and will continue to maintain an attitude of absolute impartiality in all matters relating to the forthcoming Nicaraguan election. The United States will favor neither any candidate nor any party in that election. All of its representatives in Nicaragua have been definitely instructed in that sense from the beginning, and this Government knows of no violation whatever of those instructions. Naturally we cannot accept any responsibility for rumors and newspaper articles of the character referred to.

ELECTORAL LAW OF 1928

On January 10, 1928, the Nicaraguan Senate passed a transitory electoral law which, it was felt by the Department of State, would assure the holding of a free and fair election such as had been contemplated by the two Governments. Even before the Senate had passed the measure, opposition thereto had arisen in certain quarters, sponsored no doubt by those who for personal or other selfish reasons did not desire that the election should represent a true reflection of the wishes of the electorate. This opposition was focused upon the alleged unconstitutionality of certain provisions of the proposed law. On January 17 the Chamber of Deputies approved a substitute electoral law which, in the opinion of the Department of State, made impossible an adequate supervision of the approaching election.

In view of these circumstances, the Department of State informed the American Chargé d'Affaires that it was satisfied that the law as originally proposed was constitutional, and that it must insist that the Stimson agreement be carried out not merely technically but also in spirit. Nicaraguan officials thereupon began to consider such changes in the project as would not modify the intent of the provisions which the Department of State deemed indispensable for adequate supervision, but which at the same time would satisfy the legislative authorities in Nicaragua.

The Nicaraguan Senate passed the amended draft of the electoral law by a vote of 16 to 8 on March 7, 1928. The Chamber of Deputies, controlled by General Chamorro, rejected the law on March 13, 1928, by a vote of 24 to 18, and immediately adjourned.

---

[5] File No. 817.00/5422.

On March 17, 1928, the Supreme Court of Nicaragua appointed Gen. Frank R. McCoy, who had in the meantime returned to Nicaragua, to be chairman of the National Board of Elections. The two other members of the National Board of Elections were Dr. Ramón Castillo C., representing the Conservative Party, and Dr. Enoc Aguado. The latter, after his nomination to the Vice Presidency, was succeeded by Dr. Cordero Reyes representing the Liberal Party. In order to fulfill the obligation which the Nicaraguan Government had assumed in requesting the supervision of the elections by impartial Americans, by a decree of March 21, 1928, President Diaz conferred on the National Board of Elections adequate powers to supervise the elections. The decree gave to the chairman of the National Board of Elections the authority to " command the services of the Guardia Nacional and to give to that force such orders as he may deem necessary and appropriate to insure a free and impartial election." [6] To assist the National Board of Elections there was an American Electoral Mission, composed of 906 Americans, likewise headed by General McCoy. American members of this mission were chairmen of the 13 departmental boards and of the 432 local boards.

NOMINATION OF PRESIDENTIAL CANDIDATES

The Liberal convention which met in extraordinary session on February 19, 1928, nominated General Moncada and Dr. J. Antonio Medrano for President and Vice President, respectively. The convention adopted two resolutions: the first approved the attitude of the Liberal representatives in Congress in their support of the transitory electoral law drafted by General McCoy; the second rejected in the preamble the proposal of a coalition government and acknowledged the obligation of the Liberal Party to carry out the Tipitapa Agreement, but avowed the intention of the party to " take part in this year's elections of high authorities of the Republic, with candidates nominated from among its own members in the form prescribed by its statutes." [7] On August 10, Doctor Medrano withdrew on account of serious illness. The following day the Liberal Governing Board named in his place Dr. Enoc Aguado, who immediately resigned his seat on the National Board of Elections.

The eligibility of General Moncada was challenged on August 20 by the Conservative member of the National Board of Elections on three grounds: the provisions of the Nicaraguan Constitution regarding the eligibility of Government officials for the Presidency, the provisions of article 2 of the General Treaty of Peace and Amity of 1923 regarding the eligibility for the Presidency of those

---

[6] Executive decree of Mar. 21, 1928, art. VIII.   [7] File No. 817.00/5480.

taking part in revolutionary movements, and the alleged but unproved fraud of General Moncada against the public Treasury. The National Board of Elections with the dissenting vote of the Conservative member accepted General Moncada's nomination on August 21. The Board held that the Constitution contained no express prohibition against the election of a Senator to the Presidency, that the Central American Treaty referred to recognition by other Governments and could not affect the constitutional eligibility of a presidential candidate, and that General Moncada's candidacy could not be rejected because of an informal accusation made against him.

The Conservative Party was split into two factions, one controlled by President Diaz, the other by General Chamorro. On May 20 the two factions met separately, each claiming to be the legitimate representative of the historic Conservative Party. The convention controlled by the Administration nominated Dr. Carlos Cuadra Pasos for President, not naming a candidate for Vice President; the Chamorristas nominated Vicente Rappaccioli and Martin Benard for President and Vice President, respectively. Both factions petitioned the National Board of Elections for recognition as the legitimate party. After full hearings, the National Board of Elections unanimously decided that neither of the Conservative factions had established the right to be recognized as representing the party to the exclusion of the other. It announced it would give sympathetic consideration to any plan which would enable the Conservative Party to participate in the election.

On the same day it issued the following statement: [8]

In announcing the decision of the National Board relative to the difficulties of the two factions of the Conservative Party the President of the Board desires to set at rest once and for all any possible misconception on the part of any portion of the people of Nicaragua to the effect that either the United States State Department or the personal representative of the President of the United States in Nicaragua is in any way committed to the candidacy of any particular individual or to the fortunes of any particular party or faction. It has been the earnest effort and hope of the American Government and of the National Board of Elections that the 1928 elections for supreme authorities might be held under conditions that would involve the full participation therein as such of the two great parties whose difficulties the agreements effected by Mr. Stimson sought to compose by peaceable means. The factional division within one of the parties has to date presented serious obstacles to that purpose; but it continues to be the desire and purpose of the Chairman of the National Board, approved and shared by the other members of that board, that the 1928 elections for supreme authorities shall be so conducted as to give any opportunity for the full and free expression of the will of the Nicaraguan people and that any such choice

[8] File No. 817.00/5803.

registered at the election shall in accordance with the Nicaraguan constitution and the Executive decree of March 21st, 1928 be duly certified to the Nicaraguan Congress in order that it may be given effect.

After protracted negotiation, the two factions agreed on July 26 to the nomination of Señor Adolfo Benard, a Chamorro partisan, as President, and Señor Julio Cardenal, a brother-in-law of Dr. Carlos Cuadra Pasos, as Vice President.

Two minor parties, the Conservative Republican and Liberal Republican, requested of the National Board of Elections the right to appear on the ballot. The National Board of Elections by unanimous vote refused both of these requests for two reasons: first, the Dodd's Law with all its amendments, by which third-party participation in elections was authorized, had been suspended by the decree of March 21, 1928; and, secondly, that neither political group had a sufficiently numerous following at that time to warrant recognition as a *bona fide* third party.

During the election campaign, the two presidential candidates exchanged letters, expressing complete satisfaction with the registrations and pledging the winning candidate to request the supervision of the United States over the next election. Translations of the letters in full follow: [*]

MANAGUA, *October 19, 1928.*

SEÑOR DON ADOLFO BENARD,
  Granada.

MY DEAR SEÑOR BENARD: From the sentiments expressed in my letter addressed to Gen. Emiliano Chamorro on August 12, 1916, which the newspapers of this capital published on the 18th of the present month of October, you will have learned the ideas which, since the revolution of October, I have held on electoral liberty and the prerogatives of citizens.

The letter referred to ends in this way:

" I understand that your (General Chamorro's) honor, that of all the leaders of the October revolution, and the honor of the American Government itself has that wide and luminous path as a channel and that the hour for deep thought and prudence has arrived for all Nicaraguans. May Liberals and Conservatives go to the civic contest with their freely chosen candidate, and may that one triumph who receives the votes of the majority, without pressure and without fraud. That will be the true day of liberty, which will deserve to be engraved in marble on the altar of the fatherland."

These ideas guided my mind at Tipitapa and are certainly the characteristic feature of my political life and of my longings in war and in peace.

As candidate of the Liberal Party, I still maintain them with unshakable faith; and by means of this letter I wish to urge you, the candidate of the Conservative Party, to adopt them also and that they may serve as a guide for you in the present solemn moments

---

[*] File No. 817.00/6096.

of the Republic. Let there be no more fratricidal wars and let freedom and order be established forever amongst us.

Now that we are witnessing the justice with which those in charge of the American supervision are proceeding, when with generous and praiseworthy earnestness they are extending to us their hand in the development of republican institutions, by means of a true and honest freedom in elections, we who desire an era of peace and industry for Nicaragua might agree to accept this same supervision for one or several further periods of constitutional government.

For my part I can now promise you that, when the occasion arises, if the Liberal Party wins, it will pledge itself to repay the kindness of the American Government by absolutely free elections, promising at this time, if it suits the interests of the Conservative Party, that in the following presidential election I will willingly accept the mediation of the United States in the same form and manner which the Stimson agreements established.

I offer that to you as candidate of the Conservative Party, to show that I always feel inclined to offer to others the same measure of justice and honesty which in every agreement has been promised to me or mine.

Very respectfully,   ———   J. M. MONCADA

GRANADA, *October 20, 1928.*

GEN. JOSÉ MARÍA MONCADA,
   Managua.

MY DEAR GENERAL MONCADA: I reply herewith to your courteous letter of the 19th instant which your agent, Mr. Pilar A. Ortega, delivered to me personally and which I take pleasure in answering.

It is extremely gratifying to me to inform you that I am entirely in accord with your way of thinking. I understand that a stable and lasting peace, founded on the conciliation of the two historic parties into which the public opinion of Nicaragua is divided, is the most solid and effective support on which the prosperity of our country can rest.

That peace which we all, as good Nicaraguans, should endeavor to obtain, will necessarily come as the logical result of a free and honest election in which each citizen may cast his vote, without restriction, for the candidate whom his sympathies favor.

Adopting that rule of conduct without deviation, we will finish once for all with those lamentable internal struggles which you mention and which have cost us so much blood and so much national wealth in the past.

The American supervision has come to give us the enjoyment of that electoral freedom which will bring with it, without doubt, a long and fruitful era of national tranquillity, to the welfare of all, Liberals as well as Conservatives.

I believe that we should place our entire confidence, without reservations of any kind, in the very worthy American representatives who are to make freedom of suffrage real and effective in the approaching elections of November. We are under the patriotic obligation of maintaining that confidence unchanged, because the fruits which we gather by strengthening our friendly relations with the United States Government have always been and always will be abundant. I have ever thought thus as a good Conservative and as a citizen cherishing the welfare of my country.

For those reasons which I have permitted myself to express to you in the course of this letter, I appreciate in all its importance and I embrace with enthusiasm the praiseworthy idea which you have deigned to disclose to me, of maintaining free suffrage for other constitutional periods, under the friendly and well-intentioned mediation of the United States, in the Nicaraguan electorate. Your proposal is therefore definitely accepted, but the chapter of those considerations between the two parties, so promising for the harmony of Nicaraguan citizens, having been opened, it seems well to me not to close it without also assuring other factors equally necessary for the strengthening of the basis of peace and order. I refer primarily to the economic phase, which is the most essential in modern politics, and I propose to you that we agree now on extending and perfecting the financial plan which is now in force, in the sense of assuring the honest administration and proper investment of public funds, so that by virtue of this system we may open up a prosperous future for the Republic, and above all, may improve its credit, so that we may be able to carry out operations on which to establish a basis for the progressive development of our resources, indemnifying all our citizens for the damages suffered in the recent emergency and carrying out works of material progress for our country.

And as the principal thing is peace, I believe that another element which will effectively aid in maintaining it is the institution of the National Guard in the nonpartisan form which it has been given by the agreement with the Department of State of the United States. Therefore, I propose also that we agree on some form that will assure the existence and the improvement of that military organization of the Republic.

Very respectfully yours,   ADOLFO BENARD

RESULTS OF THE ELECTIONS

The registration of voters, which took place during five days in September, resulted in a total registration of 148,831, an increase of 28 per cent over that of 1924. This increased registration was due to two causes: (1) the measures adopted to prevent intimidation of members of either party; and (2) the belief of both parties that the elections would be close, that the votes would be fairly counted, and that persons who failed to register would not be allowed to vote.

To maintain order and insure registration and voting free from intimidation, President Diaz issued several regulatory decrees and orders. A decree of August 9, 1928, granted full and unconditional amnesty to all bandits who surrendered before September 15, 1928.[10] On August 27 the President ordered the Director General of Communications to put the telegraph and post office facilities at the dis-

---

[10]A decree of Sept. 26, 1928, extended amnesty to common crimes committed in connection with political offenses.

posal of the electoral officials and also to the Conservative and Liberal Parties on equal terms. A decree of August 29, 1928, placed all Government liquor warehouses and depositories under the supervision of the Guardia Nacional and prohibited the sale of distilled liquors during the 24 hours before and on registration and election days. On September 1, the Minister of the Treasury ordered the disbandment of the Treasury guards, thereby centralizing the policing of the country in the Guardia Nacional. A decree of September 6 forbade the discharge of fireworks between September 17 and November 10, except on religious festivals and in cases where a permit had been granted. A decree of September 20 suspended the duties of the *jueces de mesta* and the *jefes de cantón* until November 11. In addition to these measures, General McCoy instructed the American Electoral Mission " to maintain a scrupulously neutral attitude between Liberals and Conservatives." Stringent regulations were issued to the Guardia Nacional enlisted men to abstain from political partisanship or even discussion of politics.

The elections on November 4 took place without any disorder. President Diaz, General Moncada, Señor Benard, and others set an example to voters by appearing at the polls early and dipping their fingers in the stain provided to prevent repeating as they cast their ballots. The voting resulted in the election of General Moncada by a majority of nearly 20,000, his vote being 76,676 to 56,987 for Señor Benard. The Liberals elected 5 Senators and 17 Deputies; the Conservatives, 4 Senators and 8 Deputies. More than 89 per cent of those who registered voted. The total voting increased 57 per cent over 1924.

The National Board of Elections approved the election returns by unanimous vote with the exception of that of the Department of Bluefields, in which case the Conservative member of the National Board of Elections refused to vote for the approval of the report of the departmental board, although the Conservative member of the latter had concurred therein. On December 28, 1928, Congress in a joint session, acting under the authority conferred on it by the Nicaraguan Constitution with only one dissenting vote, approved the election of General Moncada and Doctor Aguado. General Moncada assumed the Presidency on January 1, 1929.

APPOINTMENT OF DOCTOR SACASA AS MINISTER AT WASHINGTON

Among President Moncada's first acts was the appointment of Doctor Sacasa as Minister of Nicaragua in the United States. The appointment of Doctor Sacasa, whose representatives had concurred in the Tipitapa settlement, was interpreted as signifying the intention of the Liberals to continue their support of the policy of the

United States, which had been directed toward assisting in the reestablishment of a constitutional government and of peace.

In presenting his letters of credence to the President of the United States on April 15, 1929, Doctor Sacasa said in part: [11]

Throughout the unfortunate and complex vicissitudes with which patriotic efforts toward social and political organization in my country have met, there always has been felt in one or another form, the generous impulses of the heart of your great people and the ideals of true fraternity which it upholds.

It was no doubt at the inspiration and impulse of this high spirit that the American Government saw fit to lend Nicaragua its valuable cooperation in order that, toward the latter part of last year, absolutely free elections might be held, indicating thereby a sure road to the development of democratic institutions and cementing order and peace with the guarantees of Law.

This worthy action strengthens in the spirit of the Nicaraguan people its own disposition, at all times sustained, toward a fraternal association of our two countries which will make more effective the interchange of ideas and aspirations and the development of those international relations which are to contribute to the restoration and welfare of Nicaragua.

The Government of the President, General José Maria Moncada, established by the free vote of and identified with this frank attitude of our people, ardently desires that the bonds of cordial friendship existing between both nations be augmented without impairment of any kind. And surely because of my concurrence in these laudable purposes, I have received from my Government the honor and the trust of being designated representative of Nicaragua before Your Excellency's Government—a mission very pleasing to me because it affords me the opportunity to place my energies at the service of the common interests of my beloved country and the great American confederation to which I am bound by sentiments acquired in the unforgettable associations of college and university.

---

[11] File No. 701.1711/244.

FINANCIAL AFFAIRS, 1928–1932

Financial and Economic Survey, 1928

Shortly after the Tipitapa Agreement, the Nicaraguan Government, with the approval of both parties, requested the Department of State to select an expert to make a financial and economic survey of the country. On November 29, 1927, the Department of State acceded to this request by designating Dr. William W. Cumberland, formerly Financial Adviser-General Receiver of Haiti. Although the Department of State paid Doctor Cumberland's salary and expenses, it was made clear that the report, when rendered, would represent Doctor Cumberland's personal views and not those of the Department of State. He was requested to investigate the country's resources and requirements in order that the Nicaraguan Government and the Department of State might have the benefit of his recommendations regarding the advisability of a loan.

Doctor Cumberland's report, which was the result of a 3-months' study during the early part of 1928, recommended (1) the assurance of sufficient financial support for the Guardia Nacional, (2) certain fiscal reforms, such as the unification of the collection of customs and internal revenues and the establishment of a more effective High Commission and of the office of Auditor General, (3) the construction of a highway to the Atlantic coast, (4) a loan to refund all outstanding indebtedness, and (5) the sale of the Government-owned National Bank. When releasing the report, the Department of State repeated its dissociation from the ideas and recommendations contained therein. In a press conference, the Secretary of State specifically stated that "no part of the report had been approved by the Department." [1]

As a result of these recommendations, the Nicaraguan Government carried on negotiations during the summer of 1928 for a loan sufficient to provide funds for the settlement of legitimate claims against Nicaragua arising out of the civil war, for the necessary surveys and construction work on a railroad or highway to the Atlantic coast, for the purchase of the Corinto Wharf, for other public works, and for the payment of certain governmental debts. A loan for these purposes met with the approval of both political parties. Negotiations were not completed during the summer and,

---

[1] Memorandum of press conference, Friday, Nov. 23, 1928.

thereafter, because of the approaching presidential elections, were discontinued. As a result of the rapid economic recovery of Nicaragua during 1928, the negotiations were not resumed. The basic customs revenues of 1928 were the largest ever collected up to that time, exceeding by over $600,000 those of 1927. Upon the resignation of the incumbents of the offices of the Collector General of Customs and resident member of the High Commission, an important economy was effected by uniting the two offices.

The Claims Commissions

A claims commission organized under a law of December 3, 1926, convened on July 1, 1927, for the tabulation and consideration of claims arising out of revolutionary activities from October 25, 1925, to June 30, 1927. The scope of the Commission was eventually enlarged by presidential decree to receive claims of all kinds arising against the Government between these dates. The Commission was composed of one Liberal and one Conservative and the Resident American High Commissioner. December 31, 1927, was set as the final date upon which claims would be received for consideration. The Congress later authorized an extension of time in certain cases. The Congress passed legislation for the adjournment of the Commission on March 31, 1928, because no provision had been made for the payment of awards.

Since the Commission had not adjudicated or paid awards on any of the claims presented, a provisional claims commission was established by an Executive decree of July 30, 1929, to receive and pass upon all claims arising out of the civil war from October 25, 1925, until the date when the Executive should officially declare peace in the country. Claims presented to the former Commission were to be passed upon also. The Commission was composed of one Liberal, one Conservative, and an American appointed by the President of Nicaragua after nomination by the State Department. No decision was valid unless concurred in by the American, who was also the president of the Commission. Mr. J. S. Stanley, who had served on the Mixed Claims Commission in Haiti, was appointed by the President on July 31, 1929, took the oath of office on October 8, 1929, and presided over the first meeting of the Commission the following day. The Commission fixed March 31, 1930, as the final date for filing claims. This date was subsequently extended to June 30, 1930, to the inhabitants of the bandit-infested provinces and of the Atlantic coast, and to January 14, 1931, to persons who had claims based on documents which had previously been submitted to the High Commission in order to determine the amount of the floating debt. A law of February 6, 1930, transformed the provisional claims commission into a permanent one and determined that claims arising prior to March 5, 1930, would be received. It also authorized the payment of awards. Up until June 30, 1930, 18,010 claims were registered of a total face value of $19,772,933, of which over 11,000 were for not more than $1,000. The Commission agreed that claims not exceeding a face value of $1,000 should be considered first, in as much as most of the smaller claims were presented by inhabitants of the bandit-infested provinces, who were in urgent need of financial aid. Between February 6, 1930, and February 1, 1931, the Commission adjudicated a total of 3,631 claims of a nominal value of $1,286,526.28. On those claims the total awards amounted to $165,593.85, or about 12 per cent of the nominal value. Adjudicated claims were paid in cash out of a reserve fund of $800,000, which had been built up from the proceeds of a 12½ per cent surcharge on import duties and a 50 per cent surcharge on liquors and tobacco in addition to the duty already levied.[2] Due to the loss of its records in the Managua earthquake of March 31, 1931, the Commission adjourned until September. A law of May 23, 1931, assigned the proceeds of the 12½ per cent surcharge on import duties to a fund for the reconstruction of Government buildings destroyed by the earthquake.[3] At the suggestion of the Commission, President Moncada issued a decree on September 2 establishing new periods for the resubmission of claims previously submitted but not adjudicated prior to the earthquake. By presidential decrees effective November 26, 1931, and February 17, 1932, these periods have been extended. Due to the prevailing economic distress, the Nicaraguan Government has requested the Commission to continue its policy of giving first consideration to claims not exceeding $1,000. It is anticipated that these claims will be adjudicated during 1932 and the major claims during 1933.

THE CORINTO WHARF, THE PACIFIC RAILWAY, AND THE NATIONAL BANK

On March 1, 1929, the Nicaraguan Government, acting by right of an option granted by the first Mixed Claims Commission, purchased the Corinto Wharf from the owner, Mr. Samuel Zemurray, of New Orleans. The purchase price was $300,000, obtained from a special dividend of the Pacific Railway, the Government also receiving equipment and accessories valued at $35,000. The transfer of this

[2] *La Gaceta*, No. 20, Jan. 26, 1927. A law of Feb. 21, 1929, reaffirmed these surcharges (*La Gaceta*, No. 46, Feb. 23, 1929).
[3] *La Gaceta*, No. 108, May 28, 1931.

property which has paid from 14 to 40 per cent per annum on a capitalization of $300,000 marked the liquidation of the last of the concessions originally granted by Zelaya.

Due to disagreements over the place of deposit of the Pacific Railway funds and the loan policy of the National Bank, in October, 1929, the American members withdrew from the Board of Directors of the Pacific Railway and the National Bank, and Messrs. Brown Bros. & Co. and J. & W. Seligman & Co. resigned as "bankers" under the Financial Plans. At the same time the J. G. White Co. terminated its contract to manage the Pacific Railway. Since January 1, 1930, the management of the Pacific Railway has been under the direct supervision of the Nicaraguan Government. The Government is at present building two railroad lines, one from San Jorge on Lake Nicaragua to San Juan del Sur on the Pacific coast, and the other a branch of the Pacific Railway from León to El Sauce. It was estimated that the earnings of the Pacific Railway would pay for the construction of these two lines as well as for a part of the highway plan.

The management of the National Bank was turned over to the Nicaraguan Government on December 26, 1929. On April 19, 1930, the Nicaraguan Government appointed the International Acceptance Bank of New York City as the American depository and fiscal agent of the National Bank. This bank did not assume any of the functions of the "bankers" under the Financial Plans. Mr. Hans Sitarz, an Austrian who had had experience as a bank manager in Colombia, was appointed manager of the National Bank.

A result of the reorganization of Nicaraguan finances was the establishment in December, 1930, of the Mortgage Bank of Nicaragua, with an initial capital of $300,000. There had long been need of a mortgage bank. The seasonal nature of Nicaragua's principal export crop, coffee, has made it difficult for planters to obtain long-term bank advances. During the first six months of its existence, 78 per cent of the mortgage loans were made on coffee and cattle farms in the outlying districts. The law establishing the bank provides for an authorized capital of $1,000,000. No dividends are to be paid until the capital and legal reserve reach $1,500,000. The directors of the Mortgage Bank are the same as those of the National Bank.

In November, 1930, the Nicaraguan Government secured a revolving credit of $250,000 from the reserves of the National Bank on deposit in New York with the International Acceptance Bank in order to expedite railway construction. As a result of the killing on December 31, 1930, of eight marines who were ambushed while engaged in repairing a telephone line near Ocotal, Nueva Segovia, President Moncada took the initiative in raising additional funds to push energetically the pacification of the northern departments as well as to provide employment by highway construction for an additional number of laborers. In January, 1931, the National Bank increased the amount of the $250,000 credit to $1,000,000, of which $80,000 was to be advanced each month. For the repayment of the loan, the Government allocated the returns from five taxes and revenues (road taxes, taxes on the revenues of the Pacific Railway and of the National Bank, revenues of the Corinto Wharf, and a first lien on the Pacific Railway revenues to the extent of $15,000 monthly). Since these sources of income provided $350,000 during 1930, the Government in effect received only $650,000 of new money. The credit bore interest at 8 per cent and its duration was for one year renewable at the request of the Government.

THE ECONOMIC SITUATION, 1931

The reorganization of Nicaragua's finances, as outlined in the so-called Dawson Pacts of 1911, brought stability of currency and the consolidation of the national indebtedness. The cordoba was the only Central American currency to maintain its exchange at par during the World War. During the 20-year tenureship of the Collector General of Customs, 1912–1932, the Ethelburga Syndicate loan has been decreased from £1,000,000 to £525,940. Moreover, by the agreement of 1912, which reduced the interest rate from 6 to 5 per cent, over $928,000 has been saved to the Nicaraguan Government. The guaranteed customs bonds of 1918, issued to pay the awards of the first Mixed Claims Commission and the Commission on Public Credit, have been reduced from the original amount of $3,744,150 to $1,276,750. The Commission on Public Credit, under whose supervision the bonds were issued, believed that all the bonds would be redeemed by 1953. In 1930, it appeared that the bonds might be entirely retired in 1938 or 1939, instead of 1953, the revenues hypothecated for amortization having been unusually large during the previous years.[4] By this operation the High Commissioner estimated that the Government would save $2,000,000 in interest.[4]

The economic depression has seriously curtailed Nicaragua's foreign trade and, consequently, the Government's revenues. The value of coffee exports, which are about one-half of the total export trade, dropped in one year, 1929–30, from $5,902,754 to $3,792,217. The total trade in 1930 was the lowest since 1923. For the first six months of 1931, the customs revenues, which accounted for about 50 per cent of the Government's income, were only a little more than

---

[4] *Report of the Collector General of Customs and High Commission.* 1930. p. 57.

one-half of those for the similar period of 1929. In the latter part of 1930, the banks, reflecting the pessimistic attitude of the commercial interests, began building up large gold balances in foreign countries by buying drafts from the National Bank. In the past, their practice had been to sell their drafts on foreign accounts to the National Bank. Moreover, the withdrawal of about 4,000 United States marines between November, 1928, and June, 1931, cut off an important source of the country's income. The Nicaragua earthquake of 1931 precipitated a crisis. The Government was desperately in need of funds to clear the city of débris and to begin reconstruction. The reserves of the National Bank were too depleted to permit another large advance to the Government. The Government was disinclined to cut down its budget, since this would have added more persons to the thousands already made jobless by the earthquake. The cessation of public works would have created serious labor unrest. Finally, the International Acceptance Bank, the Government's fiscal agent in New York, agreed to loan Nicaragua $100,000 for this purpose.

This advance did not cover the payments for materials necessary to the rebuilding of the city. The Government was compelled to draw heavily upon the already decreased reserves of the National Bank. Moreover, merchants who had heavy remittances due abroad on account of heavy imports of manufactured commodities were having difficulty in securing foreign exchange. The National Bank was reluctant to sell, desiring to protect its reserves. The situation became so critical that on November 13, 1931, the President, by an Executive decree, placed the transaction in foreign exchange under the administration of a Commission of Control, composed of the Minister of Finance, the Manager of the National Bank, and the Collector General of Customs. The Commission of Control was empowered to restrict or prohibit all transaction in foreign exchange, including gold coins and foreign currency. The National Bank was excluded from the restriction of this decree, thereby giving to it a monopoly of exchange transactions.

In consequence of the difficult financial position that threatened the curtailment of vital governmental functions, Nicaragua negotiated an arrangement with representatives of the Ethelburga Syndicate loan and of the guaranteed customs loan for a partial remission of amortization charges during the calendar year 1932, thereby releasing for governmental needs approximately $335,000. The agreement signed between Nicaragua and the Council of Foreign Bondholders, dated May 25, 1912, which lowered the interest rate from 6 to 5 per cent, provided in article 9 as follows:[5]

---

[5] File No. 817.51/447.

ARTICLE 9. In case of failure on the part of the Republic to make duly and punctually any of the payments herein provided or recognized, whether of interest or sinking fund, the coupons of the Assenting Bonds of 1909 are *ipso facto* restored to their full rate of 6%.

However, in view of Nicaragua's excellent record in the past, not only in meeting the debt service promptly but also in amortizing the outstanding bonds more rapidly than was provided for in the agreement of May 25, 1912, the Council of Foreign Bondholders did not insist, when agreeing to the partial suspension of amortization payments, upon the interest rate being raised from 5 to 6 per cent.

THE MILITARY SITUATION, 1927–1932

THE GUARDIA NACIONAL

The Tipitapa Agreement provided for the disbanding of the Nicaraguan National Army, its functions to be assumed by a Guardia Nacional to be organized under the direction of American officers. On May 8, 1927, President Diaz requested the appointment of an American officer to instruct and command the Guardia. This was immediately agreed to by President Coolidge. On May 12, 1927, a colonel of the Marine Corps was appointed as Director in Chief of the Guardia. The work of organization, enlistment, and training immediately began. By August, 1927, the first newly trained detachment of the Guardia entered upon active duties outside of Managua.

The terms of an agreement for the establishment and maintenance of the Guardia Nacional de Nicaragua were drawn up and the agreement was signed at Managua on December 22, 1927, by the American Chargé d'Affaires at Managua and the Nicaraguan Minister of Foreign Affairs.[1] It provided for:

1. The creation of a Guardia Nacional of 93 officers and 1,136 enlisted men, or a total of 1,229 [2] officers and men at a cost of $689,132 per annum.
2. The Guardia to be considered the sole military and police force of the Republic and to have control of arms, ammunition, and military supplies, forts, prisons, etc., throughout the Republic, subject only to the direction of the President of Nicaragua.

This agreement was approved by the Nicaraguan Senate on January 10, 1928. The Chamber of Deputies, however, delayed approval of the bill for more than a year. The agreement was amended and finally passed by both Houses of the Nicaraguan Congress on February 19, 1929, and was approved by President Moncada. The alterations do not affect the number of officers or men nor the expenses of the Guardia, but have to do with certain matters of administration; these alterations have not been accepted by the Department of State.

---

[1] For complete agreement, see Appendix E, p. 131.
[2] Under art. I of the Convention for the Limitation of Armaments, signed by the five republics of Central America at Washington, Feb. 7, 1923, Nicaragua was limited to a standing military force of 2,500 " except in case of civil war, or impending invasion by another State."

The strength of the Guardia, as determined upon in the Guardia agreement of December 22, 1927, was based upon the belief that after the termination of the civil war peace would follow in Nicaragua. When one of the revolutionary generals, Augusto Sandino, fled to the wilderness of the Department of Nueva Segovia and began his career of banditry, a new and unforeseen situation was created. In order to cope with these depredations, the Guardia was increased, until on October 1, 1930, the total personnel of the Guardia numbered 2,256, an increase of about 85 per cent over the number provided for in the original agreement. Furthermore, the total annual cost of the Guardia, due to this expansion in numbers, grew to a total of $1,116,000.

In view of the economic depression and the resulting decrease in revenues, the Government of Nicaragua in 1930 expressed the desire to cut down the cost of the Guardia. It specifically wanted to reduce the salaries of the American officers serving with the Guardia. Although the Department of State did not consent to a reduction in the salaries of officers who had gone to Nicaragua on the basis of a stipulated salary, it consented on November 24, 1930, to a reduction in the pay of those officers joining the Guardia in the future. At the same time it agreed to a reduction by 500 men in the total Guardia personnel. On this basis the Guardia would total 1,810 men (160 officers and 1,650 enlisted men) and its annual expense would be $854,652. The Department of State insisted, however, that the Nicaraguan Government make no reduction whatsoever in the assignment of 72 officers and 1,000 enlisted men to the bandit-infested provinces; all reductions in personnel were to be made in the forces policing the tranquil portions of the country.

This reduction in the Guardia was contingent upon the establishment of local police to relieve in part the existing Guardia forces in the Nicaraguan municipalities. Every city and town had a Guardia detachment for which they made no contribution. President Moncada tried unsuccessfully to secure financial aid from them. On previous occasions the Department of State had questioned the advisability of establishing local police forces, in view of the likelihood of their being employed for partisan purposes. The new arrangement, however, while making their support dependent upon the municipalities, incorporated them as an integral part of the Guardia Nacional and subject to the control of that organization. The members of the so-called Guardia Municipal are recruited not by the local municipal authorities but by the Guardia Nacional which also trains them. Instead of being quartered at public expense, they live principally in their own homes. Although the municipalities meet the expenses of these local police forces, they pay the necessary amounts directly to a disbursing officer of the Guardia Nacional who makes the required payments. The scheme has the dual advantage of making the municipalities responsible for their own police protection and at the same time of making the Guardia Municipal an integral part of the Guardia Nacional, thereby removing it from partisan control. There are about 250 municipal police in service to-day.

Following the regrettable killing of eight marines on December 31, 1930, President Moncada took the initiative in raising additional funds primarily to increase the Nicaraguan personnel of the Guardia. From the $1,000,000 revolving credit obtained from the National Bank, $15,000 per month was allotted to increasing the Guardia by 500 men, all of whom were to be assigned to the bandit-infested provinces. Moreover, the budget of the military school, which trained the Nicaraguan officers for the Guardia, was increased by $2,000 per month. With this expansion it was considered possible to train and prepare sufficient Nicaraguan officers to replace the American officers in the Guardia upon their retirement after the 1932 elections.

As a further military measure, $17,000 [3] per month was allotted to road construction in the Department of Nueva Segovia. The Guardia had been seriously hampered in suppressing banditry in that department by the lack of roads passable the year round. During the rainy season the Guardia was forced to suspend extensive patrol activities, which enabled the bandits to reestablish themselves. Moreover, road construction furnished employment to the population of that area, thereby stabilizing men who might otherwise be tempted or driven to banditry. It also encouraged agriculture and grazing which had been little practiced in the past for lack of adequate transportation facilities.

The Guardia Nacional numbers about 200 officers and 2,150 men. Implicit in the Department of State's announcement of February 13, 1931, regarding the withdrawal of the marines after the 1932 elections is the concomitant turning over of the Guardia to Nicaraguan officers. The increased appropriation for the military school was intended to make possible the training of sufficient personnel by that time. It is planned to turn over commands below that of departmental commander to the Nicaraguan officers on December 15, 1932, and the higher commands to the officers designated by the newly elected President upon his assuming office.

---

[3]After the Managua earthquake, this amount was reduced to $5,000 per month, the difference going to meet the general expenses of the Government.

BANDITRY

Although the isolated and comparatively uncultivated parts of Nicaragua have for decades suffered from chronic bandit depredations, the situation since May 27, 1927, has been substantially different. During the earlier period, the bandits usually raided coffee plantations and cattle ranches, carrying off what they could but seldom killing the inhabitants. This booty they took across the Honduran border where it was exchanged for arms and other materials. They seldom endangered the lives or property of foreigners.

The presence in the country of the United States marines, who were sent during the civil war to protect American life and property and later stayed to disarm the combatants of both sides and to organize the Guardia Nacional, has been used as a pretext by the bandits to justify their devastating raids against foreigners. The bandit depredations arose out of the repudiation by a revolutionary general, Augusto Sandino, of his word, pledged to General Moncada in a letter, that he would lay down arms. His letter read as follows:

May 9, 1927.

ESTEEMED GENERAL MONCADA: I take pleasure in informing you that, having arrived at this place, I have found myself in a difficult position due to the fact that all of my followers have not joined me, since I have found but a few chiefs, the rest of my troops having gone to Jinotega, the place from whence they came. For this reason I feel that my remaining at this place will avail me nothing, all of my followers having disbanded.

I have decided to go to Jinotega again to assemble my men, in order to collect all the arms. In this case I shall remain there awaiting your orders.

I likewise delegate my rights in order that you may arrange the matter as may suit you best, informing me of the results at Jinotega, which I shall occupy with my troops.

The disbanding of my men is due to their not finding anything to eat, and for this reason they have left. However, I assure you that as soon as I arrive they must all come where I am and then I shall collect all the arms. . . .

A. C. SANDINO

Instead, he withdrew with a small band to the mountain fastnesses of the Department of Nueva Segovia, from which he sallied forth to pillage the country and terrorize the inhabitants.

Peaceful methods to persuade him to lay down arms were unavailing. On a number of occasions, before extensive military measures were adopted, efforts were made by appealing to Sandino's patriotism to persuade him to discontinue armed resistance. These efforts met with defiant replies. After Sandino held for ransom the managers of certain French and German concerns near Ocotal in June, 1927, the commander of the American forces in Nicaragua considered it necessary to treat him as an outlaw, which Nicaraguans generally considered him to be.

During the summer of 1927, Sandino augmented his small band with malcontents, to whom he held out the prospects of booty from pillaged farms and towns. After the failure of his attack on Ocotal, his force as a whole broke up into small bands, each under a leader owing nominal allegiance to him. These roving bands, unimpeded by baggage, have carried on their raids by quick sallies from the mountains of the north close to the Honduran border down to the more settled areas.

The amount of banditry has varied according to climatic, political, and economic conditions within the country. During the rainy season, when roads and trails are impassable, the bandits retire to the mountains in the northern provinces. During the dry season, they make their incursions into the cattle and coffee-growing sections of the southern and western sections.

Political excitement, particularly that of elections, has been the signal for renewed activities. During the registration period of 1928, the bandits committed several horrible murders in the Department of Jinotega. The Marine and Guardia forces were immediately augmented in this and the other provinces, and patrols were sent out to protect outlying towns so that the elections passed off without disorder of any kind. This policy was employed with the same success in 1930.

As a result of the unsatisfactory economic conditions, many of those unable to find employment have turned to thievery and even to banditry. Such persons joined the bandits only to take part in a raid and then return to their own community. Partly in order to alleviate this situation, the Government inaugurated two railroad projects and extensive road-building activities in Nueva Segovia. After the Managua earthquake it gave temporary employment to many thousands clearing the city of débris and carrying on the reconstruction activities. Existing labor unrest was a contributing cause of the raids on the east coast in April and on the towns in the Department of Chinandega in November, 1931.

Despite their protestations to the contrary, the unpatriotic and mercenary motives of the bandits were never more unmistakably shown than in their surprise attack on the small towns of the east coast in April, 1931. This occurred only two weeks after the country had been prostrated by the Managua earthquake catastrophe. At that time all available military forces, both Marine and Guardia Nacional, were engaged in reconstruction work, leaving the east coast with a minimum of protection forces. Although the bandits sacked Cabo Gracias a Dios, they were not successful in capturing Puerto Cabezas or other coast towns and withdrew to the mountains of the interior. During this raid nine Americans lost their lives.

At the time of this raid, the Secretary of State telegraphed the American Legation at Managua and the American Vice Consul at Bluefields as follows: [4]

In view of outbreak of banditry in portions of Nicaragua hitherto free from such violence, you will advise American citizens that this Government can not undertake general protection of Americans throughout that country with American forces. To do so would lead to difficulties and commitments which this Government does not propose to undertake. Therefore, the Department recommends to all Americans who do not feel secure under the protection afforded them by the Nicaraguan Government through the Nicaraguan National Guard to withdraw from the country, or at least to the coast towns whence they can be protected or evacuated in case of necessity. Those who remain do so at their own risk and must not expect American forces to be sent inland to their aid.

The Secretary of State subsequently expanded on the foregoing announcement in the following statement: [5]

The problem before the Government to-day is not a problem of the protection of its citizens in Nicaragua from a war, but from murder and assassination. In that respect it is totally different from the problem which existed in 1926.

In 1926, two armies, consisting of two or three thousand men each, were fighting in Nicaragua on the east coast. Both armies professed to be carrying out the rules of warfare and to be protecting neutrals and neutral property. So the problem of this Government was solved by establishing neutral zones in which, by agreement with both armies at that time, hostilities did not enter. These neutral zones, as I recall it, were established with the consent of both the Liberal and Conservative commanders of the contending armies. There was no organized attempt to murder private citizens of any country. The problem was only to protect them from the inevitable catastrophes of war.

Now we have a situation where small groups of confessed outlaws—treated as outlaws by the Nicaraguan Government—are making their way through the jungle to the east coast, with the avowed intention of murdering and pillaging the civilian inhabitants of the country. The terrain where this is taking place is one of the thickest jungles in the world. The rainfall on the east coast of Nicaragua is something more than double the rainfall on the west coast and, as a result, this is very thick jungle country, a region where it would be almost impossible for regular troops to operate effectively even if it were attempted.

Another point of difference which is vital is that in 1926 there was no Nicaraguan constabulary. Since that time, for nearly four years, our officers have been helping the Nicaraguan Government train a

---

[4] Press release of Apr. 17, 1931.　　[5] Press release of Apr. 18, 1931.

force of constabulary especially for fighting in this kind of terrain, the very object being to produce the most appropriate kind of force to meet tropical and jungle conditions of warfare. That force has been recently raised from 1,850 to over 2,100 and is reported by its officers as being highly efficient. Purely from the standpoint of protection, the most effective way to protect the American and foreign civilians who have been suddenly exposed to this danger in the forests of eastern Nicaragua is to give them warning of the danger and an opportunity to escape to the protection of the coast towns; and then for this specially trained constabulary to operate in the jungle against the bandits. If the number of constabulary now on the east coast is not sufficient for that purpose, there are certainly enough elsewhere to reinforce them against these comparatively small bands of outlaws. American naval vessels are standing by at all the threatened east-coast ports with orders to protect life and property at these ports. These ships will remain until the danger is over.

By assisting the Government of Nicaragua in organizing and training a competent Guardia, we are not only furnishing the most practical and effective method of meeting the bandit problem and the protection of Americans and foreigners in Nicaragua from its attendant perils, but we are at the same time recognizing that it is a problem with which the sovereign Government of Nicaragua is primarily concerned and a problem which it is primarily the right and duty of that Government to solve. There has been no change in the determination of the American Government not to send American troops into the interior.

The events of this last week have pretty thoroughly torn the mask off the character of the mythical patriot Sandino. Two of his lieutenants have been recognized as leaders of these outlaw bands, and, both from their work and from the evidence of captured papers, they are shown to have been engaged in a deliberate plan of assassination and pillage against helpless civilians of various nationalities, including Nicaraguans, working in mines and logging camps. The movements of these outlaws from the northwestern provinces to the eastern coast of Nicaragua came just after the terrific earthquake which prostrated the center of that country, when every humane impulse was to assist those who were suffering from the catastrophe and when all forces, including marines and constabulary, were engaged in the alleviation of distress. It was in the hour of his country's desolation that Sandino chose to send his outlaws across the country to attack the region which he believed to be left unguarded.

Considering the many adverse factors that handicap its attempts to suppress banditry, the Guardia has made substantial progress. It is true that, originally, banditry was confined to the departments bordering Honduras, and that subsequently it has broken out in other sections of the country. This was the result of Sandino's followers dispersing into small bands which can travel swiftly and without attracting attention. The Guardia has systematically combed the settled departments for bandits and, as a result, has made it extremely dangerous for small bandit groups to operate.

Due to the increasing efficiency of the Guardia operations in the northern departments, the bandits, in order to reach the richer and more cultivated areas, have been compelled to take many chances, which accounts for the sensationalism of recent raids. The growth of an *esprit de corps* in the Guardia and the improvement of means of communication have sapped the strength of the smaller and made hazardous the operation of the larger groups of bandits.

WITHDRAWAL OF THE MARINES

Armed forces of the United States were sent to Nicaragua in August, 1926, to protect American lives. At the request of both President Diaz and General Moncada, they facilitated the disarming of both the Government and the revolutionary forces in accordance with the terms of the Tipitapa Agreement. Due to the outbreak of banditry, their number was increased to prevent interference with the 1928 elections, which the United States agreed to supervise also under the terms of the Tipitapa Agreement. In November, 1928, the marine and naval forces totaled 5,480. As the Guardia developed into a fighting force and took over the patrolling of the bandit-infested provinces, the marines were withdrawn, so that by June, 1930, they numbered only 1,248. Beginning in July, 1930, additional forces were sent to assist in the conduct of the elections of that year, bringing the total in November to 1,763.

On February 13, 1931, the Department of State announced its intention of withdrawing from Nicaragua " all of the Marine Brigade who are now on combatant duty probably by June next, leaving in Nicaragua only the Marines who are still engaged in instruction in the Nicaraguan National Guard and an instruction battalion to support such instruction and an aviation section which is being used for the present to carry supplies in the bandit provinces which are entirely without roads." [6]   At the same time, it announced that the step contemplated, together with the increase in the Guardia Nacional and the road-building activities, made feasible by the $1,000,000 credit, " have paved the way for the ultimate removal of all of the Marine forces from Nicaragua immediately after the election of 1932." [6]

In February, 1931, the total armed force of the United States in Nicaragua numbered 1,500 men. Despite the Managua earthquake catastrophe and the bandit raid on the east coast in April, 1931, there was little deviation from the withdrawal program, which was effected by June 3, 1931. The aviation force was slightly increased at the time of the outbreak on the Atlantic coast, to make it easier to

---

[6] File No. 817.00/7004; press release of Feb. 13, 1931.

reinforce the Guardia there. On April 1, 1932, the marine and naval personnel in Nicaragua totalled 753, exclusive of the 205 officers in the Guardia Nacional.

From May 7, 1926, when marines were landed at Bluefields, until January 1, 1932, 30 officers and men have been killed in action and 15 died of wounds received in action.

NICARAGUAN-HONDURAN BOUNDARY DISPUTE

Under the terms of the convention signed on October 7, 1894, Nicaragua and Honduras appointed a Joint Commission to demarcate the boundary. The Joint Commission thereupon established the boundary from the Gulf of Fonseca to the Gap of Teotecacinte. When a dispute arose over the marking of the boundary from that point to the Atlantic Ocean, the matter was referred under the terms of the convention to arbitration. In due time, the King of Spain was named as arbiter, and on December 23, 1906, handed down his award. The Honduran Congress accepted the award unconditionally, but the Nicaraguan Congress, when accepting it, announced that some obscure and contradictory points in the award required clarification. International wars and internal political disturbances in both countries delayed the demarcation of the boundary. In 1912 Nicaragua refused to recognize the award, claiming that it was no longer in effect because in the choice of an arbiter the original convention had not been fulfilled.

In 1914 the Department of State endeavored unsuccessfully to secure Nicaragua's cooperation with Honduras in settling the dispute.[1] When in 1918 the conflict became acute, threatening to involve the two countries in war, the Department of State invited representatives of the two countries to confer with it in an attempt to work out a friendly solution. The two Republics, in accepting this offer, agreed to withdraw their troops into the zone occupied by them previous to June 1, 1918, and to observe this return to the *status quo ante* during the time which the Department of State was exercising its good offices.[2] On November 17, 1920, they agreed to respect and maintain the *status quo ante* to which they had consented when accepting the good offices of the Department of State.

After a series of conferences during 1920 and 1921 between delegates of the two countries and the Department of State, the latter on October 27, 1921, wrote identic notes to the Honduran and Nicaraguan Legations in Washington suggesting:

(1) That the following question, "Is the award defining the boundary rendered by the King of Spain in 1906 valid?" be sub-

---

[1] *Foreign Relations*, 1918, pp. 13–20.   [2] *Ibid.*, pp. 32–33.

mitted for determination to the Chief Justice of the United States, and that

(2) In the event that the arbitrator should hold the award of the King of Spain to be invalid, and the boundary line fixed by that award consequently inapplicable, the Chief Justice of the United States be entrusted with the duty of determining the boundary which shall be established between the two Republics, taking into consideration all facts, circumstances and antecedents relating thereto, with the prior understanding that both the Government of Honduras and the Government of Nicaragua shall accept the decision rendered as final and conclusive.[3]

Nicaragua accepted the bases proposed by the Department of State, but Honduras did not.

During the Conference on Central American Affairs in 1923, a protocol was drawn up by the delegates of Honduras and Nicaragua and cabled to their respective Governments. This protocol read as follows:[4]

The Governments of Honduras and Nicaragua having accepted the friendly mediation which the Department of State of the United States offered in 1918, in the controversy which had arisen between them regarding the arbitral award of the King of Spain rendered on December 23, 1906, and having been unable to reach an agreement as to the manner of settling the controversy, have determined to ask that the mediation of the Department of State be transformed into arbitral proceedings and have decided to request the Secretary of State of the United States to take into consideration all of the antecedents of the matter in dispute and determine the just solution of the controversy.

The Governments above named agree that they will accept the solution proposed by the Secretary of State of the United States as final and without appeal.

The Nicaraguan Government instructed its delegates to accept the protocol as proposed, but the Government of Honduras failed to reply.

Negotiations were carried on intermittently but without success during the next seven years. Finally, on January 21, 1931, the Governments of Nicaragua and Honduras signed a boundary protocol providing that the two Governments accept the arbitral award of the King of Spain rendered in 1906 and appoint a commission to mark the boundary from the Gap of Teotecacinte to the Atlantic Ocean. The protocol provides that the Commission shall be composed of three engineers: one appointed by Nicaragua; one by Hon-

---

[3] File No. 715.1715/258a. For the Spanish text of this note, see *Exposicion sobre la Cuestion de Limites entre Nicaragua y Honduras y Protocolo de Arreglo Suscrito el 21 de enero de 1931* (Managua, 1931), pp. 11–12.
[4] *Ibid.*, pp. 12–13.

duras; and one, the chairman, by the United States. The protocol was ratified by Honduras on February 9, 1931.

On May 25, the Nicaraguan Congress rejected the protocol because it regarded the award of the King of Spain " as invalid by reason of the multiple defects of form and substance with which it was prepared and pronounced." [5]   It redefined the boundary in a new protocol, upon which Honduras has taken no action.

---

[5] *La Gaceta*, No. 161, Aug. 3, 1931.

THE MANAGUA EARTHQUAKE

On March 31, 1931, Managua, the capital of Nicaragua and a city of 60,000 inhabitants, was shattered and virtually destroyed by earthquake. Fire broke out immediately, which raged for five days, consuming 33 blocks in the richest and most important area of the city before it was brought under control. Every large Government building except the National Bank, and virtually all the archives of the Nicaraguan Government were burned. Over one thousand people were killed, many thousands were injured, and nearly the entire population temporarily rendered homeless. The property loss was estimated at $15,000,000.[1]

To meet the emergency, the American Marine forces and the Guardia occupied the destroyed city immediately after the earthquake and restored order. Medical officers of the United States Navy established an emergency hospital and dressing station; the United States Army engineers engaged in the canal survey successfully prevented the fire from consuming the entire city, and the Marines and Guardia set up field kitchens where many thousands of refugees were fed daily. The American Red Cross, upon learning of the disaster, immediately appropriated $10,000 for relief, which was subsequently increased to $100,000. These funds were expended under the direction of a Central Relief Committee with the American Minister as its chairman. As many as 8,000 persons were given cooked food twice daily for two weeks, milk was distributed, the water system restored, markets established, the hospitals repaired, and relief extended to labor by giving it employment in clearing the city of débris. Special relief missions were also sent from Mexico, Panama, and the other Central American republics. President Moncada manifested on many occasions the appreciation and gratitude of the Nicaraguan people for the assistance so spontaneously rendered. On June 1, 1931, he formally conferred the Presidential Medal of Merit on 19 officers of the United States Army, Navy, and Marine Corps; and on September 8, 1931, he conferred the same medal upon the American Minister for his services in directing the relief activities of the American Red Cross in Managua.[2]

---

[1] Estimate of Col. Ernest J. Swift, Director of American Red Cross relief activities in Managua (*Washington Herald*, Apr. 30, 1931).
[2] See official report of the Central Relief Committee of the American Red Cross, Oct., 1931.

THE NICARAGUAN CANAL SURVEY

On March 2, 1929, the Congress of the United States passed a joint resolution providing for a new study of interoceanic canal routes.[1] The resolution, approved by the President on March 4, 1929, expressed special interest in the possibility of the enlargement of the Panama Canal and in the project for a new canal through Nicaragua. Under the command of Maj. Dan I. Sultan, of the Engineer Corps of the United States Army, field work on the survey of the Nicaraguan route began on August 29, 1929, and, except for a continuation of the hydrographic and meteorological work, was finished before July 1, 1931. At the time of the Managua earthquake, the survey engineers placed their services at the disposal of the Nicaraguan Government, assisting it in fighting the fire and rehabilitating the waterworks.

The report of the Interoceanic Canal Board, presented to Congress on December 10, 1931, states that an interoceanic ship canal across Nicaragua from Greytown on the Atlantic Ocean to Brito on the Pacific Ocean by way of the Deseado and San Juan Rivers and the great Lake of Nicaragua is practicable and involves no problems that can not be solved successfully. This canal would be 172.8 miles long with a set of 2-way triple-flight locks near each coast. The Interoceanic Canal Board was of the opinion that none of the past earthquakes in Central America were " of sufficient magnitude to seriously damage massive well founded canal structures at either Panama or Nicaragua." [2] A Nicaraguan canal could be constructed in 10 years and would cost $722,000,000, including $25,000,000 for acquiring rights, franchises, and land. Despite the advantages of such a canal, including a saving in time and increased dependability to shipping and an increase in trade and commerce, the recommendation of the Interoceanic Canal Board states: [3]

73. The present conditions of world trade, the necessity for economy in expenditure of public funds, and the facts that traffic through the Panama Canal now requires only about 50 per cent of its capacity and that full capacity when demanded by traffic will be assured

---

[1] Public Resolution No. 99, 70th Congress; Senate Joint Resolution No. 117, approved by Congress, Mar. 2, 1929.
[2] *Report of the Interoceanic Canal Board*, Nov. 30, 1931, p. 16.
[3] *Ibid.*, p. 24.

by the additional water supply from the Madden reservoir (at Alhajuela) with the indication that thus the Panama Canal can serve the needs of interoceanic traffic for some time to come, lead to the conclusion that no immediate steps must be taken to provide increased facilities for passing water-borne traffic from ocean to ocean.

RECENT ELECTORAL DEVELOPMENTS

THE CONGRESSIONAL ELECTIONS OF 1930

Shortly after President Moncada assumed office, the Acting Minister of Foreign Affairs addressed a note to the American Minister at Managua, a translation of which follows:[1]

MANAGUA, *February 12, 1929.*

EXCELLENCY: Under special instructions from His Excellency the President I have pleasure in informing Your Excellency that my Government being desirous of laying the foundation for peace in the Republic in a firm and stable manner, by the practice of free institutions, has arrived at an agreement with the Honorable Supreme Court of Justice, by which this High Tribunal, in the exercise of the powers which are conferred on it by the Electoral Law of March 20, 1923, will appoint a citizen of the United States of America, previously designated by His Excellency the President of the United States, as Chairman of the National Board of Elections, in order to assure complete impartiality of this official, and as the primary part of a general plan aiming at the attainment of truly free elections in the future.

The President desires to obtain in a permanent way the valuable cooperation of the United States in the stability of the Republic in Nicaragua; and to this end, I venture to request that Your Excellency be so kind as to bring to the knowledge of the enlightened Government at Washington the aims above mentioned and to opportunely urge the designation of the American citizen to preside over the National Board of Elections.

I am also authorized to advise Your Excellency that the Government of the Republic will pay to the said President a salary of eight thousand dollars a year.

With confidence that Your Excellency's enlightened Government will agree to continue lending us its assistance for such noble ends, I am pleased to convey to Your Excellency in advance the deep appreciation of my Government.

I avail [etc.]   M. CORDERO REYES

After considerable negotiation to elaborate the details of the arrangement, the Department of State accepted the invitation on May 8, 1930, when President Hoover designated Capt. Alfred Wilkinson Johnson, United States Navy, to the position of chairman of the National Board of Elections. The Supreme Court of Nicaragua

---

[1] File No. 817.00/6218.

on May 23, 1930, accepted the resignation of Dr. Segundo Albino
Román y Reyes, who had been chairman of the National Board of
Elections since the resignation of General McCoy, and appointed
Captain Johnson as his successor.

The seats of one-third of the Senators and of one-half of the
Deputies were to be filled in the congressional elections of 1930.
Article IX of the electoral decree of March 21, 1928, stated that
upon the proclamation of the result of the 1928 elections, the electoral law of March 20, 1923, and its amendments, should be auto-
matically restored. On July 26, 1930, the President, by Executive
decree, modified the electoral law of 1923 in certain administrative
details. Article III of this decree declared that these reforms should
be effective when an American citizen was chairman of the National
Board of Elections and when the elections were for supreme authorities (President, Vice President, Members of Congress).

Captain Johnson was also the chairman of the American Electoral Mission, comprising 672 persons. The Mission followed the
same procedure as in 1928 in order to make possible fair and free
elections. A decree lifting the state of martial law in the bandit-
infested provinces, an amnesty decree, a decree restricting the sale
of liquor, etc., were declared by President Moncada. The two major
parties, Liberal and Conservative, were the only contestants, as the
Liberal Republican Party did not qualify under the terms of the
electoral law. The elections, which were held on November 2, 1930,
resulted in the election of 7 Liberal Senators and 16 Deputies and
2 Conservative Senators and 6 Deputies. The total vote cast was
approximately 70 per cent of that in the same districts in 1928.

THE MUNICIPAL ELECTIONS OF 1931

The Conservatives threatened to abstain from the 1930 elections
unless the appointive municipal officials in the Department of Chontales be replaced by elective authorities. The former elective officials in this Department, as well as in the other four departments,[2]
placed under martial law because of bandit disturbances, had been
replaced by local boards appointed by the President. This demand
was not insisted upon by the Conservatives, and the elections took
place as scheduled in all parts of the country. In view of the bearing of the controversy over the reconstitution of the legal municipal
authorities, as evidenced in the 1930 elections, the Department of
State on July 11, 1931, designated Maj. Charles F. B. Price as
electoral observer of the municipal elections held on November 1,
1931. Major Price was instructed to observe the conduct of these

---

[2] Nueva Segovia, Esteli, Jinotega, and Matagalpa.

elections and to make recommendations and plans for the supervision of the presidential elections in 1932.

The municipal elections of 1931 did not settle the vexatious problem of the municipal governments in the five departments under martial law. President Moncada and the Conservative leaders attempted to reach some common understanding without success. On August 31, 1931, the President issued a decree suspending the elections in the five departments in question until the Congress meeting in regular session on December 15, 1931, could pass a law prescribing the date and other details for a special election. On September 10, 1931, the Conservative Party issued a decree of abstention from the municipal elections. As a party, the Conservatives did not participate, but in a number of municipalities where the local Conservatives felt they had a good chance of success, they formed independent groups and nominated candidates by petition.

On December 16, 1931, President Moncada introduced into Congress a project to cover the election of authorities in the places where appointed local boards existed, these elections to be held during the spring of 1932. Neither party has pushed this project. In view of the approaching presidential elections, both parties apparently prefer not to deplete their resources at this time in minor political contests.

THE PRESIDENTIAL ELECTIONS OF 1932

On January 4, 1932, the Department of State, in nominating Admiral Clark Howell Woodward, United States Navy, for appointment as chairman of the National Board of Elections, made the following announcement: [3]

One of the bases of the so-called Tipitapa Agreement of May 11, 1927, which put an end to the civil warfare then existing in Nicaragua, provided that the presidential elections of 1928 in that country should be held under the supervision of the United States in order to assure free and fair elections. In compliance with this stipulation, President Coolidge named Brig. Gen. Frank R. McCoy, U.S. Army, as his Personal Representative in Nicaragua, whom the Nicaraguan Supreme Court also appointed as chairman of the National Board of Elections. General McCoy supervised the elections held on November 4, 1928, which resulted in the election of General Moncada as President of Nicaragua. Prior to the elections, the candidates of the two contending parties, General Moncada and Señor Adolfo Benard, agreed by an exchange of letters that the one who was successful would request the supervision of the next presidential elections in 1932 by the United States.

Shortly after his inauguration in 1929, President Moncada addressed a formal communication to the Government of the United

---

[3] Press release of Jan. 4, 1932.

States stating that the Government of Nicaragua, "being desirous of laying the foundation for peace in the Republic in a firm and stable manner, by the practice of free institutions, has arrived at an agreement with the Honorable Supreme Court of Justice, by which this High Tribunal, in the exercise of the powers which are conferred on it by the electoral law of March 20, 1923, will appoint a citizen of the United States of America, previously designated by His Excellency, the President of the United States, as president of the National Board of Elections, in order to insure the complete impartiality of this official, and as the primary part of a general plan aiming at the attainment of truly free elections in the future," and requesting the designation of the American who should serve in this capacity.

In accordance with the desires of the Government of Nicaragua, the President designated Capt. Alfred W. Johnson, U.S. Navy, who was appointed by the Nicaraguan Supreme Court on May 23, 1930. In this capacity, Captain Johnson, who was also chairman of the American Electoral Mission, supervised the congressional elections in 1930. Because of his detail to sea duty, Captain Johnson tendered his resignation as chairman of the National Board of Elections, which the Supreme Court accepted on July 21, 1931. Since that time Dr. Enoc Aguado, Vice President of Nicaragua, has served as chairman of the National Board of Elections, it being understood that when the time came for holding the presidential elections in 1932, Doctor Aguado would resign in order that, in accordance with President Moncada's request for American supervision of the presidential elections, an American citizen could again be named chairman of the National Board of Elections.

In a letter to the American Minister in Managua, dated June 18, 1931, President Moncada reiterated his request made prior to the 1928 elections for the cooperation of the United States in the 1932 presidential elections. The President of the United States has therefore designated Rear Admiral Clark Howell Woodward, U. S. Navy, as his personal representative in Nicaragua to be appointed by the Supreme Court of Nicaragua as chairman of the National Board of Elections. Admiral Woodward, accompanied by his aide, Lieut. Floyd A. Stephenson, U.S.M.C., will arrive in Managua by airplane on January 10, 1932, to spend a few days on a preliminary visit in order to pay his respects to President Moncada and to meet the political leaders of the country. He will then proceed to Panama to rejoin the command of Cruiser Division No. 3, United States Fleet. After completion of his duties in connection with the winter fleet maneuvers in the Pacific, he will return to Nicaragua at the end of May or the first part of June to remain until the termination of his mission in connection with the supervision of the elections.

Admiral Woodward is familiar with local conditions in Nicaragua, where he was detailed for a few months in 1927. For his services in Nicaragua he was awarded by the Navy Department the Distinguished Service Medal and by the Nicaraguan Government its Medal of Merit with silver star and diploma.

President Hoover yesterday received Admiral Woodward and discussed with him the mission to Nicaragua in connection with the forthcoming presidential elections.

The sole interest of the United States as regards these elections is that by means of fair and open elections, at which everybody who is entitled to vote has an opportunity of doing so, the preference of the Nicaraguan people may freely be expressed. The United States Government of course will not support nor will it oppose the candidacy of any person for the nomination or for election to the presidency.

Admiral Woodward was cordially received by the Nicaraguan Government, the political parties, and the press of both parties during his visit. On January 10–12, 1932, the Supreme Court accepted the resignation of Dr. Enoc Aguado as chairman of the National Board of Elections and nominated Admiral Woodward in his stead, Doctor Aguado continuing to function pending the assumption of office by Admiral Woodward.

CONSTITUTIONAL REFORM

In the fall of 1931, President Moncada, in a conversation with the American Minister, expressed his views as to the advisability of completely amending the Constitution at the next session of Congress. Shortly afterwards, in a letter to the Secretary of State, he advanced his belief that the electoral laws, the agreement establishing the Guardia Nacional, and the Bryan-Chamorro Treaty of August 5, 1914, were in conflict with the Constitution. In January, 1932, he adduced as an additional reason for constitutional reform the bitter animosity between the Liberals and Conservatives which he thought might be allayed by an amendment providing for proportional minority representation in the Government. In order to carry into effect the various reforms, President Moncada proposed, as provided in the Constitution,[1] to call a Constituent Assembly in order to effect a complete amendment to the Constitution. At all times President Moncada denied the rumor freely circulated in Nicaragua that he intended to prolong his own term of office after January 1, 1933.

While Nicaragua was considering these matters, the Department of State, having previously consented to supervise the presidential elections, proceeded with the initial organization of the American Electoral Mission by the appointment of Admiral Woodward. Presumably because the proposal to amend completely the Constitution involved the election of a Constituent Assembly, to the supervision of which the Department of State had not consented, President Moncada in February, 1932, sent Doctors Morales and Arguello to Washington as his personal representatives to consult with the Department of State. After several meetings the two delegates were informed on March 23, 1932, of the views of the Department of State in the following memorandum:[2]

The Secretary of State has given careful and sympathetic consideration to the two memoranda dated March 2 and March 10, 1932, presented by Doctor Carlos A. Morales and Doctor Horacio Arguello Bolaños, regarding the desire of the political entities which they represent to revise the Constitution of Nicaragua.

The Secretary of State has been very gratified to receive the statements of Messrs. Morales and Arguello that their parties deem that peace is the highest consideration in the welfare of Nicaragua, and that the Tipitapa Agreement closed the chapter of Nicaragua's civil discord and opened a new era for the Republic by means of the

---

[1] Arts 160, 163, and 164.
[2] File No. 817.011/89A.

free election of supreme authorities, and the establishment of a National Guard as a foundation of peace and a guarantee of public liberties.

Mr. Stimson desires in the first place to state that the question of amending the Nicaraguan Constitution is, of course, one for decision by Nicaragua itself. It is understood that the Department of State is being consulted because of the fact that the United States has consented, at the request of Nicaragua, to supervise the elections for supreme authorities in November, 1932, and that it is now desired to ascertain the views of the Department of State as to the extension of this electoral supervision to comprise elections for representatives to a Constituent Assembly for the purpose of effecting a total revision of the Constitution. This plan, it may be noted, would eliminate the scheduled elections for the regular Congress.

The memoranda of Messrs. Morales and Arguello set out four reasons for desiring a total amendment of the Constitution:

(1) The situation created by the ratification of the Canal Treaty of August 5, 1914;
(2) The establishment of the National Guard on a firm basis;
(3) The establishment of proportional representation in certain branches of the Government; and
(4) The extension of the term of office of certain Government officials.

With regard to the Canal Treaty Mr. Stimson is gratified to note the following statement from the memorandum of March 10, 1932, presented by Messrs Morales and Arguello:

We believe it proper to declare, that we hold the considerations which we offered incidentally in our Memorandum of the 2nd of the current month of March on the approval of the Canal Treaty of 1914 to be eliminated from the discussion on the problem now before us, since we frankly acknowledge that Mr. White's reply on that point is technically and legally correct and the Treaty has all its constitutional effectiveness.

Mr. White, in the conference of March 7, 1932, in which he set forth the views alluded to by Messrs. Morales and Arguello, referred to the letter of the Secretary of State to President Moncada dated December 9, 1931, in which it was pointed out that it was self-evident that the provisions of the Canal Treaty were not regarded by the Nicaraguan Government which negotiated it as being in conflict with the Constitution. Mr. White then went on to say that since this matter was brought up again now, it would be well to dispose of it by pointing out that Article 162 of the Nicaraguan Constitution provides that the treaties or compacts referred to in the last part of Article 2 of the Constitution (with the exception of those treaties looking toward union with one or more Republics of Central America) shall be ratified by a two-thirds vote of each House, and by this act the Constitution shall be considered as amended, notwithstanding the other provision of Title XXIII of the Constitution. In other words, the Canal Treaty having been ratified by the Senate of Nicaragua unanimously and by the Chamber of Deputies by 28 votes in favor and 7 against, it was therefore ratified in accordance with Article 162 of the Constitution and by that act the Constitution was amended. Mr. White pointed out that there was, therefore, no occasion to make any further amendments to the Constitution on this score. The Secretary of State is gratified to take note that Messrs. Morales and Arguello agree with this point of view.

With regard to the question of the National Guard, the Secretary of State desires to refer to the letter which he wrote on December 9, 1931, to President Moncada, in which he stated:

> I have asked my legal advisers to examine the various points raised in your letter and in your memorandum of September 10 respecting the constitutionality of the Guardia and the regulations issued for its governance. Without entering upon a lengthy discussion of the matter, I may say that their advice confirms what has always been my understanding since the question of the formation of a single, non-partisan military force was discussed at Tipitapa, where it became one of the bases of the settlement reached, namely, that under the Constitution of Nicaragua the President enjoys sufficient authority to establish the Guardia as the sole military force of the Republic for the assurance of the rights of the nation, the enforcement of law and the maintenance of public order, and to issue the necessary regulations to govern the Guardia.

Should the Congress of Nicaragua feel that there are amendments to the Constitution which would be desirable in order to give the National Guard greater prestige through provisions therefor in the Constitution, Article 160 of the Constitution would seem to provide means by which this may be done. It would not appear to be necessary to reform completely the Constitution for this object.

As respects the questions of minority representation and the extension of the term of office of Government officials, it would also seem that the method of partial amendment in Article 160 of the Constitution provides a means for accomplishing desired reforms without resorting to the extraordinary procedure of completely revising the Constitution.

In the first section of the March 10 memorandum, Messrs. Morales and Arguello set forth a *résumé* of their understanding of the views expressed by Mr. White in the conference of March 7. It might be pointed out that this *résumé* does not in all points represent exactly what was said by Mr. White. For instance, under a sub-paragraph (*f*) the *résumé* states that Mr. White said that:

> in order to ascertain whether the country desires absolute amendment of the Constitution, a referendum must first be taken, in the November elections, by providing a special square in the ballot for this purpose . . .; that in case of securing favorable public opinion, the Constituent Assembly would be convoked the following year.

Mr. White, of course, did not say that in his view this procedure " must " be followed. He merely suggested that if it were desired to consult popular opinion in Nicaragua as to the advisability of a complete reform of the Constitution, this could perhaps take the form of a popular expression of opinion at the time of the regular elections in November 1932 and if an affirmative opinion was expressed the regular Congress in 1933 could then take appropriate action in accordance with the Constitution. This suggestion was made, moreover, in view of the fact that the State Department's information seems to indicate that the desire for a complete reform of the Constitution is by no means general in Nicaragua.

In considering the supervision of Nicaraguan elections by the United States it would seem well to bear in mind the antecedents of the matter.   One of the bases of the Tipitapa agreement of 1927 was that the presidential elections of 1928 should be held under the supervision of the United States in order to assure free and fair elections.   Prior to holding the 1928 elections, the candidates of the two parties, General Moncada and Señor Benard, agreed by an exchange of letters that the one who was successful would request the supervision of the next elections for supreme authorities in 1932 by the United States.   President Moncada, shortly after his inauguration in 1929 and in pursuance of this agreement, formally requested the United States to supervise the 1932 elections.   The United States Government has consented to this and is now making appropriate arrangements to that end.   The elections which the United States Government has consented to supervise, however, are for " supreme authorities ", namely, for President, Vice President, one-half of the membership of the Chamber of Deputies and one-third of the Senate. What is now proposed by Messrs. Morales and Arguello is a very different election, namely, an election for President and for a Constituent Assembly, thus eliminating the elections for the regular Congress.

The Secretary of State has given most careful consideration to this proposal.   He cannot escape the conviction that a situation might be created through the election of a Constituent Assembly which would jeopardize the induction into office on January 1, 1933, as well as the constitutional authority of the President elected at the same time.   Messrs. Morales and Arguello have not indicated, either in their conversations with Mr. White or in their memorandum of the 10th instant, how this difficulty—which frankly appears insurmountable—might be overcome.   Indeed, the views they expressed in conversation were to the effect that the Constituent Assembly would embody the sovereign authority of Nicaragua and would in itself constitute the executive, legislative and judicial organs of the Government.   Moreover, it appears to be somewhat doubtful whether, in view of the pertinent provisions of the Nicaraguan Constitution, a Constituent Assembly could legally be chosen during the present year.   The Secretary of State is, therefore, confirmed in his view of the unwisdom of considering such action at this time.   Nicaragua has made admirable progress through the holding of free and fair elections in 1928 and 1930.   The course of wisdom would seem to be to consolidate this progress and to add another step to it through holding the 1932 elections in the form and manner scheduled and thus continuing on the pathway of regular and orderly procedure under the Constitution.   To do anything else would seem to prejudice the progress heretofore realized, and certainly no friend of Nicaragua would wish to lend support to that end.

In view of the foregoing, therefore, the Secretary of State desires to reply to Messrs. Morales and Arguello as follows:

(a) The United States is prepared, upon the issuance of the decrees deemed necessary to insure a fair election, to supervise the normal and regular elections for supreme authorities in November, 1932, namely, elections for President, Vice President, one-half of the membership of the Chamber of Deputies, and one-third of the Senate of the regular Congress;

(*b*) The United States cannot consent, for the reasons given, to lend its assistance in supervising elections of any other nature than those set forth above;

(*c*) The question of whether or not Nicaragua should amend its Constitution is one for Nicaragua alone to determine. Article 160 of the present Constitution provides a method for accomplishing a partial amendment. If Nicaragua desires a complete amendment of the Constitution through the convocation of a Constituent Assembly, this could be accomplished after 1932, through appropriate action in accordance with the Constitution. If, however, Nicaragua should decide to elect a Constituent Assembly in the present year the United States would be unable to continue with its plans to supervise the November elections.

In terminating, the Secretary of State desires again to express his pleasure at the assurances given in the two memoranda under acknowledgment of the desire for peace and the aspiration for constitutional life in Nicaragua. These are sentiments which the Secretary of State heartily reciprocates and in which he extends his best wishes to Nicaraguans of all Parties. Mr. Stimson's associations in Nicaragua have been so intimate in the past, and his interest is so enduring, that he sincerely hopes that the regular elections in November, if held as scheduled, will advance the Republic one more step toward the goal which all Nicaraguans and all friends of Nicaragua desire, namely, towards peace, order and stability; the development of a tradition of holding free and fair elections; and the maintenance of order through the existence of a non-partisan constabulary. Nicaragua is well embarked on this program and carries the sincere and cordial good wishes of the Secretary of State for its complete realization.

APPENDIXES

A. The So-called Dawson Pacts, Signed October 27, 1910 [1]

[Translation]

Agreement No. 1.

After numerous conferences the undersigned have agreed upon the following political and economic bases for the reorganization of the country:

1. The convocation of the people of the Republic to proceed to hold elections with the object of electing the members of a Constituent Assembly, in November next, and that they will assemble in the following December and will elect a president and vice-president for a period of two years, on the basis of a democratic Constitution.

2. To lend all support in the said Constituent Assembly to the candidacy of General Juan Jose Estrada for president *pro tempore* and to that of Adolfo Diaz for vice-president for the said term of two years.

3. The Constituent Assembly will adopt a constitution tending to the abolition of monopolies, guaranteeing the legitimate rights of foreigners; and in addition will convoke the people for the election of constitutional president corresponding to the period following upon that previously mentioned.

Signed in triplicate at Managua, October 27, 1910.

Juan J. Estrada
Adolfo Diaz
Luis Mena
E. Chamorro.

Agreement No. 2.

1. We have likewise agreed that all unsettled claims proceeding from the annulment of contracts and concessions, associated with the previous regime of Nicaragua, will be submitted to the impartial examination of a mixed commission appointed by the Government of this Republic, in harmony with that of the United States.

2. The election and number of its members and the plan of its proceedings will be in conformity with the agreement with the American Agent, after submitting it to the consideration of the Department of State, which must be done before signing it.

3. In the same way we obligate ourselves to pursue and punish the executioners and accomplices in the death of Cannon and Groce. Concerning the indemnity that must be paid to the families of both victims, it will await the result of these proceedings.

Signed in duplicate at Managua, October 27, 1910.

Juan J. Estrada
Adolfo Diaz
Luis Mena
E. Chamorro.

---

[1] File No. 123.N81/29B; *Foreign Relations*, 1911, pp. 652–653.

Agreement No. 3.

In order to rehabilitate the public finances and to pay legitimate claims, both foreign as well as national, the good offices of the American Government will be solicited, with the object of negotiating a loan, which will be guaranteed by a certain per cent of the customs receipts of the Republic, collected in accordance with the terms of an agreement satisfactory to both Governments.

Signed in triplicate at Managua,

JUAN J. ESTRADA,
ADOLFO DIAZ
LUIS MENA
E. CHAMORRO.

Agreement No. 4.

The signers, desirous of duly complying with the programme of the Revolution of October 11th, have agreed to designate at their opportunity and by majority, a candidate for constitutional president of the Republic and another for Vice-President, corresponding to the period following the Presidency *pro tempore* of General Estrada, obligating themselves to take into consideration that the one chosen must represent the Revolution and the conservative party.

The subscribers obligate themselves in order that, in addition to the established laws guaranteeing a free election, there will be no concentration of armed forces of the Government in any point of the Republic, other than shall be necessary for the preservation of order and proper policing.

They add that General Estrada can not be candidate for the new period, or that which follows the provisional one.

Also it is agreed that the Government to be established in Nicaragua must not permit, under any pretext, the Zelayista element in its administration.

Managua, October 27, 1910.

JUAN J. ESTRADA,
FERNANDO SOLORZANO
LUIS MENA
E. CHAMORRO
ADOLF DIAZ

(This "Agreement No. 4", being one affecting Nicaraguan politics but not international relations is not referred to in the note of the Minister of Foreign Affairs, which touches only the first three "Agreements". Signed originals of all were left in the Legation archives.) T. C. DAWSON.

B. LOAN CONVENTION BETWEEN THE UNITED STATES AND NICARAGUA, SIGNED JUNE 6, 1911 (KNOX-CASTRILLO CONVENTION)

The Republic of Nicaragua, being now established on a firm political and constitutional basis, after eleven months of civil war and after seventeen years of administrative abuses resulting in the illegal diversion of public property and revenue, the accumulation of debts and claims in the hands of both natives and foreigners, and the existence of ruinous and disputed concessions in many of which foreigners are beneficiaries, finds the financial and economic situation of the country in urgent need of radical reconstruction; and believing that this needed reconstruction on account of the circumstances above set forth will be difficult and complicated, especially as it involves the necessity of obtaining a loan adequate in amount yet on terms commensurate with the national resources, the Republic of Nicaragua has indicated its desire for cooperation on the part of the United States for the refunding of its debt and the placing of its finances and administration upon a sound and stable basis with a view to meeting its foreign obligations, and to securing the tranquillity, prosperity, and progress of the country; and the Government of the United States, animated by a desire to promote the peace and prosperous development of all the Central American countries, and appreciating the wish of Nicaragua to contribute to such development by establishing on a firm footing its own material strength; and it being recognized as necessary, in view of the present conditions of Nicaraguan finances and resources, that, to afford efficient and legitimate security and to obtain the special benefits sought, the Governments concerned should assume a special relation thereto; and the two Governments being convinced that some contract should be negotiated and concluded between the Government of Nicaragua and some competent and reliable American banking group, said contract to afford a beneficial, just, and equitable accomplishment of the purposes in question, have, with these objects in view, named as their plenipotentiaries.

The President of the United States of America, Philander C. Knox, Secretary of State of the United States; and

The President of Nicaragua, Dr. Salvador Castrillo, junior, Envoy Extraordinary and Minister Plenipotentiary of the Republic of Nicaragua near the Government of the United States;

Who, having communicated to each other their respective full powers, found in good and due form, have agreed upon the following:

ARTICLE I.

The Government of Nicaragua undertakes to make and negotiate a contract providing for the refunding of its present internal and external debt and the adjustment and settlement of claims, liquidated and unliquidated; for the placing of its finances upon a sound and stable basis; and for the future development of the natural and economic resources of that country. The Governments of the United States and Nicaragua will take due note of all the provisions of the said contract when made, and will consult, in case of any difficulties, with a view to the faithful execution of the provisions of said contract, in order that all the benefits to Nicaragua and the security of the loan may at the same time be assured.

ARTICLE II.

The loan which shall be made by the Government of Nicaragua pursuant to the above undertaking shall be secured upon the customs of Nicaragua, and the Government of Nicaragua agrees not to alter the import or export customs duties, or other charges affecting the entry, exit, or transit of goods, during the existence of the loan under the said contract, without consultation and agreement with the Government of the United States.

ARTICLE III.

A full and detailed statement of the operations under this contract shall be submitted by the Fiscal Agent of the loan to the Department of State of the United States and to the Minister of Finance of Nicaragua at the expiration of each twelve months, and at such other times as may be requested by either of the two Governments.

ARTICLE IV.[2]

The Government of Nicaragua, so long as the loan exists, will appoint from a list of names to be presented to it by the fiscal agent of the loan and approved by the President of the United States of America, a collector general of customs, who shall administer the customs in accordance with the contract securing said loan and will give this official full protection in the exercise of his functions. The Government of the United States will in turn afford such protection as it may find requisite.

ARTICLE V.

This Convention shall be ratified and the ratifications hereof shall be exchanged at Managua as soon as possible.

In faith whereof, the respective plenipotentiaries have signed the present Convention in the English and Spanish languages and have hereunto affixed their seals.

Done in duplicate, at Washington, this sixth day of June, one thousand nine hundred and eleven.

[SEAL]   PHILANDER C. KNOX.
[SEAL]   SALVADOR CASTRILLO.

C. CONVENTION BETWEEN THE UNITED STATES AND NICARAGUA REGARDING A NICARAGUAN CANAL ROUTE (BRYAN-CHAMORRO TREATY)

Signed at Washington, August 5, 1914; ratification advised by the Senate, with amendments, February 18, 1916; ratified by the President, June 19, 1916; ratified by Nicaragua, April 13, 1916; ratifications exchanged at Washington, June 22, 1916; proclaimed, June 24, 1916.

BY THE PRESIDENT OF THE UNITED STATES OF AMERICA.

A PROCLAMATION.

WHEREAS a Convention between the United States of America and the Republic of Nicaragua granting to the United States the exclusive proprietary rights for the construction and operation of an interoceanic canal by a Nicaraguan route, the lease of certain islands, and the right to establish a naval base on the Gulf of Fonseca, was concluded and signed by their respective Plenipotentiaries at Washington, on the fifth day of August, one thousand nine hundred and fourteen, the original of which Convention, being in the English and Spanish languages is, as amended by the Senate of the United States, word for word as follows:

The Government of the United States of America and the Government of Nicaragua being animated by the desire to strengthen their ancient and cordial friendship by the most sincere cooperation for all purposes of their mutual advantage and interest and to provide for the possible future construction of an interoceanic ship canal by way of the San Juan River and the great Lake of Nicaragua, or by any route over Nicaraguan territory, whenever the construction of such canal shall be deemed by the Government of the United States conducive to the interests of both countries, and the Government of Nicaragua wishing to facilitate in every way possible the successful maintenance and operation of the Panama Canal, the two Governments have re-

---

[2]As amended by the Nicaraguan Assembly, June 14, 1911.—EDITOR.

solved to conclude a Convention to these ends, and have accordingly appointed as their plenipotentiaries:

The President of the United States, the Honorable William Jennings Bryan, Secretary of State; and

The President of Nicaragua, Señor General Don Emiliano Chamorro, Envoy Extraordinary and Minister Plenipotentiary of Nicaragua to the United States;

Who, having exhibited to each other their respective full powers, found to be in good and due form, have agreed upon and concluded the following articles:

ARTICLE I.

The Government of Nicaragua grants in perpetuity to the Government of the United States, forever free from all taxation or other public charge, the exclusive proprietary rights necessary and convenient for the construction, operation and maintenance of an interoceanic canal by way of the San Juan River and the great Lake of Nicaragua or by way of any route over Nicaraguan territory, the details of the terms upon which such canal shall be constructed, operated and maintained to be agreed to by the two governments whenever the Government of the United States shall notify the Government of Nicaragua of its desire or intention to construct such canal.

ARTICLE II.

To enable the Government of the United States to protect the Panama Canal and the proprietary rights granted to the Government of the United States by the foregoing article, and also to enable the Government of the United States to take any measure necessary to the ends contemplated herein, the Government of Nicaragua hereby leases for a term of ninety-nine years to the Government of the United States the islands in the Caribbean Sea known as Great Corn Island and Little Corn Island; and the Government of Nicaragua further grants to the Government of the United States for a like period of ninety-nine years the right to establish, operate and maintain a naval base at such place on the territory of Nicaragua bordering upon the Gulf of Fonseca as the Government of the United States may select. The Government of the United States shall have the option of renewing for a further term of ninety-nine years the above leases and grants upon the expiration of their respective terms, it being expressly agreed that the territory hereby leased and the naval base which may be maintained under the grant aforesaid shall be subject exclusively to the laws and sovereign authority of the United States during the terms of such lease and grant and of any renewal or renewals thereof.

ARTICLE III.

In consideration of the foregoing stipulations and for the purposes contemplated by this Convention and for the purpose of reducing the present indebtedness of Nicaragua, the Government of the United States shall, upon the date of the exchange of ratification of this Convention, pay for the benefit of the Republic of Nicaragua the sum of three million dollars United States gold coin, of the present weight and fineness, to be deposited to the order of the Government of Nicaragua in such bank or banks or with such banking corporation as the Government of the United States may determine, to be applied by Nicaragua upon its indebtedness or other public purposes for the advancement of the welfare of Nicaragua in a manner to be determined by the two High Contracting Parties, all such disbursements to be made by orders drawn by the Minister of Finance of the Republic of Nicaragua and approved by the Secretary of State of the United States or by such person as he may designate.

ARTICLE IV.

This Convention shall be ratified by the High Contracting Parties in accordance with their respective laws, and the ratifications thereof shall be exchanged at Washington as soon as possible.

In witness whereof the respective plenipotentiaries have signed the present treaty and have affixed thereunto their seals.

Done at Washington, in duplicate, in the English and Spanish languages, on the 5th day of August, in the year nineteen hundred and fourteen.

WILLIAM JENNINGS BRYAN [SEAL]
EMILIANO CHAMORRO [SEAL]

AND WHEREAS, the advice and consent of the Senate of the United States to the ratification of the said Convention was given with the following proviso: "*Provided*, That, whereas, Costa Rica, Salvador and Honduras have protested against the ratification of the said Convention in the fear or belief that said Convention might in some respect impair existing rights of said States; therefore, it is declared by the Senate that in advising and consenting to the ratification of the said Convention as amended such advice and consent are given with the understanding, to be expressed as a part of the instrument of ratification, that nothing in said Convention is intended to affect any existing right of any of the said named States; "

AND WHEREAS, the said understanding has been accepted by the Government of Nicaragua;

AND WHEREAS, the said Convention, as amended by the Senate of the United States, has been duly ratified on both parts, and the ratifications of the two governments were exchanged in the City of Washington, on the twenty-second day of June, one thousand nine hundred and sixteen;

Now, THEREFORE, be it known that I, Woodrow Wilson, President of the United States of America, have caused the said Convention, as amended, and the said understanding to be made public, to the end that the same and every article and clause thereof may be observed and fulfilled with good faith by the United States and the citizens thereof.

IN TESTIMONY WHEREOF, I have hereunto set my hand and caused the seal of the United States to be affixed.

Done at the City of Washington this twenty-fourth day of June in the year of our Lord one thousand nine hundred and sixteen, and of the

[SEAL] Independence of the United States of America the one hundred and fortieth.

WOODROW WILSON

By the President:
    ROBERT LANSING,
        Secretary of State.

D. AN AGREEMENT BETWEEN THE UNITED STATES AND COSTA RICA, SIGNED AT WASHINGTON, FEBRUARY 1, 1923, BY WHICH THE TWO GOVERNMENTS ENGAGE THEMSELVES TO ENTER INTO NEGOTIATIONS WITH EACH OTHER TO SETTLE THE PLAN AND THE AGREEMENTS WHICH MAY BE FOUND NECESSARY TO ACCOMPLISH THE CONSTRUCTION AND TO PROVIDE FOR THE OWNERSHIP AND CONTROL OF AN INTEROCEANIC CANAL ACROSS COSTA RICAN TERRITORY

It is agreed between the two Governments that when the President of the United States is authorized by law to acquire control of the rights which Costa Rica possesses in the San Juan River, or in Salinas Bay, and such portion of the territory now belonging to Costa Rica as may be desirable and necessary on which to construct and protect a canal of depth and capacity sufficient for the passage of vessels of the greatest tonnage and draft now in use, from a point near San Juan del Norte on the Carribbean Sea via Lake Nicaragua to Brito on the Pacific Ocean, they mutually engage to enter into negotiations with each other to settle the plan and the agreements, in detail, found necessary to accomplish the construction and to provide for the ownership and control of the proposed canal.

This Agreement shall be ratified by the President of the United States, by and with the advice and consent of the Senate thereof, and by the President of Costa Rica, in accordance with the Constitution and laws of that Republic, and the ratifications shall be exchanged at Washington as soon as possible.

In witness whereof, the undersigned have signed this protocol and have hereunto affixed their seals.

Done in duplicate at Washington, this 1st day of February, 1923.

[SEAL]   CHARLES E. HUGHES.
[SEAL]   J. RAFAEL OREAMUNO.

E. AGREEMENT FOR THE ESTABLISHMENT OF THE GUARDIA NACIONAL OF NICARAGUA, SIGNED DECEMBER 22, 1927

Whereas the Republic of Nicaragua is desirous of preserving internal peace and order and the security of individual rights, and is desirous of carrying out plans for the maintenance of domestic tranquillity and the promotion of the prosperity of the Republic and its people;

And whereas the assistance and co-operation of the Government of the United States is deemed essential to an early realization of the measures to be adopted;

And whereas the United States is in full sympathy with these aims and objects of the Republic and is desirous of contributing in all proper ways to their attainment the undersigned duly authorized thereto by their respective Governments have agreed as follows:

I

The Republic of Nicaragua undertakes to create without delay an efficient constabulary to be known as the Guardia Nacional de Nicaragua urban and rural composed of native Nicaraguans, the strength of which and the amounts to be expended for pay, rations, and expenses of operation, et cetera, shall be as set forth in the following table:

COMMISSIONED PERSONNEL	Per Annum $ Gold
1 Brigadier General	$3,000.00
1 Colonel, Chief of Staff	2,500.00
3 Colonels (Line) at $2,400.00 per annum	7,200.00
1 Colonel, Quartermaster	2,400.00
1 Colonel, Medical	2,400.00
4 Majors (Line) at $2,100.00 per annum	8,400.00
1 Major, Paymaster	2,100.00
1 Major, General Headquarters Inspector	2,100.00
1 Major, Law Officer	2,100.00
2 Majors, Medical, at $2,100.00 per annum	4,200.00
10 Captains, at $1,800.00 per annum	18,000.00
2 Captains, Medical, at $1,800.00 per annum	3,600.00
20 First Lieutenants, at $1,200.00 per annum	24,000.00
2 First Lieutenants, Medical, at $1,200.00 per annum	2,400.00
20 Second Lieutenants, at $900.00 per annum	18,000.00
3 Second Lieutenants, Medical, at $900.00 per annum	2,700.00
20 Student Officers (Cadets) at $600.00 per annum	12,000.00
93	$117,100.00

ENLISTED PERSONNEL	Per Annum $ Gold
4 Sergeants Major, at $40.00 per month	1,920.00
10 First Sergeants, at $35.00 per month	4,200.00
10 Q.M. Sergeants, at $30.00 per month	3,600.00
60 Sergeants, at $25.00 per month	18,000.00
120 Corporals, at $18.00 per month	25,920.00
20 Field Musics, at $14.00 per month	3,360.00
840 Privates, at $12.00 per month	120,960.00
1,064	$177,960.00

BAND

		Per Annum $ Gold
1	Leader	1,200.00
1	Assistant Leader	900.00
10	Musicians, 1st class, at $30.00 per month	3,600.00
10	Musicians, 2nd class, at $25.00 per month	3,000.00
15	Musicians, 3rd class, at $20.00 per month	3,600.00
37		$12,300.00

ENLISTED MEDICAL PERSONNEL

		Per Annum $ Gold
1	First Sergeant, at $35.00 per month	420.00
4	Sergeants, at $25.00 per month	1,200.00
20	Corporals, at $18.00 per month	4,320.00
10	Privates, at $12.00 per month	1,440.00
35		$7,380.00

OPERATIONS AND MAINTENANCE

Civil employees; uniforms and clothing; Arms equipment and target practice; remounts and forage; Motor vehicles and maintenance; repairs and replacements; Transportation of Supplies and Troops; Maps, stationery and office supplies; Intelligence service; rent, repairs and construction of barracks; Gasoline, kerosene; Lights; Tools and miscellaneous expenditures for operations and maintenance of the Constabulary _____ $200,000.00

RATIONS

Expenses of procuring and preparing rations for 1136 enlisted at $0.30 per diem _____ $124,392.00

PRISONS AND PENITENTIARIES

Operation and Maintenance _____ $40,000.00
Medical Supplies and Maintenance of Constabulary Hospitals, Prison Dispensaries, etc _____ 10,000.00

GRAND TOTAL	$689,132.00

The foregoing provisions shall be regarded as the minimum requirements for the Guardia Nacional de Nicaragua. If the condition of the Nicaraguan Government's finances shall so warrant, the strength of the Guardia Nacional, commissioned and enlisted, and the expenses thereof may be increased upon the recommendation of the Chief of the Guardia Nacional and upon the consent in writing of the President of Nicaragua.

If the condition of the Nicaraguan Government's finances shall so warrant a suitable Coast Guard and a suitable Aviation Unit may upon the recommendation of the Chief of the Guardia Nacional de Nicaragua and upon the consent in writing of the President of Nicaragua be made a part of the Guardia Nacional de Nicaragua, similarly officered and manned with appropriate ranks and subject in the same manner to regulations and discipline as provided herein for the personnel of the Guardia Nacional de Nicaragua.

II

The Guardia Nacional de Nicaragua shall be considered the sole military and police force of the Republic, clothed with full power to preserve domestic peace and the security of individual rights. It shall have control of arms and ammunition, military supplies and supervision of the traffic therein throughout the

Republic. It shall have control of all fortifications, barracks, buildings, grounds, prisons, penitentiaries, vessels, and other government property which were formerly assigned to or under the control of the Army, Navy and Police Forces of the Republic. It shall be subject only to the direction of the President of Nicaragua; all other officials desiring the services of the Guardia Nacional de Nicaragua shall be required to submit requests through the nearest official of that organization. The Guard of Honor for the Palace of the President shall be a company of selected men and officers from the personnel of the Guardia Nacional, and will wear distinctive insignia while employed on this service.

III

All matters of recruiting, appointment, instruction, training, promotion, examination, discipline, operation of troops, clothing, rations, arms and equipment, quarters and administration, shall be under the jurisdiction of the Chief of the Guardia Nacional.

IV

Rules and regulations for the administration and discipline of the Guardia Nacional de Nicaragua, Prisons and Penitentiaries, shall be issued by the Chief of the Guardia Nacional after being approved by the President of Nicaragua. Infraction of these rules and regulations by members of the Guardia Nacional may be punished by arrest and imprisonment, suspension from duty without pay, forfeiture of pay, or dismissal, under regulations promulgated by the Chief of the Guardia Nacional and approved by the President of Nicaragua.

V

Other offenses committed by members of the Guardia Nacional de Nicaragua shall be investigated by officers of the Guardia Nacional as directed by the Chief of the Guardia Nacional. If it should appear upon investigation that an offense has been committed, the offender will be turned over to the civil authorities.

VI

Courts-martial constituted under the rules and regulations of the Chief of the Guardia Nacional may try native Nicaraguan officers and enlisted men of the Guardia for infraction of the rules and regulations. The findings of the courts-martial of the Guardia Nacional after approval of the Chief are final, and not subject to appeal or review except by the Supreme Court of Nicaragua and then, only in questions of excess of power or questions of jurisdiction.

VII

Persons violating the Regulations (if there is no civil law) or the Laws (if there is a civil law) governing traffic in arms, ammunition and military stores, shall be punished by a fine of from fifty to one thousand cordobas or imprisonment of from ninety days to five years, or both; for which purpose the Government of Nicaragua will present to Congress a project of law to amend the criminal laws in the sense indicated.

VIII

The Guardia Nacional de Nicaragua shall be under the control of the President of Nicaragua and all orders from him pertaining to the Guardia

Nacional shall be delivered to the Chief thereof. All other civil officials desiring protection or the services of the Guardia Nacional will make application to the senior officer of the Guardia Nacional in that locality.

IX

An adequate amount as provided in Article I of this Agreement shall be appropriated annually to defray the expenses for pay, allowances, equipment, uniforms, transportation, administration and other current expenses of the Guardia Nacional de Nicaragua. Allotments for the various needs of the Guardia Nacional shall be made from this sum by the Chief of the Guardia Nacional.

X

Reports of expenditures shall be made by the Chief of the Guardia Nacional as directed by the President of Nicaragua and audited in accordance with the law.

Savings effected under any title may be expended under any other title upon written approval of the Chief of the Guardia Nacional.

XI

The laws necessary to make effective the above provisions shall be submitted to the legislative body of Nicaragua.

XII

In consideration of the foregoing the Government of the United States in virtue of authority conferred on the President by the Act of Congress approved May 19, 1926, entitled "An Act to authorize the President to detail officers and enlisted men of the United States Army, Navy and Marine Corps to assist the governments of the Latin-American Republics in military and naval matters" undertakes to detail officers and enlisted men of the United States Navy and Marine Corps to assist the Government of Nicaragua in the organizing and training of a constabulary as herein provided.

All American officers serving with the Guardia Nacional of Nicaragua shall be appointed from personnel of the United States Navy and Marine Corps by the President of Nicaragua upon nomination of the President of the United States. They will be replaced by Nicaraguans when the latter have successfully completed the course of instructions prescribed by the Chief of the Guardia Nacional de Nicaragua and have shown by their conduct and examination that they are fit for command.

Officers and enlisted men of the United States Navy and Marine Corps serving with the Guardia Nacional will not be tried by Nicaraguan civil courts or courts-martial but will be subject to trial by court-martial under the laws of the United States for the government of the Navy.

In witness whereof, the undersigned have hereunto signed their names and affixed their seals in duplicate, in the city of Managua, this twenty-second day of December, 1927.

[SEAL]   DANA G. MUNRO
[SEAL]   CARLOS CUADRA PASOS.